Desert Springs in the City
A Concise History of the Carmelites

Leopold Glueckert, O. Carm.

CARMELITE MEDIA

This book was originally published as a series of articles in *The Sword*, from 2010, no.1-2 until 2012, no. 2.

Layout and Cover design by William J. Harry, O. Carm.

© 2012 by Carmelite Media
Printed in the United States of America

Carmelite Media
8501 Bailey Road
Darien, Illinois 60561

Phone: 1-630-971-0724
Email: publications@carmelnet.org
Website: carmelites.info/publications

Printed Book: ISBN: 978-1-936742-05-9

TABLE OF CONTENTS

Appendices :

Introduction

This small book has been a long time in the making, but I believe it will serve a genuine need. Carmelite history has seen a very welcome revival in the last 50 years, but not all of the best work is available to people of the general public. Much of the most worthy scholarship is either very weighty, or in languages other than English. So for the general readers in the English speaking world, a short and understandable narrative of the Carmelite story is not easy to find.

It is my intention that this present, thin volume will serve as a sort of "ignition key" to some of the other and more detailed sources, rather than the last word on the entire Carmelite story. Of necessity, a survey of eight centuries of tradition must be "miles wide, but only inches deep." Many readers may be disappointed at how much is left out, or only treated superficially, but that is the nature of a survey. The best thing that a reader must do with a quick-reading book is to read it quickly; then one must move on to something more substantial. Fortunately, more is available.

The intended audience for this work is the general, intelligent reader, who is not a specialist of any sort, but who has a healthy curiosity about what makes up the somewhat contradictory fabric of the Carmelite ethos. Any person who may be considering a more reflective and prayerful attitude toward a lifetime of joyful service to others will find a home in this house. Secular and Lay Carmelites, as well as Carmelite students in formation, will be able to read this story as a helpful first step on their journey.

This short excerpt of the very long Carmelite story is humbly presented to all people who seek peace, love, and joy, as well as an appreciation of holiness as a means to a more perfect world.

Chapter 1
Hermits in the Wadi

Sunrise. About the year 1200. Just south of the crusader fortress at Acre, a dry river valley leads down from a green mountain to the sun-washed shores of the eastern Mediterranean. The head of a lean, bearded man pokes out of a natural cave. He looks at the sun. He is wearing a rough woolen cloak of alternating light and dark stripes. He says nothing, but raises his eyes to heaven in a silent prayer to God and tries to estimate from the angle of the sun how long it will be before he joins his fellow hermits in their Eucharistic worship at the makeshift chapel in the center of the wadi.

Details of exactly who he was, where he came from, or why he had chosen to be in the Holy Land at this time are lost and unrecorded in history. But this hermit and many like him were heralds of a new movement in the Church. Their spontaneous community in a *wadi*, a dry gulch along the slopes of Mt. Carmel, became the cradle of the Carmelite Rule sourcing an utterly unique spirituality in Western Christianity.

Hermits they were. Silence and solitude seemed especially significant here in the place of Elijah, the fiery prophet of Carmel. Here they wrestled and argued with God, as Elijah himself had done, struggling to find the most perfect and direct way to live as Jesus taught. Their diet was simple, their clothing homespun, their reflection accomplished in silence. Hermits had always spent long hours contemplating the presence of God, but this band living on the slopes of Carmel also prayed the psalms in a manner similar to the monks in established monasteries. But their prayer of the psalms was largely private. Once a day they did leave their individual cells, located a respectful distance apart, to share the Eucharist in their common chapel.

Their leader, the Prior, was one like themselves, a European who had come to the land of Jesus during the Crusades. Some had come as soldiers, others pilgrims, or merchants, or sailors. All had been captivated by the beauty of the land made holy by Jesus and his apostles. All had seen the slopes of Carmel as a spiritual refuge where they could follow Elijah's passionate dedication to heroic virtue and the love of God. The Prior had been chosen from among them by their consensus, and he guided them with brotherly concern. It was expected that the Prior would help them to maintain a balance between mutual help and respectful solitude. The Prior was also the first to meet visitors to the community and to see to their needs.

Religious Traditions

While this community in the *wadi* was relatively young, other religious communities in Europe had been well established. Following Constantine's legalization of Christianity in 313, the martyrs who had given witness to Christ by their blood gave way to hermits who elected to become living martyrs. Discouraged by the evils of society and the corruption of some church leaders, they chose a solitary life with God in its most dramatic form. After a few centuries, some hermits banded together in communities for mutual support and inspiration. These earliest monks attempted to integrate the details of their lives, sharing common meals, common sleeping quarters, and common prayer.

Medieval monasteries were huge, self-sufficient communities, sometimes with hundreds of monks who were committed to forming an alternative to secular society. Because of their vast land holdings, monks did not depend on outside sources of income and were free to live their lives according to a spiritual formula. The Rule of St. Benedict called for the monk's day to be balanced between work, prayer and study for a harmonious life founded on the gospel instead of self-interest. By the time of Charlemagne, many monasteries had become highly centralized and regularized. Some of the openness of Benedict's original system had been lost, and obedience to the rules became ever more important.

Monks would rise in the night to begin chanting God's praises long before dawn. This was the first of eight times of prayer established by Benedict. After the night office (Matins), came the glorious morning prayer at dawn (Lauds). The so-called "little" hours through the daytime fell at the first, third, sixth, and ninth hours of daylight (Prime, Terce, Sext, None). A solemn evening prayer at the end of the day (Vespers) and a night prayer (Compline) closed the monk's day of prayer.

Between prayer times were periods of work. Most monks worked at raising food for the community and developed some of the best farming techniques anywhere in Europe. More specialized scholarly work might include studying ancient classics, copying of books and manuscripts, and original writing in such fields as liturgy and theology. Without the monks' diligent attention to the reproduction and preservation of ancient texts, many of the flames of knowledge would have gone out in Europe.

Elijah, Spiritual Father of the Carmelites, pictured in a bas relief of the slaying of the prophets of Baal, a story in the Book of Kings. This series hangs in the Discalced Carmelite Church on Mt. Carmel, Israel. *(Photo courtesy of Carmelite Media)*

Hermits in the *Wadi*

But for the hermits on Carmel, life was focused on extreme simplicity in imitation of Elijah. His story in the Books of Kings speaks of intimate conversations with God as well as the confrontation with evil, personified by unjust kings or false prophets. Those who took up residence in the *wadi* treasured the silence of the place and their chance to be alone with God. Their awareness of the presence of God was constant, whether alone with Him in their caves, or together with one another in chapel. The night-time hours were of special value to hermits. What might otherwise become a time of temptation was sublimated into a restful vigil of reflection on the scriptures, leading to spontaneous prayer and praise.

No one can be certain how long people of faith had inhabited the *wadi* in imitation of Elijah's virtue. There may have been Greek hermits or monks there as early as the fifth century. But we do know that Latin crusaders from the West adopted this tradition and settled on Carmel in substantial numbers before 1200. Many of those who had come to fight, or to visit the holy places, found their greatest fulfillment on the slopes of Carmel. Near to places where Jesus had walked, they had a safe haven with adequate food and water. The mountain seemed created by God as a place of prayer.

Impact of the Crusades

The First Crusade began in 1096 as a heroic effort to take back the Holy Land from Muslim control. After a lightning campaign which surprised the Muslim forces, the western-dominated Kingdom of Jerusalem and several other states were created. But the Crusades were hard to sustain. The Crusaders were for- eigners who came to fight and pray, but then went home. Unless new crusaders came to replace them, the Muslim armies could quickly re-conquer Jerusalem and the other cities.

The entire situation began to deteriorate after the battle of Hattin in 1187. The Crusader armies suffered a serious defeat and no longer had enough fighting men to hold on to everything that they had conquered. Many Christians found it necessary to fall back toward the coast. We assume that some hermits and solitaries from other places fled to the *wadi* for refuge. But there was no relief in sight. At no time were there more than 1000 Christian knights in the entire Holy Land. And often, there were far fewer.

It is ironic that the military woes of the Crusaders actually intensified the reli- gious activity on the slopes of Carmel. As a place to find God, the mountain had a long and noble history. More than just a mountain peak, Carmel is a green and fertile ridge, which rises dramatically from the Bay of Haifa and thrusts southward and eastward toward Megiddo for about 21 miles. Although rugged to climb, the mountain affords ample ground water and dense vegetation, as well as breathtaking views from the upper reaches. Every spring, torrential rains feed fast rushing streams, which carve deep ravines and natural caves into the soft rock. These creased valleys are dry for most of the year, although cool springs keep bubbling continuously from underground sources. One such spring, the "Fountain of Elijah," blesses the *wadi* called 'Ain-es-siah with fresh water all year long. Olives, grapes, figs, and pomegranates grow there and provide a ready source of food.

This *wadi* is only two miles south of the promontory, and faces westward toward the sea. The position would become increasingly important as the Crusades staggered along toward their final conclusion. For most of the remaining years, the western slope of the mountain was protected against raids by brigands and Muslim partisans. And the *wadi's* location put the hermits squarely alongside the coastal road, which became the principal route of communication between Acre and Caesarea. Since the disaster at Hattin, the Patriarch of Jerusalem had chosen to live safely at the fortified port of Acre, rather than in Jerusalem itself. Many hermits and solitaries from all over the Holy Land found life in the open countryside too dangerous and fell back to the relative safety of the coast. Some associated themselves with the existing brotherhood in the *wadi*, where they found friendly support for their prayer and reflection.

Renewal of Eremitical Life

Although the earliest hermits had declined in numbers with the rise of monas- teries, there was a surprising rebound in the eremitical life during the eleventh and twelfth centuries. These latter-day hermits found that life in the monaster- ies had become too complicated and confining for their rather free and open

The wadi 'Ain es-siah, near the font of Elijah, looking out to the Mediterranean Sea, where the early Carmelites first settled. Ruins from the early monastery survive to this day. *(Photo used with permission of Julia Goren)*

style of prayer. So they again sought direct contact with God in wild or remote places, like the wadi 'Ain-es-siah. They were, in effect, lay preachers who lived on the fringes of society. They rejected the materialism of the culture, and the wealth and corruption of both Church and State. In their efforts to immerse themselves in the Word of God, they embraced the poverty and humanity of the suffering Jesus in their own lives.

Ironically, the hermits maintained a better relationship with ordinary lay people than did the monks. Monks, by necessity, were confined to their monasteries and made their own life within its walls. Hermits, on the other hand, had no reliable source of income, and often needed to support themselves by selling or bartering the products of their labor. During these occasional contacts with ordinary folks in the countryside, they often proved to be a surprisingly good source of wisdom and sage advice. Sometimes a visitor would express his gratitude by leaving an offering, but it was certainly not required. Spiritual advice from one Christian to another was a normal occurrence.

There is archeological evidence that hermits lived in the *wadi* as early as the fifth century. They were probably Greek or Syrian ascetics who followed the classic pattern of living simply in God's presence, and praying continually, as the Spirit prompted them. On one side of the *wadi*, there is a small stable-chapel, carved out of the natural rock, which dates from this time. Although it has the look of a stable, it is unlikely that animals were actually kept there. It is too cramped for a large animal, like a horse, and the feeding troughs and tethering rings are too high for smaller animals, like sheep. More likely it was a place of prayer, designed as a reminder of Bethlehem, as a Nativity chapel celebrating the Incarnation. During that same fifth century, the Councils of Ephesus (431) and Chalcedon (451) had clarified the Church's teaching on the nature of Jesus, on how he could be both human and divine. That small cave-chapel in the *wadi* resembles one built in Nazareth during the same period. If it was in fact designed to honor Mary as God's own channel into the human race, then it imprinted a special Marian character on the place.

The archeologists have also recorded a nearly unbroken trail of ceramic evidence from the fifth through the thirteenth centuries. So there is strong evidence that someone was living in the *wadi* during most of that period, as safety considerations allowed. We are not able to verify who those people were for certain, but the place was often unsafe for anyone other than hermits or mystics. Pilgrims and travelers have left us periodic accounts of holy men encountered along the *wadi* and the coast road, but the details of their way of life and their organization have been lost to recorded history. But at last this long tradition of quiet and humble contemplation took on a formal aspect, when some of the hermits requested formal approval from ecclesiastical authorities. This straightforward step led directly to the Carmelite Rule, a document as concise and powerful as a mustard seed.

The Need for a Rule

Sometime shortly after 1200, the hermits from Carmel contacted Albert, Latin Patriarch of Jerusalem, to request his help in drafting a Rule which would capture and preserve their way of life. Tradition tells us that the leader of the hermits was called Brocard. Albert later refers to him as simply "Brother B." Since Albert's residence at Acre was less than a day's journey from the *wadi*, he may very well have made a personal visit. The resulting Rule, rather than being a lofty discourse on ideals, was simply a description of what the hermits were actually doing in their daily life: silence and solitude, prayer and fasting, hospitality to visitors from the coastal road, and whatever other pastoral activity the Spirit motivated. By his official endorsement of their lifestyle, Albert "baptized" it as a formula which others might follow with merit. "It is to me, however" he wrote in Chapter 3 of the Rule, "that you have come for a rule of life in keeping with your avowed purpose...." The "avowed purpose" was already a living entity, expressed in the activity and spiritual path that the hermits had developed and were already observing in the *wadi*. Albert, as the most senior prelate in the Holy Land, gave that way of life – that path – official status. But the Carmelite Rule remains unique in that it sprang from an existing method, rather than serving as a starting point for something which was to follow.

To compose a Rule for a religious family was not something to be taken lightly. Rules had a great sense of permanence and stability about them. Once approved, they could only be changed or modified by the pope.

Albert was also aware of how complicated religious legislation could be. The Benedictine Rule, for example, was based on rather simple principles, but the statutes are very detailed. Benedict laid down specific decrees, with very precise difficulties in mind. Being both an intelligent and provident person, and also a legal-minded Roman, he tried to anticipate every conceivable situation and propose a solution for it. It was a very detailed rule book for a well-ordered life.

St. Albert, Patriarch of Jerusalem, from a fresco of the 1400s in the Carmelite church in San Felice del Benaco, Italy. *(Photo courtesy of Carmelite Media)*

By way of contrast, the Carmelite Rule is a masterpiece of simplicity. Including the introduction and conclusion, there are only 24 "chapters" which we would call paragraphs. In addition to its brevity, it shows a remarkable sense of perspective, based on common sense. Albert understood that all hermits consider simplicity of life to be a return to the basic principles of the Gospel. His Rule, created to reflect that same spirit of simplicity, has been more flexible, and thus more durable, than a collection of tightly worded legalities. The Carmelite Rule has been changed only twice in eight centuries (1247 and 1432).

Significance of Albert's Rule

Even before he became Patriarch of Jerusalem, Alberto Avogadro of Vercelli had built a very impressive career as a pastor, diplomat, mediator of disputes, and lawgiver. Years earlier, he had invested much time and energy in setting down a way of life for a group called the Humiliati. Like the earliest Franciscans, the Humiliati were a vigorous lay movement who promoted radical poverty and simplicity of life. The Cathars and Albigensians had been condemned for similar militant views in earlier times, and violently stamped out. When the Humiliati showed interest in joining the mainstream of the Church, they were allowed to reorganize their regimen. Albert was one of the legates who composed new constitutions for them, with reasonable success. Perhaps Albert was dissatisfied with his elaborate legislation for them, and concluded that simplicity might be better.

Dating the Rule is not difficult. The traditional date is 1209, and that may be exactly correct. But it could not have been earlier than 1206, when Albert arrived at Acre, nor later than 1214, when he was murdered by an official whom

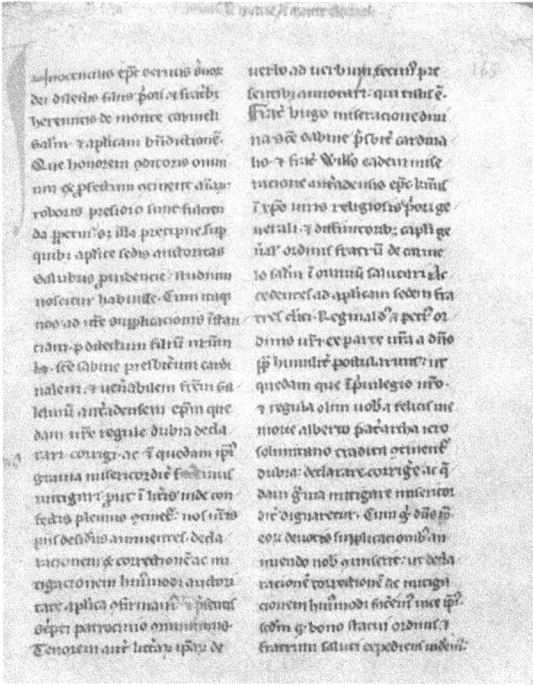

Quae conditionis, the earliest known copy of the Rule.

he had rebuked. The timing is important. The Fourth Lateran Council (1215) placed a ban on new religious orders, and the granting of any new Rules. So anything sanctioned by Albert could not have been included under the ban. As if to emphasize its legality, Pope Honorius III gave formal approval to the same Rule in 1226. Despite all the other achievements of a fine career, Albert's legislation for the Carmelites was probably the greatest success of his life.

Later in the same century, the Second Council of Lyon (1274) confirmed the prohibition on new orders, and actually suppressed several orders which did not meet the time standard. The Franciscans and Dominicans were formally approved, while the Carmelites and Augustinians were given temporary approbation, since their legality seemed to be well founded.[1] Boniface VIII gave the final approval in 1298.

Albert begins with a greeting and an introduction, and states that he has been asked to formulate a Rule. After the first three paragraphs, he moves immediately to leadership. Chapter 4 states that there should be a leader, a Prior, elected by either common consent or "by the greater and more mature part of you." In other words, a general consensus is best, but a majority will be adequate if consensus is not possible. The simple fact that the Prior is being chosen by the community is significant. He is the "first among equals" and not in any sense a spiritual sage or abbot. The democratic process was taken for granted among hermits, even as it was falling into disfavor in the Church at large. (Chapters 5, 7, and 13 were not added to the Rule until 1247.)

Central Importance of the Cell

Chapter 6 states that each member of the community should have a separate cell, allotted by the Prior with the consent of the rest. This regulation highlights

---

1. In its original form, the Albertine Rule had no chapter numbers at all. The numbers were added in 1247, when Pope Innocent IV authorized the Rule's first change or "mitigation." In 1999, a revision of the chapter numbers was by authorized a joint meeting of the General Councils of the Carmelites and Discalced Carmelites; the revised numbers are used in this book, and in the text of the Rule which appears in Appendix I.

the importance of sacred space in the hermit's spiritual environment. Each one was to have his own place, which would be his primary point of contact with God. He should remain there and develop a sense of belonging in God's presence. It is difficult to over-emphasize the importance of the cell for the early Carmelite. It was not just a separate room in a larger building, but a very individual space, not even touching any other. In the *wadi*, at least, it could be a small cave, or another shelter like a hut, tent, or lean-to, always some distance from all the others.

Albert then goes on to describe what should happen in the cell. Chapter 8 specifies that there be no change of cells without the Prior's approval. Cells belong to the community, not the individual. Chapter 9 requires that the Prior's cell be located near the entrance to the place. He is to be the first person to meet visitors coming in from outside, so that he can make suitable arrangements for them. This disposition was not intended to be a barrier in any sense. The Prior was not the sentry of the community, since there was no formal monastic enclosure in the *wadi*. He is the "front man" both physically and psychologically. His cell is in front because it is his task to offer hospitality to visitors, not keep them out. He judges how to assist those seeking help or advice, desiring to visit individual hermits, or simply satisfying their curiosity about this place and its residents. The archeological remains of the *wadi* community support this conclusion. The ruins of the Prior's cell show an elaborate two-chambered structure, which was, in effect, a rather large reception area.

Although the *wadi* was quiet and somewhat secluded, the principal road between Acre and Caesarea ran along the coast, not far from the entrance. Its location near this major highway brought visitors to the community's doorstep, and all indications are that the community was open to these visitors. The hermits were not in any sense people who were trying to hide, or to close themselves off from the outside world. They certainly valued their peace and quiet highly, and made the space for it, but the area was still accessible to outsiders. The ruins reveal that the hermits did more than accept visitors grudgingly; they were interested in accommodating them, even at considerable cost. The remains of some very high quality masonry testify to a keen interest in taking care of people who were not of their group. Crusaders and pilgrims mention the Carmel community as a normal stop on their way from Acre to Jerusalem.

Prayer as a Way of Life

The ruins also include a simple stone chapel, which was doubled in size on at least one occasion. The later construction included a bell tower, indicating that they were allowed to call outside people to worship. The exact dating of the construction is still uncertain, but we can assume that the most significant building took place throughout the thirteenth century, ending suddenly in 1291, when the fortress of Acre was finally captured by the Muslims. After that event, there was no future for Christians in the Holy Land, especially those living as a religious community.

But the physical layout of the ruins follows the Rule exactly. Albert describes the Prior's cell as being near the entrance of the place. He also talks about the oratory, or chapel, being in the midst of the cells. This place of public worship was not on the periphery, but in the center of the dwellings. The individual cells are harder to trace, since they tended to be light free-standing shelters constructed wherever space permitted, or else small, natural caves along the sides of the *wadi*. There is evidence that makeshift huts probably ranged along the walls of the chapel and elsewhere, since burned remnants of wood and other flimsy materials remain just below ground. A wealth of additional evidence has also been found: pottery, buckles, coins, pins, religious articles, even a small clay oven, ordinary physical items reminding us of the nameless, mysterious hermits and their radically spiritual lives.

Some scholars consider Chapter 10 to be the central element of the Rule. It exhorts the brethren to remain in their cells, or near them, unless they are kept away by other legitimate duties. In these holy spaces, they are to "ponder the Lord's law day and night, and keep watch in prayer." This precept is the basis for the entire way of life which the hermits followed. The hermit's natural condition is presented as a life of reflection and silence in or near the solitude of the cell. "Pondering the law of the Lord" is a picturesque way of saying that the individual should reflect not only on the Scriptures, but on God's entire loving relationship with the human family.

Chapter 11 deals with vocal prayer. In Albert's original version, there is a distinction between those who can read, and those who can not. Those who know how to read the psalms "should say those which our holy forefathers laid down, and according to the Church's approved custom" for each of the canonical hours of the monastic day. Those who do not know how to read will say 25 Our Fathers for the night office, except for Sundays and feasts, when the number is doubled to 50. The Our Father is said seven times in the morning, in place of Lauds, and seven times for each of the other hours, except for Vespers, which is celebrated with 15 Our Fathers. What is said here is almost as important as what is not said. The prayer timetable is roughly similar to that of a monastery, but this prayer is offered privately, not in common. It seems more like an around-the-clock vigil than the monastic office. Meeting in the chapel was reserved for the Eucharist, not the hours of the office.

Albert's Rule also assumes that full choir books were not commonly available on Carmel. The monastic orders in their large chapels would normally combine the psalter with readings and other prayers which were proper to the day or the season. But that meant having additional, specialized choir books. The men on Carmel very likely had some copies of the psalter on hand, but not all the other books needed for the full office. The psalter was the most familiar part, since it was repeated over and over each week. Some hermits knew it by heart after a while, so they could replicate much of the office without need of the very heavy and expensive choir books. And so the prayer that ascended from the *wadi* community to God was united in its content, but individualized by the

Simon Stock and the community at prayer. This painting is one of a series by renowned artist Adam Kossowski giving the history of the Carmelite foundation in Aylesford, England. *(Photo courtesy of Carmelite Media)*

solitude of the petitioner.

Policy of Common Life

Chapter 12 reminds the community that they should have no claim on any personal property, but only what they hold in common. The Prior is charged with seeing to it that goods are shared fairly, special attention being given to those with special needs because of age or other circumstances.

We are not certain how many of the original Carmelites would have been priests. It is safe to assume that some of the hermits were ordained, but probably not many. However in Chapter 14, Albert exhorts them to come together in the oratory each morning to celebrate the Eucharist, so there doubtless would have been enough priests to make that regulation possible. There is no other distinction of any sort between priests and brothers. The difference between readers and non-readers seems more significant, indicating that there were probably quite a few who were not literate. Also noteworthy is the daily gathering for Mass, which was unusual for hermits living alone. Daily Eucharist was normal for monks in an established monastery, but not for those leading otherwise detached lives. So this precept must have reflected a very important value for them, and was yet another indication of their determination to combine the spiritual benefits of both solitude and community.

Chapter 15 requires a meeting of the community every Sunday (or whenever necessary) to discuss matters of discipline and spiritual welfare. This gathering

Hermit's cell at the Putri Karmel foundation of Lembah Karmel in Cicanjur, Indonesia. *(Photo courtesy of Carmelite Media)*

was also a time for fraternal correction, which was always to be done lovingly. This Sunday meeting for practical matters highlights the importance of the community as an element of balance. Hermits who keep to themselves for too long can become a bit unbalanced, if not stark raving mad. This very sensible regulation offers the mutual support of the community, so that each individual can go forward on his spiritual path in a healthy way. The call to fraternal correction also enables members of the community to grind down their own rough edges, so that no one becomes too extreme. Here too, we see an example of Albert's experience with the Humiliati working to good advantage.

On the subject of fasting, Albert says in Chapter 16 "You are to fast every day except Sundays, from the feast of the Exaltation of the Holy Cross (September 14), until Easter, unless bodily sickness or feebleness, or some other good reason, demand dispensation from the fast; for necessity overrides every law." What does fasting mean? He does not specify any guideline except common sense. Fasting can be very severe, or simply eating less than one might like. How much or how little is left to the judgment of the individual.

In the original Rule, Chapter 17 establishes abstinence from meat as a permanent condition. In other words, the community in the *wadi* ate a vegetarian diet, whenever possible. Exceptions were possible for the sick and infirm, of course. This regulation was one of the first to be relaxed by the pope.

Spiritual Combat

Chapters 18 and 19 compare the hermit's life to active warfare against evil. In this section, Albert borrows freely from Chapter 6 of Paul's Letter to the Ephesians. The image of the virtues as spiritual armor made good sense to people living in a war zone, especially if some of them were veterans of combat. Chapter 20 recommends physical work as an essential discipline, especially to those who might otherwise allow idleness to lead them into sin.

In Chapter 21, silence is presented as an essential element of contemplation. The original exhortation states that silence helps to keep thoughts clear and uncluttered, and is also a means to foster holiness. Too much idle chatter can block spiritual progress. Depending on the time of day, speaking is either kept to a minimum, or avoided altogether. In Albert's version, the so-called Grand Silence lasted from Vespers until about mid-morning of the following day.

Chapter 22 exhorts the leaders of the community to see themselves as servants of the rest, just as Jesus had taught. By the same token, Chapter 23 tells the other brothers to identify the Prior with the will of Jesus himself, and give loyal service to him. Finally, Chapter 24 encourages all to go beyond the basic obligations, and do even more than is strictly required. Albert concludes with another appeal to common sense as the regulator of not only law, but of virtue as well.

Simplicity of the Rule

As a straightforward formula of life, the Rule draws heavily on words and images from the Bible. Albert uses as many as 150 direct or indirect references to the Scriptures, since in many cases, the Bible would be the only authoritative book many of the hermits had ever seen.

Most of the Rule is self-explanatory. It is simple, direct, adaptable, and benefits from Albert's flexible attitude. His use of phrases like "when this can be done" or "necessity has no law" reveals his faith in common sense and simplicity. Even more important than clear legislation is his sane attitude toward following that legislation. Albert's Rule allowed the community in the *wadi* to structure their simple world. The simplicity of the Rule, with its inherent suppleness, saved much rewriting and revision over the many centuries which followed, when Carmelites found themselves in places and situations never dreamed of in the Holy Land. The flexibility had been there from the first day.

Instead of legalism and rigidity, Albert painted a beautiful icon of prayer, reflection, and concern for God's people. But he also reminded us that, as good as ideals are, even those beautiful ideals are not God. The one true God who cares for his children is best served by calmly seeking his will in silence and awe.

+   +   +

Chapter 2
A Migration Through Cultures

Sicily, 1240. A brisk sea breeze ruffled the beard of the man in the striped cloak. He scuffed his foot on the deck of the cargo ship, as he looked at the pier, piled high with casks and bales of every variety. There were no familiar faces on the waterfront; in fact there were no familiar sights of any kind. He did not remember Trapani looking so shabby, or so unfriendly. He missed the fragrance of the Aleppo pine near his cave in the wadi, and wondered if the pine was still there. Was anything still there? The lean man asked himself whether he really wanted to go ashore at all. Given a choice, he would never have left the wadi, but indeed there had been no choice. And now there was no going back.

The almost idyllic life of the hermits in the wadi was on borrowed time. The heroic efforts to sustain the Crusader kingdoms would fail sooner or later. The small community had to face an unwelcome choice: transfer their way of life to another place, or see it die altogether. In the hot fires of that debate, their resolve to go on was toughened, even if the details of their life together had to be changed. Those changes, even though traumatic, added a fresh, creative energy.

Uncertainty in the *Wadi*

Following the disaster at Hattin in 1187, Jerusalem and most of the Holy Land fell to the armies of Islam. It was only the Third Crusade (1189-92) which restored Acre and the coast to the Christians. The treaty of 1191 between Saladin and English King Richard the Lion Hearted specified that the coastal strip between Tyre and Jaffa would be under Christian control. This zone included the wadi 'Ain es-Siah. By 1229, the Holy Roman Emperor Frederick II had added a corridor between Jaffa and Jerusalem for pilgrims, and had also regained Nazareth and western Galilee. This settlement, sealed by a 10-year truce (1230-40), helped stabilize ordinary life to some extent. Nevertheless, with existence in the wadi and the rest of the Christian territory so uneasy, at best, some community members began to speak of returning to Europe permanently, because of the turmoil.

That option was distasteful to most, since their way of life had recently become a source of great hope. Albert's Rule had been confirmed by Pope Honorius III in 1226, and again by Pope Gregory IX in 1229. Most of the brothers now wore the same style of undyed wool habit, consisting of a tunic with a belt, together with a long scapular over the tunic, and a large hood. Over it all was a large woolen cloak with 7 vertical stripes of alternating bleached and unbleached fabric, a common local fashion. Their small chapel, dedicated to the Virgin Mary, had become a popular landmark for other Christians living in the enclave. The hermits were known locally as the "Brothers of Our Lady on Mount Carmel." Their numbers grew steadily, as their disciplined way of living became more widely known.

Although the dates of foundation are uncertain, the Holy Land Carmelites established houses in both Acre and Tyre, and possibly elsewhere on the mainland. Additional houses were built on Cyprus which was considered an offshore annex to the Crusaders' territory. One of these was a hermitage at Fortamia, established in 1238. Other houses on Cyprus would follow. Even before the expansion of the order to Europe, it was possible to speak of a "Holy Land Province" of houses within the Carmelite family.

Emigration Begins

Meanwhile, traveling back to Europe was relatively simple, since ships docked continually at ports like Acre and Jaffa. The truce of 1230 meant that merchants could resume their commerce in safety, and that pilgrims were again free to visit the places made holy by the presence of Jesus. The Pisans, Genoese and Venetians, ferrying new contingents of crusaders to the Holy Land for a price, did not want to return home with empty space on their ships. Anyone who could pay the price of passage could return to Italy or beyond. Returning to their various homes in Europe was easy enough. But it would be far more difficult to transplant their new way of life, and then to introduce and live it out in the places where they had originated. The hermits who returned from the wadi to Europe were vastly different individuals from the men who had left years earlier.

As early as 1235, it is likely that a hermit named Pierre de Corbie journeyed to the town of Valenciennes in Flanders with a companion. A local merchant gave them land for a church in the tanners' quarter, and they settled there amid the working poor. What a very different place from the wadi! How could they merge one way of life with another?

With the end of the truce in 1240, fighting resumed all along the frontier. An expedition of English knights, led by Richard of Cornwall, brother of King Henry III, landed at Acre in October of that year. In less than a year, he had won back all of Galilee, but then returned home. Some Englishmen from the Carmel community, including Ralph Fresburn (or Fryston), befriended several of his knights and made the journey back to England with them. By Christmas of 1241, the king had quickly granted permission to make foundations. Sir William Vescy, one of those knights, donated land for a hermitage at Hulne, in Northumbria, near the Scottish border. His companion Sir Richard Gray of Codnor endowed a similar settlement at Aylesford in Kent. Hulne was, and remains today, a very remote district, but Aylesford lies east of London, along the pilgrims' road to Canterbury. Like the foundation at Valenciennes, Aylesford made the new arrivals face the hard question of whether their solitary approach to prayer and charity could adapt to busy European conditions. Only a few years later, the same Sir Richard offered the hermits land for a foundation in London itself. His generosity helped bring the whole issue to a significant moment of truth.

Among the other early settlements in Europe, port cities and areas close to them trace the migratory pattern of the earliest Carmelites. Messina in Sicily was probably founded in the 1230's, and Trapani, at the western end of the island, would not be long afterward. A house in Pisa, a principal Italian maritime port, was founded by 1249. French hermits established a hermitage called Les Aygalades, near Marseilles, some time after 1241. St. Louis IX, King of France, returned from his crusades with six Carmelites, and built them a house in Paris in 1254. Whenever possible, these earliest communities built according to the physical layout of the wadi, with a central chapel, and individual cells surrounding it. In imitation of the original foundation, these new chapels were often dedicated to Our Lady of Mount Carmel.

Efforts to Carry On

Even as some of the brothers set off for European ports, life continued in the wadi, bolstered by some active construction. In 1263, Pope Urban IV issued a call for support to build an impressive monastery in the wadi. One immediate result of this request was the construction of a large vaulted room close to the two-chambered prior's cell, together with an expanded chapel, and other walls and chambers still visible today in the ruins. The hermits' friendship with the Knights Templar was very helpful in this construction. The Knights had previously built a small but powerful fortress just south of the wadi. This fort was called 'Atlit, or "Castle of the Pilgrims."

The Templars had already been generous donors to the wadi community, and now they lent their masons to the new project, as well as a liberal quantity of dressed building stone. Even today, it is obvious to the visitor that the impressive walls are built from a type of stone not native to Carmel. Carefully shaped blocks of brilliant white stone exhibit regular mason's marks which perfectly match the construction of 'Atlit's powerful walls. While it is not known whether the walls were ever defended, archers' loopholes bear witness to the ever-present Muslim threat. Sadly for the soldiers of the cross, the military situation had already deteriorated badly.

The expiration of the truce in 1240 had marked the beginning of the end for the crusaders. Jerusalem fell to the Muslim forces again in 1244, due largely to the increasing strength of troops from Egypt. For a brief instant, Christians hoped for military help from a most unlikely source: the Mongols. These terrible and almost unbeatable raiders from Asia had already attacked the Muslim world from the east, where they slaughtered appalling numbers of people in Persia, Syria, and the entire city of Baghdad. But in 1260, a strong Mongol force was stopped in its tracks at Ain Jalut by the Egyptian Mamelukes. This pivotal victory encouraged the Mamelukes to consider themselves invincible, at the same time that their ranks were being swelled by angry refugees from the Mongol depredations. The new Egyptian sultan, Baibars, invaded the Crusaders' state in 1265 with a formidable army. He surprised the defenders of the fortress of Caesarea and the town fell at once. He raced up the coast toward the 'Atlit fortress, which proved to be too strong for him, so Baibars swept past it to maintain his momentum. He found no resistance in the wadi and probably burned most of the flimsy shelters of the hermits. He then went on to destroy the city of Haifa, killing all those who did not flee. By the time he arrived at Acre, he found it well-defended and decided not to attack. So he returned to Egypt in 1268, leaving soldiers to garrison points along the coast.

Although most of the hermits survived to return to their ruined home, they saw how easily they had been turned out of their familiar abode. They might be forced to run for their lives again very soon. A handful tried to resume their former life as though nothing had happened, and prayed for the best. But others undoubtedly saw an urgent need to make their way to safety, and looked elsewhere.

The End on Carmel

Another determined push from Egypt in 1291 sealed the fate of the Crusades forever. The entire coastal strip was occupied by the Muslim forces and Acre fell after a long and bitter siege, with most of the survivors slaughtered. Other coastal cities followed in short order, since they were unable to stand on their own. We are uncertain of the fate of the community on Carmel, but tradition tells us that the surviving hermits were slain together, as they sang God's praises. Those who were able to get away probably fled to the 'Atlit fortress, which once again held open a door for the last survivors. When 'Atlit was evacuated on August 14, the crusading movement was truly at an end, and the burned ruins in the wadi remain desolate and silent to this day.

Problems of Adaptation

The relocation of communities to Europe had been proceeding quickly, but the transfer of an entire way of life proved to be more problematic. European Christians found the newcomers odd and even alien. Their striped cloak was

Gathering of the Carmelites by St. Louis in 1248 (Abholung der Karmeliten durch Ludwig den Heiligen 1248), a fresco by Jörg Ratgeb (1516-1517) in the refectory of the Carmelite monastery in Frankfurt am Main, Germany. Although a story without basis, the scene illustrates the reality of the Carmelites leaving the Holy Land and its eremetical lifestyle for Europe to become mendicants.

a common enough style in the Holy Land, but looked outlandish in Europe, and even became a source of ridicule. The preferred location of communities in desolate places sometimes made them almost invisible. The Rule demanded that they avoid meat in their diet, so even in a harsher climate they continued to eat simple meals in the solitude of their cells. Their prayer had been loosely structured around the Psalms, and seemed out of step with every other religious community, who prayed the full Divine Office. They tried to support themselves by begging, but ordinary working people hesitated to give anything to such strange creatures.

Since the new Carmelite communities were located so far apart, they needed to communicate every few years by general meetings called chapters. The chapter provided a chance to regulate policy and elect superiors. So it was that in 1247, the hermits gathered at a chapter held at Aylesford, England. There they addressed the need to adapt Carmelite life to urban society. At the request of the chapter, Pope Innocent IV assigned two Dominican scholars to help adjust the Carmelite Rule to the new conditions.

Among the sweeping changes which resulted was the permission to make foundations in places other than wasteland (now Chapter 5). The Carmelites would also now eat their meals in a common refectory (Chapter 7) and pray the Canonical Office rather than just the Psalms (Chapter 11). The period of the

Presentation of the Rule to Pope Innocent IV to have it mitigated for life in Europe. Above, Mary is presenting the Brown Scapular to Simon Stock. This painting hangs in the Carmine Maggiore in Naples, Italy *(Photo courtesy of Carmelite Media)*

night silence was shortened. Those who were traveling or begging were allowed to eat meat whenever necessary, and have asses or mules for transportation (Chapter 13). Since all these changes were approved by the pope, this first mitigation of Albert's Rule in 1247 represented a substantial and legally-binding revolution in the order's way of life. But at least for the time being, the reflective tradition of the desert continued to dominate much of the spiritual practice of the transplanted hermits.

Transition to Mendicants

This "minor" legislation, however, was actually a profound change of life. The First Mitigation effectively put the Carmelites on the fast track towards becoming a mendicant order. The mendicants were tremendously popular. They had infused new life into the church with the rebound of cities and the increasing pace of urban life. The first mendicants were Dominicans and Franciscans who had responded to a need to minister to the urban poor on their own terms. Mendicant friars built simple houses and chapels in the towns, and lived alongside merchants, artisans, and the working poor. Unlike monks, whose monasteries were outside the cities in remote places, the friars intended to serve God by serving ordinary people, and living among them. They supported themselves, not by large land holdings, but by begging, or by working as teachers or preachers. Their smaller communities, with a more central organization, were grouped into provinces which gave them greater flexibility and freedom of movement than the large abbey communities. Friars were not bound by vows of stability, and were able to move quickly to meet the needs of the growing towns and those who lived there.

The mendicants had already established a good reputation as skillful preachers, wise confessors, and learned teachers in the new medieval universities. By joining the ranks of the mendicants, Carmelites assured that their way of life would merge into an already popular trend. Much of what made the mendicants so well-liked by the common people was their dynamic style of preaching and their independence from the established parish structure. Sermons often took place outside of Mass, as a sort of spiritual revival. It was not unusual for them to last well over an hour, requiring careful planning and rhetorical skill to hold the attention of the listeners. Mendicants' chapels were normally not parish churches, but alternate sites for confessions, preaching, and devotional prayer. Their piety, learning, and zeal sometimes made them popular enough to draw donations and revenue away from parish priests. It is no surprise that many bishops felt that mendicants needed to be reined in and placed under their own control.

The Struggle for Legality

Twice during the 13th century members of the hierarchy attempted to suppress the mendicant orders at Church councils. But the popularity of the new orders, together with the support of several strong popes, allowed them to survive. At the Fourth Lateran Council (1215), a ban had been issued on the writing of any new rule. From that point on, any new community had to adopt an existing rule, and those who could not do so were to be disbanded. The Second Council of Lyons (1274) repeated the ban on new orders and strengthened its enforcement with the suppression of several mendicant communities which had grown up in spite of the 1215 law.

Although the Dominicans and Franciscans were clearly legal, the Carmelites and Augustinians had only been given provisional approval since the date of their foundation was still in some dispute. Such popular communities as the Pied Friars and Sack Friars were broken up because they could not demonstrate that they had been recognized before 1215. Several of their houses and churches were then transferred to the Carmelites and other surviving orders. The Carmelites also chose this moment to replace their original (and expensive) Palestinian striped mantle with the trademark white cloak of the Pied Friars. The general chapter at Pavia (1284) made a formal request to change the cloak, and the pope agreed. Henceforth, the name White Friars was commonly applied to the sons of Carmel.

Beyond mere legal survival, however, was the issue of the Order's purpose and mission. The original motivating force of the crusade-driven hermits had been spiritual combat with the Evil One, as chapters 18 and 19 of the Rule attest. But under their new living conditions, the needs of neighboring people in the towns had a way of becoming the principal focus of their activity, and the old eremitical practices of silence and solitude were likely to become neglected and all but forgotten. To the 13th century mind, there was no conflict between contemplation and active ministry, since a religious needed to engage in both of them. Everyone assumed that a pious Christian could go out to the desert to pray and contemplate, but then returned to the city to serve the needs of others.

Even on the slopes of Carmel, there had been occasional ministry to outsiders, but the balance there had been heavily weighted in favor of silent prayer. It is important to remember that this new transition toward apostolic activity was gradual, and not at all premeditated. But the transition was very real indeed, and needed to be addressed sooner or later.

Chapters and Constitutions

Albert's original Rule had been crafted for a single community, in a well-established location, with a single elected prior. The dispersion of old and new hermits to so many new places meant that communication between communities had to take another form, and that the Rule's basic principles had to somehow be applied to circumstances that no one had foreseen. To a certain extent, the regular gathering of the General Chapters took care of some of that communication. Another fairly simple expedient was the devolution of leadership among local, provincial, and general superiors. Each local community continued to have its own prior, but these communities were grouped into regional or national provinces, led by an elected provincial prior. The general prior of the entire order was selected by representatives of each of the provinces when they met every few years at the General Chapter. It was no longer assumed that a general should be elected for life, but for a specified term of office, and possibly more than one term.

Another principal function of the General Chapter was the publication and revision of "Constitutions," regulations which attempted to apply the Rule to the actual circumstances of community life. Throughout the 13th century, the constitutions were revised nearly every time a Chapter met, indicating the great concern over being faithful to founding principles despite the turmoil of the times. The constitutions of 1281 are the oldest which still exist, although we know at least partial contents of earlier ones from other sources. For that matter, there are no surviving copies of the original version of the Rule, as it was composed by Albert. That document would have to be carefully reconstructed by later scholars, using fragments and secondary sources.

The earliest touchstone issue was whether or not the Carmelites were to remain primarily hermits, with the rugged virtues of the desert community, but no practical need for more formal education in the ways of city life. Or should they merge into the mendicant mainstream, retaining only lip service to a ceremonial memory of their past life in the wadi. Was the "desert" of Carmel an **attitude** behind the way their ministry was carried out, or an actual physical **place** of prayer and solitude? At the outset, the "desert" was generally accepted as a true place of quiet seclusion, but the trend had swung toward urban ministry and scholarship by about 1300.

As yet there was no formal program of studies or religious formation, even though the other mendicants were already engaging with the great universities. Most of the earliest communities of Carmelites struggled to maintain in-

Fresco of St. Albert of Sicily and St. Angelus accompanying Mary and Christ Child. The fresco, in the Carmelite sanctuary in San Felice del Benaco, Italy, dates to the 1400's. *(Photo courtesy of Carmelite Media)*

dividual cells at some distance from one another, but some allowed personal cubicles within a single building. The rapid growth in both new houses and new members meant that, after a few decades, only a small sprinkling of the old hermits from the wadi remained within the much larger Carmelite family. We can assume that the novices were enthusiastic in embracing their new way of life, but not altogether certain of how to be faithful to its fundamental ideals. But the physical presence within a town usually meant active engagement with the affairs of that town. So the end result was a trend toward vigorous ministry, at the expense of silence and solitude. The sequence of Carmelite saints reflects this transition. Those before about 1300 are austere solitaries; those afterward were talented leaders, scholars and preachers.

Drawing of St. Albert and St. Angelus with St. Ann, the mother of Mary, holding Mary and Jesus in her lap. This drawing is conserved in the Bamberg Library *(Photo courtesy of Rafael Leiva, O. Carm.)*

Early Saints

The earliest named holy men of this period, Angelus and Albert, both from Sicily, are very much transplanted hermits. Reliable details are hard to come by, as they are in most stories from this age. Angelus is known as a saintly and austere figure who was martyred near Licata. There is a legend that he met personally with both Francis and Dominic, but that legend is impossible to verify. Alberto degli Abbati lived at Trapani, and was celebrated among local people for his holy life, wise preaching, and healing of the sick. He probably died about 1307. Yet another rough account tells of Franco of Siena, a former soldier who lived the last years of his long life as a repentant sinner, dying about 1291. It is likely that he was an early lay affiliate of the Order, but one who never professed vows. These shadowy figures are real people, but details of their lives are so obscure that it is nearly impossible to distinguish fact from legend.

Another hermit launched the most famous challenge to the drift toward towns and cities. He was Nicholas "the Frenchman" of Narbonne, who was prior general from 1266 to 1271. His passionate treatise was entitled *The Flaming Arrow* (*Ignea Sagitta*), and appeared in 1270. It is a call to abandon the distractions of the modern city for that life with God which the desert represents. He does not criticize the apostolic ministry as such, only those who blunder into it without the solid preparation which flows from a well-founded spirituality.

Nicholas points out that preaching, confessing, and advising are serious tasks, which demand a distinctive spiritual maturity which can only come from study and prayer. Any individual who assumes that he can dispense spiritual pearls simply because he wears a religious habit is acting irresponsibly. Serious and conscientious care of God's people must flow from the unique character of a Carmelite: one who struggles with God in seclusion. He loses no opportunity to pillory those who spout folly amid many words, yet have nothing substantial behind their brave façade. The mature Carmelite must return first to the desert, where everything speaks of God, and not assume that the citadel of Carmel is the walled town. For Nicholas, ministry is indeed a good thing, but only when it rests on the spiritual grounding which Elijah's mountain represents.

A Search for Roots

Nicholas was heard with respect, but his words did not halt the headlong move toward the cities. There may have been a brief reevaluation of the impetuous rush into the active life, and the value of quiet contemplation as a source of apostolic strength. The Constitutions of 1281 repeat the recommendation of solitary cells in all foundations, but that guideline is gone by the end of the century. The call to identity which Nicholas voiced also had an immediate effect. Most agreed that Carmelites should be seen as a distinct group, and not just one more gathering of mendicants. This stance presented a problem, however, since most other orders could name their founders, and point to a firm date of establishment. The hermits from the slopes of Carmel could do no such thing, since their coming together was as close to a spontaneous foundation as one can imagine. Elijah was indeed the inspiration for their movement, but any actual chronological connection with the fiery prophet remained very vague indeed.

This perceived deficiency led to a decision, late in the 13th century, to introduce a section to the constitutions explaining the origin and mission of the Carmelite tradition. This so-called *Rubrica Prima* became a fixture in subsequent constitutions, and the root of the rich Elian legend which sprang up in much later writing.

Certain Brothers, new in the Order, do not know exactly how to answer those who ask, from whom, when, and how our Order took birth, or else why we are called: Brothers of the Order of Blessed Mary of Mount Carmel. So we wish to recommend the way for them to reply in suitable words.

In order to witness to the truth we say that from the time of the prophets Elijah and Elisha, pious dwellers on Mount Carmel, Holy Fathers of the Old and New Testament, intensely fond of this solitary Mount for the sake of contemplation, lived there unquestionably in a praiseworthy manner, near the fountain of Elijah while observing a holy penitential life which they continued unremittingly with saintly progress.

Their successors, after Christ's Incarnation, built a church there in honor of the Blessed Virgin Mary, took her for their patroness and from that time forward called themselves by apostolic privilege: Brothers of the Blessed Virgin of Mount Carmel.

Albert, Patriarch of the Church of Jerusalem, gathered them together into one family, writing for them, before the Lateran Council, a Rule which was afterwards approved by the Sovereign Pontiffs who piously confirmed it, their bulls giving proof of this.

It is in this profession that we, the descendants of these Fathers serve the Lord to this present day, in different parts of the world.

The text implies that those who found their way to the wadi during the crusading period were joining a much older, and well established,

Nicholas of Narbonne from a book of sketches of each Carmelite Prior General. The book was compiled by Carmelite historian Marianus Ventimiglia in 1773 and republished in a facsimile edition in 1923.

tradition of prayer in that same place. That tradition itself, rather than a precise individual, is seen as a "founder" of the Carmelite way of life. Insofar as that tradition is seen as informal, it might indeed have merit. But the many later attempts to fill in specific details, and even to trace an unbroken line of succession from Elijah to Brocard, are difficult to accept, and even harder to demonstrate.

Early Leaders

Apart from historical fantasy, it is difficult enough to list the real leaders of the period immediately after Albert's Rule. A prior general named Godfrey was probably the leader from at least 1249, but maybe even earlier. His immediate successor was most likely an Englishman named Simon, known to history as Simon Stock. Simon was probably elected at the London chapter of 1254. Therefore he was not the one who requested the first mitigation in 1247, although he certainly might have been a member of that earlier chapter. By all accounts, Simon led a very holy life and promoted prayer among the communities, especially a love for Mary as patroness of the Order. He died in 1266 while visiting the newly founded Carmelite house at Bordeaux, and was buried in their chapel in that city.

Simon Stock is commonly associated with the use of the Carmelite scapular as a

symbol of dedication to Mary. That may be entirely correct, even if there is little evidence to support it. But it is also possible to conclude from the existing documents that the devotion began with another devout Simon, a holy Carmelite, but who was not prior general at all. In any case, it was not until a century later that the scapular devotion developed into a popular and widespread religious observance.

Simon was succeeded by Nicholas of Narbonne (the one called the Frenchman, mentioned earlier). He saw himself primarily as a motivator and a symbol of unity for the increasingly diverse order. He presided over the chapter of 1269 at Messina, which included members of the Holy Land province from Acre. The obvious anxiety about the safety of those heroic hold-outs also highlighted the concern for the future of those who had moved to Europe. For Nicholas, only the strict observance of the hermits' virtues could (or should) assure a happy future for the struggling community. After the publication of his *Flaming Arrow*, Nicholas seems to have become increasingly frustrated, and resigned in 1271, in order to retire to his beloved seclusion. In his own mind, Nicholas probably felt great discouragement at his inability to halt the transformation of his eremitical brotherhood into a busy mendicant order. Yet throughout the industrious times that followed, the spiritual stance of the Carmelites would continue to be that of the desert…that place of stark silence and utter dependence on God for everything. Nicholas must receive at least part of the credit for that enduring theme. He certainly merits the reward set aside for those who are faithful even in times of trial and frustration.

The generals for the remainder of the century were solid and resolute men, genuine hermits, who guided the growth and adaptation of the new community to European towns. Nicholas was followed by Ralph, an Englishman who may be the same Ralph Fresburn who helped to found the hermitage at Hulne. Peter of Millau was a Frenchman who presided over the dramatic transition to the medieval universities, and attended the pivotal Second Council of Lyons (1274), where he probably had to defend the Carmelites against suppression, since Albert's Rule was accepted before 1215. Yet he never abandoned his great simplicity of life and his contemplative comportment. He was followed by Raymond de l'Ile, also noted for his spiritual manner and love for contemplation, a hermit at heart. It seems that each of the generals during the 13th century came from a contemplative background, and lived out a strong spirituality in spite of all other demands. The changeover from hermits to friars was not accomplished without struggle and uncertainty, nor was it done quickly. But the transition proceeded with remarkable success, judging from the popularity and growth of this novel religious family.

Status after the Crusades

By 1300, there were 150 houses, divided among 12 distinct provinces. The Holy Land province, by this time, represented only the communities on Cyprus, since those in Acre, Tyre, and the wadi of Mount Carmel had all been lost.

The province of Sicily represented a significant number of communities on that large island and in southern Italy. The province of Tuscany included Pisa, Rome, and others in central Italy, while the new province of Lombardy covered the north. In France, Provence embraced the many houses in the south, Aquitaine the west, and Francia the center-north. A recent partition had divided Upper (Alpine and southern) Germany from Lower (Rhineland and northern) Germany. England remained a single province, but a very large one, providing a good source of energy and leadership. The new province of Scotland and Ireland had recently detached the communities in the Celtic speaking regions. Finally, the province of Spain was largely confined to Catalonia and the north at this stage. Although it is tempting to speculate about how many friars there might have been, there are no reliable records to tell us. Still, the number had to be considerable to allow 150 viable communities to flourish.

Another important development which made this growth possible was the entry of the Carmelites into the flourishing universities in Paris and elsewhere. Nicholas of Narbonne had complained about the poor quality of preparation and scholarship among his brothers. It was just about the time that he resigned that local superiors were beginning to send their students to schools where they might benefit from a better quality of formation and intellectual development. By 1281, the general chapter held at London set out guidelines for central houses of studies in scripture, philosophy, theology, and other worthy learning. The earliest *studium generale* was to be in Paris, which always remained the most important center of learning. By 1291, other houses of study were established at Toulouse, Montpellier, Cologne, and London. Within a very few years, others followed at Bologna, Florence, Avignon, and other places. Each province was expected to set aside members for advanced studies, including those among the best and brightest who would go to Paris. These friar-scholars were encouraged to speak Latin fluently, so that their national origin would not be a barrier to the formation of an international circle of avid learners. Provinces were urged to send more than just the minimum numbers of students, if they could, and to help support those who might be less fortunate. A special prior was to be appointed for the students, and a high intellectual character was to be encouraged alongside the prayer and community duties.

It is natural that as soon as these students received their academic decrees, some of them would move off to preaching and writing, but others would remain at the houses of study to teach the next students in sequence. So it was in Paris and elsewhere that masters and doctors of theology and related studies became important contributors to the life of their communities.

Since they came somewhat belatedly to the universities, these scholars never developed a specific Carmelite "school" of theology, but remained free to play a more eclectic role in adopting the ideas of Dominicans, Franciscans, Augustinians, or others. Yet there were soon to be some very fine and original thinkers from the ranks of the White Friars, as we will see. The dramatic success of the program of studies in Paris forced the move in 1319 to a newer and much larger house at Place Maubert in the heart of the University district.

One event signaled a representative watershed in the trend toward advanced studies: the general chapter at Bruges (1297) elected Gerard of Bologna to be the next prior general. Gerard was one of the best of those early new scholars, having only earned his doctorate in theology at Paris two years before. The next century would certainly have a different flavor from the one that was just ending.

+ + +

Chapter 3
Roots and Branches

London, 1300. The sandy-haired student stumbled through the rubbish accumulated on the street corner, barely holding onto his bundle of stiff papers. He was always embarrassed when he was late for a lecture, but he just could not get away in time. The older friar had been grumbling about all the noise the students made in the corridors, and he had to listen long enough to be polite. Actually, he didn't feel they'd been all that loud, especially since they had so much to be excited about. Had they really disturbed anyone's recollection? He was sure that learning good theology and good preaching would make a much bigger impact. Wouldn't it?

From about 1300 onward, Carmelites entered the life in towns and cities with great fervor. Their popularity as preachers and confessors had overcome the initial uncertainty of many townsfolk. Their obvious connection to Mary matched the piety of most medieval working people. And their simple living habits made them easy to approach, since they never seemed to act as though they were "above" the status of a smith or a baker.

City Life

The typical Carmelite house in a 14th century city might be arranged around a large hollow courtyard. It could be a pleasant, colonnaded cloister walk, sometimes with a lush garden, a fountain, or a small pool in the center. The courtyard was designed to be an enclosed place of tranquility, symbolizing spiritual refreshment. On one side of the courtyard was the main church, facing toward the east. Most churches combined the nave area for the general public with a large choir section for members of the community behind or beside the main altar. This choir segment was very likely to be a busy place, since the community assembled frequently there for prayer, both day and night. Each friar would likely have an assigned place in one of the choir stalls, which grew to be a sort of spiritual "home." Choir books there would be in constant use, and were certainly among the most highly valued of the community's possessions.

Along another side of the cloister yard would probably be the refectory, where the community members ate together at long tables, either in silence or listening to reading from the Rule, the Bible, or some other spiritual book. There was some sort of podium or book stand for the reader. Nearby rooms were used for storing, preparing, and serving the food, as well as others for washing and storing dishes. But the actual kitchen might be more remote, or even detached, because of the danger of fire. If space permitted, gardens for fresh fruit and vegetables could be located nearby, and even shelters for poultry or livestock. A meatless diet was still the norm, but animals could provide eggs and milk, and sometimes meat for those whose health made it necessary. When appropriate, there might also be outbuildings for producing butter and cheese.

On yet another side of the cloister, there was probably a large chapter room or assembly hall. Community meetings were mandated by the Rule for Sundays or whenever needed. The chapter hall allowed the community to assemble for extended conferences or discussions without closing the chapel to use by people from the neighborhood. Other large rooms on the ground floor might include a library or an infirmary. In a few cases, there might be a separate wing added onto the main house as a novitiate annex with cells and classrooms for the formation of new candidates.

Most of the cells for members of the community would be grouped together in a single section, often on the upper floor above the common rooms. The shortage of space within a walled town usually meant that a house could only expand in one direction, by adding another floor. Even after the move to the cities, cells continued to be distinct and separate for each friar, but sometimes not as silent or private as a dedicated contemplative might wish.

Most of the time, the cell of the prior continued to be located near the main entrance, in harmony with the Rule. There was almost always a brother whose main job was to watch over the front door, which became increasingly busy in the new urban setting. There were usually parlors and visiting rooms located near the door, so that outsiders did not have to enter into the areas set aside for the community. But even with all these precautions, the noise and activity of any medieval city had a way of penetrating to the innermost heart of a religious house. The friar who wanted to keep himself free from all distraction in the heart of a town had to make a much greater effort to do so than one on a quiet mountain top.

Studies and Scholars

Formation of candidates in any Carmelite community included classes in religious studies, philosophy, logic, ethics, and the effective use of the language. The novitiate year focused on the spiritual traditions of the Order, with its

Carmelite Cloister in Florence, Italy-- a typical design containing a large courtyard with a pleasant, colonnaded cloister walk, sometimes with a lush garden, and a fountain in the center. The courtyard provided an enclosed place of tranquility, symbolizing spiritual refreshment. *(Photo courtesy of Carmelite Media)*

proper liturgy and style of prayer. Those who went on to more advanced scholarship spent another four years studying philosophical and theological principles, and their application to practical cases. These "bachelors" would spend much of their time debating with one another, and teaching basic principles to less advanced scholars. Another two years of biblical study could follow, and still another two years of debating and teaching the interpretations of authorities. The entry of the Carmelites into the world of the medieval universities meant that their improved educations would enable them to enter into the social and political life of their times, in both secular and religious realms. They would be better prepared to act as eloquent preachers or wise confessors. It also allowed some Carmelites to remain in academic work, where they became first rate theologians, philosophers, and spiritual writers.

Gerard of Bologna, the doctor of theology who was elected prior general in 1297, is representative of this transformation. Gerard guided the order competently for the next 20 years, but still continued his intellectual life, writing on a wide variety of theological topics. He also attended the Council of Vienne (1311-12) and advised King Philip IV of France. He was one of the theologians consulted by the cardinals about the Spiritual Franciscans and their radical approach to evangelical poverty, and even to the mere ownership of private property. Gerard was joined in this dialogue by two other first rate Carmelite

Painting of John Baconthorpe in the lavishly decorated library of the Carmelite house in Krakow, Poland. *(Photo courtesy of Carmelite Media)*

theologians, Augier de Spuento, provincial of Provence, and Guy Terreni, from Perpignan. Guy succeeded Gerard as prior general in 1318.

Another superb thinker from this early circle was the English theologian John Baconthorpe. John has been compared to Duns Scotus for his keen mind and his highly critical attitude toward philosophical and theological nuances. He seemed to see connections where no one else could see them, and to make distinctions in an argument which led to a clear and speedy solution. Like most other Carmelites, John took special interest in Marian theology. He often refers to Mary as a "sister" to the Carmelites. To him, the simplicity of the young woman of Nazareth -- her prayer, silence, and solitude even before the angel's visit -- resembled the life style of the hermits in the wadi.

Although it may not have been an original thought of his, John is probably the first Carmelite writer to connect Elijah's little cloud with Mary. In the passage of 1 Kings 18:44, a small rain cloud rises from the sea, and grows into the abundant downpour which ends the drought and replenishes the fruits of the earth. Through the eyes of faith, John sees a pre-figure of Mary in the small and light cloud, since she was both humble, and free of the weight of sin. Her son released floods of grace and forgiveness for sinful humanity.

John also joined in the vigorous debate about the Immaculate Conception of Mary. Although he started as an opponent of that teaching, the more he reflected, studied, and argued against it, the more he became attracted to it. In the end, he became a strong backer of the belief that Mary had been conceived without any taint of original sin. And like so many of his brothers, he felt that the finest tribute he could offer to Mary was imitation of her virtues: her obedience, poverty, prayerfulness, and especially her chastity.

It was during this same period that the distinctive Carmelite liturgy was standardized according to the Rite of the Holy Sepulcher in Jerusalem. In 1312, Sibert de Beka published a special Ordinal, a liturgical book which governed the proper antiphons, psalms, and scripture readings for each day of the liturgical year. The Jerusalem Rite was a remnant of the crusading period, adapted from the old Gallican Rite once used in Paris and northern France. Because of its relocation to the Sepulcher in Jerusalem, the rite also took on special emphasis on the Resurrection of Jesus. The Carmelites had retained this link with the Holy Land, both as a distinctive feature of their heritage, and also because of the large number of special Marian feasts, including the Immaculate Conception. Carmelites continued to use this special rite until after Vatican II.

Saints and Writers

Among the most noted saints of this century are two who served the Church as members of the hierarchy, Andrew Corsini, and Peter Thomas. They differed from the pervious century's heroes in the degree of their sophistication, education, and polish. Both served their own local communities so well that the popes asked them to go further.

Andrew, a noble Florentine who joined the Tuscan province, proved to be both scholarly and saintly. He taught theology in the *studium generale*, and was named provincial at just the time when the Black Death struck Italy. The records list more than a hundred dead in the Tuscan province. In 1350, Andrew was named bishop of Fiesole, a scenic town in the mountains above Florence. In an age when many bishops saw themselves as princes entitled to live in luxury, Andrew — who actually came from a noble family — chose to live like a friar, simply and frugally. The new bishop dedicated himself to being a true spiritual father to his people. He visited every corner of his diocese, hearing people's concerns and encouraging his priests to live holy and disciplined lives. Andrew showed special care for the poor and the sick. He was a good preacher, and paid special attention to the quality of liturgy in his cathedral. With money from his own pocket, he repaired the cathedral and many other churches. He was also a good administrator, who gave jobs only to those qualified for them, and worked to eliminate corruption among church employees. When Andrew died in 1374, he was buried in the church of the Carmine in Florence.

Peter Thomas proved to be a heroic saint of a different sort. He came from Bergerac in western France, joined the province of Aquitaine, and proved to be a brilliant university student in Paris. As he worked toward earning a doctorate in theology, he was nominated to be Procurator General in 1345, which meant that he was primarily a liaison between the Carmelites and the pope's curia in Avignon. His success in this office led to his appointment to a series of diplomatic missions for the pope. In 1353, he served as a peacemaker between Genoa and Venice, and also between Pope Innocent VI and the King of Naples. He was then sent to Stefan Dushan, King of Serbia, where he negotiated a reunion between the Serbian and Roman churches. The rest of his life was dedicated to a series of deputations to Constantinople, where he labored mightily to reconcile theological differences with the Greek Church, and to build an alliance to halt the military advances of the Ottoman Turks. Although he made only moderate gains toward these overwhelming goals, he drew great admiration and esteem among the eastern Christians because of his simple spirituality. The Byzantine Emperor John V, Paleologos, did in fact declare his loyalty to the pope, and a desire for complete union, but the Patriarch and most other Greek bishops still found too many obstacles to a comprehensive reconciliation.

Peter Thomas pressed for an alliance of Christian states to seize Alexandria in Egypt. By 1364, he had assembled forces from Venice, Cyprus, and the Knights of St. John to join the Byzantine and Papal contingents in a grand alliance for a military campaign, but it never reached the strength of a serious crusade. Although greatly disappointed, Peter Thomas vowed to struggle on. Death prevented him from doing so, however, and he was buried in the Carmelite church at Famagusta on Cyprus. Even constant travel and frequent illness never kept him from his prayer. His simplicity enabled him to speak easily with any-one, including rough soldiers and sailors. And yet, he remained a diplomat of the first quality. Throughout his life, his sincere love of peace melted a great deal of entrenched prejudice and hostility. Shortly before his death in 1366, the pope named him Archbishop of Crete, Special Legate, and Latin Patriarch of Constantinople.

An entirely different sort of scholar emerged in Germany about the same time. John of Hildesheim was a well-regarded member of the Lower German prov-ince who studied at both Avignon (where he was a pupil of Peter Thomas) and at Paris. In addition to several works on Carmelite history and traditions, he wrote one of the most popular books of the middle ages. His *History of the Three Magi* assembled all of the stories, legends, and fables he could find about the wise men of the Nativity story. John skillfully blended them into a readable saga, together with details of ordinary life and customs in the lands of the ex-otic East, and even some of his own devout reflections on the meaning of the Son of God's birth into the human race. He died in 1375.

The *Institution* and Carmelite Ideals

Even though more than a century had passed since the migration of the first hermits from the Holy Land to Europe, there was still a sense of unresolved identity in the Carmelite family. The shadowy origins of their desert spirituality did not seem to match the mendicant institutions which they had adopted. It may have been the seeming lack of a personal founder which led Philip Ribot, provincial of Catalonia, to produce a very significant work about 1380.

Philip was searching for documentation of the earliest roots of Carmelite spiri-tuality, hoping to compile a practical manual of formation for new candidates. In his quest for the origins and development of the Order, he might have want-ed to enhance the *Rubrica Prima* of the 1200s, which urged the Carmelites to identify with their long prophetic tradition at a time when they were already firmly committed to the mendicant life. He incorporated and developed earlier legends which articulated the inner spirit and character of the Order. The final outcome was a key work which became second only to the Rule as the principal spiritual reading of Carmelites until the 17th century.

Ribot fashioned an interesting product which he presented as a compendium of documents. There were ten "books" in all, which traced Carmel's earliest ideals. The first seven books were described as a single work in Greek, entitled

St. Peter Thomas— bishop, papal legate, peacemaker— in the Carmelite habit with the wide-brimmed hat he wore on his incessant journeys and praying the breviary he recited every day. The work, by the artist Francisco de Zurbarán (1598-1664) now hangs in the Museum of Fine Arts in Boston.

The Institution of the First Monks, written in 412 by John XLIV, bishop of Jerusalem. Beginning with the story of Elijah, the relentless search for a personal liaison with a powerful and loving God is traced through centuries of Hebrew and Greek tradition, until it culminates in the writing of Albert's Rule. The other three books cite shorter documents: a letter of Cyril, prior general (1221-4) speaking of the previous work, a treatise by Sibert de Beka explaining the changes to the Rule in 1247, and the chronicle of William of Sanvico, provincial of the Holy Land in 1291, and a survivor of the final massacre on Carmel. Ribot concludes with a final series of authentic papal documents praising the history and heritage of the Carmelites.

In actual fact, these documents have very little historical credibility, except for the essay of Sibert de Beka, who was an excellent scholar. Philip Ribot was far more than an editor and commentator, since he either collected documents of suspicious origin, or fabricated them himself. The true value of these manuscripts is not in their historical veracity, but in how clearly they present the aspirations of the Carmelite style of contemplation.

In the first book of the *Institution*, the Elijah story from the First Book of Kings forms the foundation of Carmel's prophetic vocation. The twin objectives of the prophet-hermit are first, to arrive at a holy heart, free of actual sin, by his own labor and virtuous action, aided by God's grace; and then, in the second phase, to savor God's presence in his heart and mind, a free gift bestowed by God. In the story (1 Kings 17: 2-4), God tells Elijah to "leave here, turn eastward and hide by the wadi Cherith, east of the Jordan." That passage is interpreted as a command to renounce earthly possessions, fight temptations of the flesh, and flee urban sinfulness, in order to grow in love for God and neighbor. The story continues as God says "you will drink from the brook, and I have ordered the ravens to feed you there." This is seen as God's promise to reveal himself to the soul of Elijah, as he continues his hermit's life of single-mindedness.

Building upon this significant foundation, books two through five trace an imaginative history of the Carmelites after Elijah, through the rest of the Old Testament and the first thousand years of the Christian era. Elijah forms a band of faithful followers whom he teaches to pray, and who do good for others as they flee Jezebel's persecution. Elisha and the company of the prophets continue their tradition in the desert through the next centuries, and are spared exile to Babylon because of their faithfulness to God's will. John the Baptist turns the sons of Carmel toward Jesus and they follow him. After Pentecost, they hear Peter's words and are baptized as committed Christians. They continue their preaching and prayer in the Holy Land throughout the following centuries. Book six connects the band of hermits with Mary, who had already been revealed to Elijah in his vision of the little cloud (1 Kings 18:42-4). After the ascension of Jesus, the Carmelites recognize and honor Mary as their spiritual sister and patroness, and build a place of prayer in her honor. Finally, book seven speaks of the Carmelite habit as their sign of dedication to God, especially the scapular as a symbol of their obedience. The scapular did not take on its formal connection with Mary until the following century.

Thus both Elijah and Mary are considered, not so much as historical figures, but as icons of the Carmelite self-understanding. Both were attentive and open to God, with hearts not bound by any idolatry. Both longed to experience God's presence in their lives, and both did in fact receive it. The *Institution* story includes a tradition that Elijah was the first man, and Mary was the first woman, to take a vow of virginity. In both cases, their actions and words renounced worldly values so that they could unite their hearts with God in perfect love. In turn, God allowed them to experience the intensity of his presence, even in this life. By emptying themselves of any other worldly attachments, they remained free to be filled with the love of God himself. Ribot really has little of merit to say about the biblical Elijah and Mary, but quite a lot about Carmelites. Although the *Institution* is bad history, it remains a good and careful delineation of Carmel's contemplative spirit, based on Elijah's prophetic vocation.

Carmel's Appeal

Unlike many other religious orders, the Carmelites still had no official structure for women. Benedict, Dominic, and Francis all established groups of women to follow their respective rules from the very beginning, but the hermits from the wadi did not. It was only after the mid-15th century that women were welcomed to join the Carmelite family. Before that time, there were certainly individual women (and men as well) who chose to connect themselves to an existing Carmel without formal vows, and to follow its traditions of prayer and simple living. Often they would receive spiritual direction from the friars, and sometimes would wear some variation of the Carmelite habit.

One such noteworthy person was Joan of Toulouse, who may have been a noblewoman from Navarre. Toward the end of the 14th century, she lived in a plain shelter alongside the Carmelite house in Toulouse as a "conversa," one who had "converted" or turned her life around toward a spiritual path. By all accounts, Joan was a pious woman who shared her religious insights with the friars and prayed for them constantly. Her way of life was austere: she ate little, slept on the ground, and wore very rough clothing resembling that of the Carmelites. She had no formal ministry, other than her prayerful support of the community, but her encouragement had a very good effect, especially on the younger friars. It seems that Joan died near the end of the 14th century. There are also reports of another woman named Anne of Toulouse who followed a similar life in the same city. Details of her existence are sketchy, but she may be typical of many other unknown holy collaborators.

Although the Carmelites continued to expand throughout Europe in the 14th century, their greatest concentration was in the South of France. Eventually there would be eight French-speaking provinces, and five of these were in the southern regions. It was during that same period that the official residence of the popes moved to Avignon, along the Rhône River. Between 1309 and 1378, a total of seven popes, all of them French, lived in southern France, all the while continuing to proclaim their desire to return to Rome. Carmelite generals also lived at Avignon during the same time, and frequently got on well with the Papal court. Most of these superiors were either French or Catalonian.

The Plague

It was during the mid-fourteenth century that the Carmelites — along with the rest of Europe — suffered the devastation of the Black Death. The plague came from the East on the same sort of commercial ships that had carried the earliest hermits back from the Holy Land. Beginning in Sicily, it traveled relentlessly northward and westward from 1348 until 1351, when it died out in Scandinavia. It is estimated that one third to one half of the population of Europe may have died from this mysterious illness. The percentage of victims among the clergy was almost certainly higher, since religious were charged with care of the sick, and because religious communities lived closely enough together in their houses to quicken the spread of the infestation.

Carmelite records list 200 friars as having died at the 1348 general chapter in Metz, or during their travel to or from the chapter. Andrew Corsini's Tuscan province lost over 100 members. All the clerical students at Toulouse died. The single house at Avignon lost 66 members from its community. English provincial Thomas Netter later reported that 24 friars died of plague in London during a single year. Other communities must have suffered similar losses, but the records are very uneven about the reporting of details. We are reminded of situations during the plague when entire villages vanished, with no one left to recount the ghastly story or bury the dead.

As a result of the sudden shortage of members, there was a subtle pressure to fill the gaps with less qualified people, or by rushing new candidates through their formation and education too quickly. Within the Carmelite sphere -- as in the Church at large -- pressure mounted to fill important posts with preachers, teachers and superiors who lacked the high qualifications and competence that had been demanded only a few years earlier. Serious study may have seemed like an unnecessary luxury, and was sometimes waived or dispensed entirely. Although the bubonic plague occurred well over a century and a half before the

Reformation, it still remains one of its principal remote causes.

The Horrors of War

Less dramatic than the plague, but more relentless, was the danger of warfare in the countryside. Perhaps one third of the 90 Carmelite houses in France were destroyed during the Hundred Years War between England and France (1337-1453). That long, intermittent conflict grew out of the weakness of the French royal family, and the willingness of several English monarchs to challenge them for the French crown. In theory, an English king owed allegiance to his French overlord because of his title of Duke of Normandy. But the incompetence of French leadership often led to war, wreaking havoc on civilians on both sides. Countless other local conflicts, especially in Germany and Italy, took their toll on churches and priories of the Order. Isolated houses were easy prey for a marauding army. Foundations within a town's walls might be damaged during a prolonged siege or even demolished by defenders to build new ramparts. Many of these houses were rebuilt, but not all.

The Western Schism

In 1378, the last of the Avignon popes, Gregory XI, decided to return to Rome just before he died. Most of the cardinals who assembled to elect his successor were French. But the angry Romans who assembled outside of their conclave loudly demanded that an Italian be chosen, and the pressure on the cardinals took on the added threat of violence. Under considerable duress, they chose an Italian, Urban VI, who almost immediately revealed himself as an angry and cantankerous bully. Although the cardinals had acted legally, they decided that they had made a mistake, and elected another Frenchman, who took the name Clement VII, and returned to Avignon claiming to be the only true pope of the universal Church. This was the opening round in the sorry episode known as the Western Schism (1378-1417). Here, as in the case of many medieval wars, the breakdown of generous and highly principled leadership led to disaster.

As if the situation of having two popes were not outlandish enough, it was worsened by the stubbornness on both sides and an unwillingness to compromise or admit any blame. Secular rulers took sides in the dispute, largely based on political considerations. Within a few years, the states of western Christendom and most of their citizens were sharply polarized over which claimant they believed was the true vicar of Christ on earth. In general terms, the states in Italy, Germany, England, and Scandinavia favored Rome, while France, Spain, Naples, and Scotland supported Avignon. Both popes excommunicated one another and their supporters, and created fresh numbers of cardinals, who elected their successors when they died. Both factions counted great saints and humble believers who trusted the popes to be what they claimed to be. But even among the most devoted supporters, patience began to wear thin as worldly prelates acted more like buffoons and swindlers than holy successors to the apostles.

The Carmelite church in Avignon. The Carmelites first went to Avignon in 1267 with the church serving as the General Curia during the Avignon papacy (1308-1377) and then of the Avignon Priors General during the Western Schism (1378-1415). The Carmelites remained there until the French Revolution suppressed all religious orders. This church building survived because it was the headquarters of the Jacobins during the French Revolution. Today it is the parish church of St. Symphorien although it is still commonly known as "the Carmelite Church." *(Photo courtesy of Patrick McMahon, O. Carm.)*

Most of the religious orders were surprised and confused by this exceptional state of affairs, and tried to maintain their integrity until the situation was resolved. The Carmelite general in 1378 was Bernard Oller, a former provincial of Provence living at Avignon, who tended to support Clement VII who was in residence there. Bernard tried to maintain the unity of the Order in the face of intense pressure to take sides. Clement ordered him to punish the Italian provinces that recognized Urban, but he failed to do so. The general chapter at Bruges in 1379 was a unified assembly of all provinces, but that would be the last one for a while. Already the communities of several houses were requesting separation from a province which did not match their preferred affiliation. Flemish houses wanted to break away from Francia, Neapolitan houses from Rome, and so forth.

But when the mercurial Urban VI summoned Bernard Oller to Rome, he did not go. Urban declared him deposed and named Michele Aiguani of Bologna in his place. Neither Oller nor Aiguani seemed to relish the idea of joining the bitter dispute which divided the entire Church, and each attempted to govern his segment of the Order with dignity and honesty. But the Carmelite family was indeed divided. Subsequent chapters perpetuated the parallel tracks of leadership within the Order over the next thirty years, and each time a chapter was held, substitutes were sometimes named to represent those provinces that did not appear.

Perhaps the most notable attempt to heal the Western Schism was the Council of Pisa (1409), which deposed both Avignon and Roman claimants (neither of whom consented), then elected a third pope to further complicate the situation. It was not until 1417 that the Council of Constance resolved to cut the Gordian knot by electing a single pontiff, Martin V, recognized by nearly everyone. But by that time, the Carmelites had already resolved their own leadership impasse. In 1411, Carmelites of both loyalties met at Bologna, and both generals agreed to resign and abide by the consensus of the reunited Order. Jean Grossi, of the province of Toulouse, was elected, and wisely hastened to begin the healing process by an appeal to common heritage and ideals. Indeed, much healing was needed.

Carmelites as Heroes

In the midst of the general atmosphere of a disintegrating society, there were still a few examples of heroic dedication and holiness among Europe's Carmelites. One case in point was a knight who became the liberator of Portugal; another was an English theologian who came to be an advisor to kings.

A truly fascinating figure in Carmelite history is Nuno Alvares Pereira, the national hero of Portugal. Nuno was a devout nobleman, born in 1360, who grew up amid stories of holy knights and their gallant struggles against evil. His career as a page at the royal court and a skilled military officer in service to the king seemed fairly typical. He served his ruler loyally, married well, and raised a daughter. But when King Ferdinand I of Portugal died in 1383, his brother John of Aviz did not automatically succeed him. The old king's daughter was married to the King of Castile, who hoped to incorporate Portugal into his growing realm. Nuno was one of a handful of nobles who recognized that such action would result in a loss of national identity, and chose to fight on behalf of John of Aviz. He won the battle of Atoleiros the following year, allowing

Carmelite Saint Nuno Alvares Pereira, distributing his wealth to the poor, in an azulejo which now hangs in the reception area of Casa San Nuno, a conference and retreat center in Fatima, Portugal. Also represented is the exterior of the sanctuary of the Carmelite church and the Carmelite monastery donated by Saint Nuno and where he would eventually live as a Carmelite. The church was heavily damaged in the Great Lisbon Earthquake on November 1, 1755 and only the skeleton remains today. Today the Carmelite residence serves as headquarters for the National Republican Guard of Portugal. *(Photo courtesy of Carmelite Media)*

his patron to be crowned as John I. In turn, Nuno was named Constable of Portugal and commander in chief of its armies. Subsequent victories against heavy odds at Aljubarrota and Valverde in 1385 confirmed Nuno's genius as a military leader. Portuguese independence was not seriously threatened again for nearly two centuries.

Despite the need for the bloody work of the battlefield, Nuno remained almost childlike in his devotion to God and his strict code of morality, even for the soldiers in his army. He attributed his stunning victories to Mary's intercession on his behalf. Although the "Holy Constable" was one of the most powerful men in the kingdom, he used his wealth and influence to promote religious devotion, and to build many churches as signs of his gratitude. Perhaps the most spectacular of his churches was the imposing Carmo in Lisbon, which he entrusted to the care of the Carmelites. At that time, there was only a single Carmelite house in Portugal, at Moura, but Nuno knew what he wanted. He personally hand-picked the members of the new Lisbon community, led by the fervent Gomes de Santa Maria. The new house and church were lavishly endowed by the Constable, who also insisted on regular prayer and strict observance of the Rule. He also retained the right to expel anyone who was unworthy of a devout community. The friars agreed to follow a particularly demanding regimen, including two periods of community meditation per day.

Cell of St. Nuno recreated today in the former Carmelite monastery he built and then lived in as a simple brother. A Carmelite habit lays on the bed. St. Nuno is the patron saint for the National Republican Guard (GNR), a national police force, housed in the building Nuno donated to the Carmelites. *(Photo courtesy of Carmelite Media)*

Nuno's wife had died in 1388, and his daughter was married to the king's son, the Duke of Braganza. So he marked his retirement from public life by giving away his considerable wealth, and returning to the simplest sort of life. At the age of 63, he petitioned to enter the community at the Carmo, and was admitted as Brother Nuno de Santa Maria. He passed his remaining days in prayer and menial tasks in the beautiful setting which he had made possible. Powerful and illustrious people continued to visit him in the monastery, causing him some embarrassment. But when he asked to be moved to a more remote house, King John gently overruled his old friend. Nuno died quietly in 1431, the same year as Joan of Arc, a different sort of military genius, but one who shared his love of God and country. After a lavish state funeral, Nuno was laid to rest in the Carmo he had bequeathed to his beloved compatriots.

Thomas Netter of Walden was another sort of exceptional Carmelite, a scholar who has been called "the only great theologian of the 15th century." Thomas was born in 1375, and joined the English province as a very young man. He studied and taught at Oxford just as the controversy with the Lollards reached its climax. John Wycliffe's teaching had aroused enormous debate among the previous generation of thinkers, including more than a score of learned Carmelites. By the time Netter composed his brilliant and systematic study of the debate, Wycliffe had already been largely discredited at Oxford by the University community. His frustrated followers withdrew from the scholars' arena and took on the character of a popular revivalist movement.

In addition to being one of the most celebrated and vigorous theologians of his day, Thomas lived his entire life as an earnest and sincere friar, much devoted to study and contemplation. By 1414 he was elected provincial of England, as he continued his forceful preaching and scholarship. He remained provincial until the end of his life in 1430, and developed a reputation as a strict but fair disciplinarian, and yet one who had a lively sense of humor.

When King Henry IV died in 1413, Thomas Netter preached at his funeral. The new monarch, Henry V, was surprised when Thomas rebuked him for his lack of discipline in religious matters. That audacity impressed the king so much that Netter became a member of his inner circle. Henry's reign was short, but brilliant, as he galvanized his kingdom to recover the initiative in the stagnating Hundred Years War. After winning the battle of Agincourt, Henry V controlled most of northern France. Netter served his king loyally as confessor and advisor during that entire period.

Thomas also attended two church councils, where his theological dexterity proved useful. In 1409, he endorsed measures at the Council of Pisa designed to end the Western Schism, but also worked to strengthen the position of ecumenical councils in relation to the popes. He represented Henry V at the Council of Constance when the Schism finally ended in 1415. He carried a royal letter defending the merit of the mendicant orders. The king trusted Thomas so completely that he later named him to lead a diplomatic delegation to Poland in 1419. His mission was to make peace between the Polish King Wladislaw II Jagellon, Grand Duke Alexander of Lithuania, and Michael Küchmeister von Sternberg, Grand Master of the Teutonic Knights.

Thomas accompanied the king to France in 1422, and was with him when he died. He not only delivered Henry's funeral oration at Westminster, but became tutor and chaplain to the young Henry VI, who was only two years old at the time of his father's death. Thomas himself died in 1430 while escorting the young king to Paris for his coronation, and was buried in the Carmelite church at Rouen.

Decline of Prayer and Community

Throughout the 14th century, the Carmelites had made impressive strides in their numbers and influence, as well as the quality of their scholarly and spiritual accomplishments. But the level of religious observance in many communities had declined to an alarming degree. This condition was not the result of any single factor, but rather a long, gradual falling off from the fervent ideals and practices of the previous century.

One root of the problem was a significant weakening of Carmelite prayer life. In far too many instances, the classical model of intense conversation with a loving God was allowed to become a routine practice with no enthusiasm, and then a legalistic obligation, to be evaded whenever possible. References in many of the 14th century constitutions urge the ordinary friar to remain faithful to regular prayer in common, not just as an individual, but as a member of the praying community. Other recommendations caution the superiors against granting too many exemptions from community prayer, even to very busy friars. In fact there were so many exhortations to fidelity that it becomes evident that prayer was being largely neglected as an essential facet of life.

Another significant source of trouble was the increasing prosperity and popularity of the Carmelites in those cities where they had taken root. Their very success ended up being corrosive of religious discipline, especially the mandate to own no personal property. Poverty was no longer taken as seriously by many religious as it had once been. The simplest understanding of poverty was that the individual owned nothing of his own, but that even his clothing and furnishings belonged to his community. Yet even in the early 1300's there were many instances of friars who asked for and received permission to keep earnings, gifts, or other items of value as though they were personal possessions. Exceptions and dispensations would become a general curse of clerics in the 14th and 15th centuries. The constitutions specifically prohibited ownership of land, buildings, or animals, but it seems that the regulation was frequently ignored. One common rationalization stated that a prosperous family which "donated" extra things of value to one of their number when he professed his vows as a Carmelite was actually helping the entire community. But it is difficult to see how community harmony could be improved by constant reminders of which brothers had greater resources than others. In any case, it was far too easy to obtain exceptions for men who wanted to retain material things for their own use.

Yet another basic flaw in the fabric of community life was the growth of a sort of sub-class within the Carmelite family. Masters and Doctors of theology were highly respected for their accomplishments, and often awarded special

Thomas Netter of Walden in a painting at The Friars, Aylesford England. (Photo courtesy of Carmelite Media)

exemptions and privileges. For example, it was not necessarily expected that they would either pray with the community in the chapel, or eat with them in the refectory at the appointed times. Professors in the houses of study might have a student assigned to them as a servant or menial helper. In time, only those with advanced degrees could be elected to some positions of responsibility or authority, or even vote in some elections. Perhaps the worst and most obvious danger to community life came from those who aspired to the privileges of the educated friars without actually doing the study required for the academic degree. Certainly the 14th century had its surplus of corrupt church functionaries, especially in the Roman Curia, who were willing to provide false diplomas, degrees, certificates, or exemptions to anyone who could pay their price.

For all their talents and excellence, there was a real danger that the intellectuals might develop more as a community unto themselves, and less as simple-living friars with gifts to share. As in the case of poverty, there seemed to be some good reasons to encourage this "aristocracy of talent." Intellectual peers might well stimulate one another to greater achievements by forming a closely knit clique among themselves, for example. But there was an equally obvious pitfall for talented men to accentuate gifts of the intellect, at the expense of their own moral and spiritual growth. There are times when the most helpful lesson might come from a lowly brother with a scrubbing bucket, and not from a rare manuscript.

By about 1400, the Order had about 300 houses -- twice as many as the century before. But the rate of growth had slowed considerably. It is not difficult to see that there were already many good reasons to promote a revitalization of spiritual values and discipline. The renewal would indeed come, but first it would be necessary to endure the dramatic convulsion of the Protestant Reformation, and its resulting purification by fire.

+   +   +

Chapter 4
Reform and Renewal

Nantes: 1460. "God bless you," said the market woman in a husky voice. She handed the pail of shellfish to her customer with a broad smile, as she tucked a few gray curls back under her cap. She hoped that all her clients remembered God's benevolence as they enjoyed the seafood from her stall. She was especially happy that her neighbors, the Carmelites, were finally paying more attention to encouraging prayer and service among hard working people like herself. Her calloused fingers quietly touched the rectangle of nut-brown cloth underneath her apron, as she remembered to utter a silent prayer for patience and sensitivity to the needs of her next patron.

Beginning in Italy around the mid-1300's, the Renaissance swept through western Christianity like a torrent. A heightened interest in the ancient cultures of Greece and Rome served to promote a renewal of the human spirit as well. The deep pessimism created by war, plague, and religious scandals had made such a rejuvenation seem all the more critical. One common perception was that the highly charged religious atmosphere of the late middle ages had not been enough to save Christendom from a truly ghastly century of misfortune. Was there a better path? The intricately ordered society of the ancients seemed to offer an alternative, based on the finest products of human talent. So there was a fairly spontaneous rediscovery of the neglected literature, art, philosophy, and architecture of the Greco-Roman civilizations.

Renaissance Carmel

Along with that modification in attitude came "humanism," a renewed emphasis on the excellence of the human spirit, with all its abilities. Properly educated humanists were expected to develop their God-given talents in art, languages, music, graciousness, and their appreciation of all possible facets of the beautiful, created world. Especially in the fields of painting and sculpture, young artists tended to stress natural forms, rather than symbolic ones. Realism, even faithful to unattractive details, was preferred to idealism. A renewed curiosity about how God created the material universe, and how it worked in detail, would eventually fuel the scientific revolution and the great voyages of discovery. The more critical attitude toward human behavior and the validity of authority would also set forces in motion which would trigger both the Protestant and Catholic Reformations. And the development of printing with movable type by Johann Gutenberg quickly enabled those same ideas to be disseminated more rapidly that at any previous time in history.

Some critics of humanism have portrayed the Renaissance as an anti-religious movement. But in fact most of the art produced by this vigorous age continued to be religious art, not disparaging God, but honoring the human race as the pinnacle of God's creation. Pope Nicholas V, for one, opposed the critics, and embraced the new art forms as a means of expression for promoting religious values, including the classic virtues, stories from the Bible, and lives of the saints. Nicholas went on to found the Vatican Library and the Vatican Museums as institutions of study and faith-driven learning, which he hoped would enrich the intellectual life of the world. Yet it was deeply distressing to him and to others that the sophistication and wisdom of the Renaissance was also accompanied with an upsurge of hedonism and neo-paganism. The libertines of that age sometimes tend to outshine the genuine Christian humanists like Erasmus and Thomas More. Among the Carmelite humanists of the time were Baptist of Mantua and Arnold Bostius. These individuals never forgot their primary obligation to be Christians, as they also tried to discover and penetrate the deepest parts of the human spirit.

Especially in the city of Florence, the cradle of the new movement, the Carmelites also joined in the attention toward the new art forms. Choir books were lavishly illustrated using the new realistic forms. The imposing Gothic church of the Carmine, after many years in the building, was finally dedicated in 1422. It was almost immediately embellished by further decoration in the new style, as well as bright frescoes on the walls of the cloister. Of the many interior chapels, the Brancacci chapel became the most renowned for the stunning frescoes celebrating the life of Peter the Apostle. Artists Masolino and Masaccio began work in 1425, and Masaccio in particular unleashed a flood of creative vigor. The chapel became a hands-on school for later artists, who came to study and copy the graceful forms and colors. The Brancacci chapel was the artistic cradle for such geniuses as Michelangelo, Leonardo, Raphael, Botticelli, and a young Carmelite from that same house, Filippo Lippi. When a disastrous fire in 1771 destroyed the nave of the church and most of its chapels, only the Brancacci and Corsini chapels were saved for posterity.

Fra. Filippo Lippi (1406-69) was a superb artist, if not a very good Carmelite. He came to the Carmine with his brother as a very young boy, and took his vows in 1421. As Masaccio worked on his masterpiece, Filippo watched closely

Self Portrait of Filippo Lippi in the fresco of the funeral of Mary, Mother of God, in the Cathedral of Spoletto, Italy, Filippo Lippi portrayed himself, his son, Filippino, and his helpers, Fra Diamante and Pier Matteo d'Amelia as mourners. The paintings were completed shortly before Lippi's death in 1469. *(Photo courtesy of Carmelite Media)*

and learned many of his techniques. He began his own sketching, and quickly became a popular and busy painter in his own right, with many offers from wealthy patrons. His beautiful Madonnas and attractive landscapes delighted art lovers of every sort. After 1432, he received permission to live outside the Carmine so that he could work more easily. The loss of his supportive community was unfortunate, since he fell into temptations of the flesh and financial difficulties, and lost his spiritual focus. After he began working on the cathedral at Prato, he fathered two children with a woman 30 years younger than himself. His son Filippino also became a fine painter, and completed the work in the unfinished Brancacci chapel in 1484.

In time, Filippo reformed his life, returned to observing religious discipline, and remained a religious until he died. He later became something of a household painter for the Medici family. His final commission was the embellishment of the cathedral at Spoleto, and he was working there with his colleague Fra Diamante at the time of his death. Lorenzo the Magnificent wanted to bring his body back to Florence for burial, but agreed to the pleas of the people of Spoleto, where his tomb remains today. Botticelli is only one of Filippo's many artistic disciples.

In this period of vigorous intellectual ferment, there were countless other Carmelite writers, scientists, and musicians who made worthy contributions to their respective fields of knowledge. Among them was Giuliano Ristori of Prato, provincial of Tuscany, whom Cosimo de'Medici named to the chair of astronomy at the University of Pisa. He later became the dean of the University, and helped Michelangelo design the fortifications of Pisa during the siege of 1530. Similar in many ways was scientist Paolo Foscarini, provincial of Calabria. He anticipated Galileo by seventeen years, as he wrote a well-reasoned essay demonstrating that it was not against scripture to accept Copernicus' heliocentric theory.

If the wealth and popularity of the previous century had eroded the fabric of an ordinary Carmelite community, the opulence of the new studies and art forms sidetracked many more friars from their commitment to simplicity and virtue. The stunning beauty of so many works of Renaissance painting, sculpture and architecture served to distract entire generations of religious from their foundational principles, even as they increased their fervor and enthusiasm with so much high quality preaching and writing.

Reform amid Riches

Giving in to secularism was relatively easy, of course. But it is surprising how many Carmelites emerged in the middle years of the 15th century to challenge the trend toward increasing self-indulgence. One prior general in particular, John Soreth (1451-71), symbolizes the struggle to return to the Order's spiritual roots and to revitalize the details of personal and community life. But even before Soreth's election, a small group of zealous friars decided to bind themselves to a stricter observance of Albert's Rule. They were the pioneers of a new style of renewal, the "reform congregation."

The so-called Congregation of Mantua began in 1413 as a nearly spontaneous movement among the rank and file of the Carmelites in northern Italy. In the beginning, a handful of friars grew more and more frustrated with their inability to live what they considered a proper Carmelite life in their existing houses. But rather than leave their communities out of disappointment, they resolved to make a courageous attempt to fix what was broken. They asked for and received permission to authorize a stricter observance at the house of Le Selve, in the Tuscan province, between Florence and Pisa. The moving force behind the proposal was Jacobo di Alberto, a former novice master and prior in Florence. Jacobo drew up a stricter set of guidelines for his volunteers in an experimental community. His more rigorous observance of silence and simplicity of life quickly attracted others of similar mind. Meticulous attention to remaining in or near one's cell was imperative. No individual was allowed to keep anything of value. All money was deposited in a common chest. Within just a few years of Le Selve's reform, two other communities asked to join the new observance, Geronde in the French-speaking Swiss diocese of Sion, and the important city of Mantua.

The Mantuan Congregation became a distinct sub-community within the Order by 1442, but not based on any geographical region, as the ordinary provinces were. Reformed houses owed their obedience directly to a vicar general, elected by members of the reform. It is significant that provincials were no longer allowed to move community members in or out of the reformed houses without the consent of the individual friars. A reform-minded provincial might ordinarily want to mix some of his more observant friars into a less rigorous community in order to spread their enthusiasm and flourishing spirituality. But now those friars would first have to agree to move, and they often preferred not to accept the extra aggravation. The reformers attracted enough new members to be able to merge with existing communities if they wished to do so. But they were more likely to simply found a totally new house, leaving the others to languish. The Mantuan Reform was certainly a good thing, but its most important disadvantage was that they became a separate and parallel track alongside the less observant houses, and frequently did not interact with them.

Friars of the new congregation wore a gray habit of unbleached wool, with approximately the same cut as the habit of other Carmelites. The quality of their religious observance remained relatively good. Eventually, there were over 30 Mantuan houses, extending throughout northern and central Italy, including the popular Marian shrine at Loreto, and the venerable church of San Crisogono in the Trastevere quarter of Rome. The Mantuan friars were also very helpful in supporting some of the earliest contemplative Carmelite women in Italy.

The reform attracted a considerable number of volunteers from other Italian and French speaking provinces, including the passionate Breton preacher Thomas Connecte. Although he became a magnet for many followers, Thomas had a bizarre, unforgiving style of preaching which to some extent anticipated the rigors of Savonarola. Although he preached against genuine abuses, Connecte came across as a vindictive bully, more eager to punish than to forgive. He finished badly when he overreached himself by hurling rash accusations and fiery rhetoric even at the pope and cardinals. Even so, many of his more sincere followers joined the new reform and became earnest contributors to its collective holiness.

Friars of the Mantuan Congregation

Other Mantuan communities also produced several fine religious, who remain on the Carmelite calendar with the title of Blessed. Angelus Augustine Mazzinghi (1385-1438) was called "the first son of the reform" because he was among the very first to join the house at Le Selve. He was a stirring and very popular preacher, especially noted for his Lenten sermons on repentance. He also served as prior at both Le Selve and Florence for many years, and was a noted counselor and spiritual adviser.

Bartholomew Fanti (d.1495) was a native of Mantua. He joined the Carmelites there, and became a spiritual leader of the Reform, as well as a fervent Marian writer and spiritual director. Among his many achievements was composing the clear and succinct statutes for a Marian confraternity in Mantua. He lavished many years of loving care on that group of lay people, and was venerated by them. Bartholomew was particularly devoted to preaching about the living presence of Jesus in the Eucharist.

Best noted of all was Baptist Spagnoli, commonly known as Baptist of Mantua (1447-1516). From his very earliest years, his brilliant mind attracted the attention of his superiors, and he built a superb record of studies at Mantua, Padua, and Bologna. He was active in university affairs for the rest of his life. He was named prior of Parma, then of Mantua. In 1488, Baptist was bold enough to preach a severe admonition on corruption to Pope Innocent VIII and the Roman Curia (who badly needed to hear such a message). By the end of his life he had served six terms as vicar general of his Congregation, and a few years as prior general of the entire Order. As general, he attempted to promote a genuine atmosphere of study, and eliminate loopholes for those who tried to evade their obligations. He was invited to attend the Fifth Lateran Council, and even to lead a mission for Pope Leo X in 1515 to make peace between King François I of France and Massimiliano Sforza, Duke of Milan. But his increasingly poor health may have prevented him from meeting those commitments.

But it was primarily in the field of literature that Baptist is remembered today. He was a personal friend of some of the most significant Renaissance writers, and never lost an opportunity to promote Christian humanistic values in his discussions with them. He dedicated several years to tutoring the children of the illustrious Gonzaga family of Mantua. Even by the exacting standards of Renaissance writers, Baptist was idolized as a poet and Latin stylist by his contemporaries. Shakespeare quotes some of "the Mantuan's" verses in *Love's Labors Lost*. It was the great Desiderius Erasmus of Rotterdam who nicknamed him "the Christian Virgil." Baptist wrote volumes of letters and commentary about war and peace, political issues, and social mores in the Italy of his day. His writings on religious and devotional subjects, especially his spiritual poetry, were some of the best of the age. An astonishing amount of his work was reprinted again and again through many editions and translations long after his death.

Just about the time the Mantuan congregation was finding its place, Pope Eugenius IV granted a second mitigation of Albert's Rule in 1432. Under the terms of the new mitigation, the abstinence from meat was cut back to only three days a week: Wednesday, Friday, and Saturday. The mandate to remain in the cells or near them was also loosened to allow more freedom of movement within the houses, or indeed outside of them. In view of the extensive ministerial commitments which most houses had taken on, many felt that the relaxation of those rules made sense, as an admission of what was already taking place in most communities anyhow. But the timing of such a relaxation of discipline was especially awkward for any religious family trying to reform itself. Some more observant communities and individuals, including the entire Congregation of Mantua, declared that they would not take advantage of the new leniency.

The Danish Province

At about the same time, another small but vigorous province emerged in Denmark. The powerful King Erik of Pomerania introduced the first Carmelites to his Baltic realm in 1410, and helped them to build their first three houses. One factor in Erik's generous patronage may have been his English queen Phillipa, who probably knew the White Friars in her homeland. Another reason may have been the Carmelites' devotion to Saint Anne, mother of Mary, who was the patroness of the merchants of the powerful Hanseatic League. Erik had engineered a union of the three Scandinavian kingdoms (Denmark, Norway, and Sweden) for the first and only time in their history. In an effort to assert Scandinavian autonomy, he hoped to break the commercial domination

Cloister Walk in Helsingør, Denmark— The Carmelite monastery of Saint Mary is one of the best preserved medievel monastic structures in northern Europe. After the Reformation the building was a poorhouse, a hospital, and a home for the distressed elderly of the town. St Mary's Parish church next door was originally the monastery's church. Hans Christian Anderson called it "the most beautiful in Denmark."

of the Hansa merchants in the Baltic and North Seas. So he imported the first Carmelite friars from Bavaria and southern Germany, rather than the northern cities where the Hansa was strongest. There were also strong links with the strongly observant Flemish Carmelites, and many Danish students were sent to study at Louvain and Cologne.

In addition to the King's patronage, several important members of the nobility and church hierarchy sponsored the growth of the Carmelites in Danish and Swedish commercial towns like Landskrona and Helsingør. The Danish Carmelites were formally separated from the Saxon province in 1462, with a native provincial of their own, Mad (Matthew) Svendsen. All sources seem to indicate that Denmark was a reformed and observant province for all of its short history. The friars maintained high spiritual and intellectual standards, especially in their studies of scripture. Their houses and churches were noted for their smartness and beauty. Especially after the foundation of a house of studies in Copenhagen (1517), Carmelite scholars fostered development of the University and the academic life of the entire Kingdom. Today the large house and church at Helsingør and the church at Saeby are among the finest medieval remnants anywhere in Scandinavia. Hans Christian Anderson called the Helsingør church and its house of studies complex "the most beautiful in Denmark."

John Soreth's Reforms

The 15th century's most successful reformer, John Soreth, was from Caen, in Normandy. He joined the province of Francia and studied at the Place Maubert *studium* in Paris. Eventually he became provincial of Francia, with an eye to helping its members return to their fervor as men of prayer. He was elected prior general in 1451 at the general chapter in Avignon. He led the Order in an outstanding manner for the next 20 years. John used both legislation and personal influence to promote his reforms. But he probably accomplished more actual renewal by his own efforts at visiting and encouragement than the reform congregations did by their legislation. It is not surprising that he was most successful in the northern French provinces, and in Germany and the Low Countries. He was an inveterate traveler and attempted to visit nearly every house which he could reach. In fact he spent so much time on the road throughout his 20 years that his adversaries called him "the Ethiopian" because of his dark tan. But visiting was important to John. He was convinced that many otherwise good communities had been allowed to decay because no one had ever visited their houses to point out weaknesses, and to encourage them to increase their fervor. Even allowing for the limitations of time and distance, he always assumed that every single priory in the Carmelite world could and should be a center of holiness and prayer.

John Soreth's program of reform is sometimes called the Calistine Observance, as distinguished from that of the Mantuan congregation, since John's plan was approved by Pope Calixtus III. Working with one community at a time, John would exhort them to commit themselves to a new beginning, and a formal renewal of their commitment to Carmel. The first step to this regeneration of life would be a formal statement renouncing all temporal goods, privileges, and exemptions which might weaken a clear commitment to the Gospel and the friar's own vows. Each individual stated voluntarily that he would eat at a common table, with no special refectories, and no food and drink in the living quarters. They renewed their pledge to stay in their cells as much as possible, even if it meant restricting some of the ministerial work outside of the houses. Visitors were to be admitted to the enclosure only with permission of the prior.

Although most Carmelites who went through this process still had valid vows, they were asked to repeat a period of postulancy. They returned to secular dress, and repeated many of the lessons of their novitiate with an eye toward making a new and stronger commitment to their vows. When the community was ready, they selected a feast day to formalize their rebirth. On the vigil of that day, everyone was encouraged to receive the sacrament of Reconciliation. Before the solemn Mass of the Holy Spirit, the friars would prostrate themselves face down on the floor of the choir, while the Seven Penitential Psalms were chanted for the forgiveness of their sins. Afterward the prior would address the community in the chapter room about religious observance and the renunciation of property. Everyone would commit themselves to the same ideals by both an oral promise and a written note. Then they would return to the church singing the *Te Deum*, and enjoy a celebratory dinner. Finally, each friar would clear everything out of his cell and bring it to a common storeroom, where things could be redistributed in the most appropriate manner.

Soreth's formalization of "starting over" might seem somewhat theatrical, but it worked remarkably well in many areas of France, Germany, and the Low Countries. Especially in the Lower German province, the reformed houses at Mörs and Enghien were powerful sources of inspiration and discipline to other communities. John's relations with the Mantuan Congregation were cool, but cooperative, since the quality of their communities was high. His main source of frustration was that their separate structure slowed the spread of the Order's general reform. He was less successful in other parts of Italy and further areas where he was not able to travel.

John issued new constitutions for the whole Order in 1462, which stressed the urgent need to observe poverty, solitude, and faithfulness to the vows. On the eve of the Reformation, one commentator stated that, in Belgium, the Carmelites and Dominicans were the only orders which were truly alive. John Soreth must get at least part of the credit for this amazing revival.

Carmelite Women

John Soreth should also receive the primary recognition for bringing women into the Carmelite family. Even from the earliest times, there were lay people, both men and women alike, who wanted to associate themselves with the Carmelites and share in their spirituality to some degree. But there had never been any official structure for encouraging these people and keeping them close. In 1452, just one year after John was elected, he attended the provincial chapter for Lower Germany at Cologne. A deputation of religious women from the Netherlands was also present, hoping to formalize a relationship with the Carmelites. The women were known as beguines, and lived an informal sort of community life without vows, devoted to prayer and charitable works. The reforming Cardinal Nicholas of Cusa had visited the area recently, and was unhappy with the unstructured nature of their lives. He ordered the beguine communities either to disband, or to regularize their practice by adopting the rule of an existing Order. The beguines of Ten Elsen were already receiving spiritual direction and support from the local Carmelite house at Guelders, so it was natural for them to adopt the Carmelite Rule as well.

John agreed that this might be right time to formalize a place for a women's sisterhood in Carmel. Working through the community in Florence, he requested authorization from Pope Nicholas V to affiliate existing female communities,

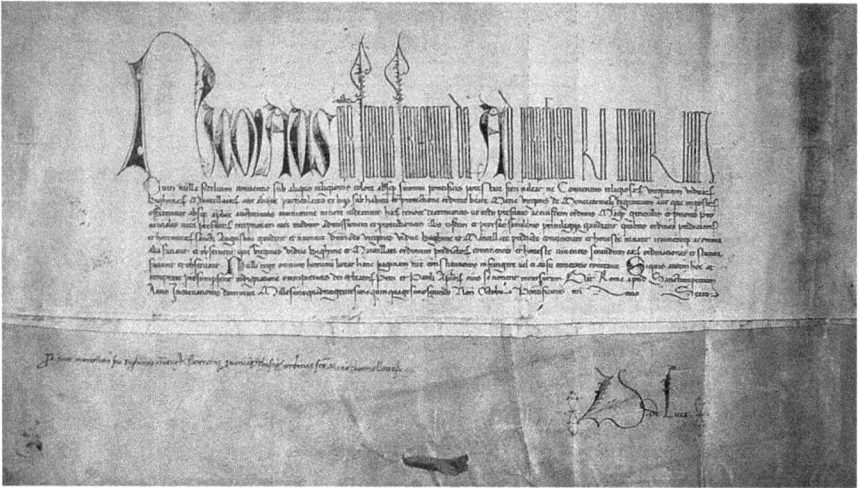

**The bull *Cum nulla (1452)* given by Pope Nicholas V, opening the possibility for female communities and lay people to be part of the Carmelite Order.

and to found additional convents for women. The pope responded with the bull *Cum Nulla* (1452) which granted papal permission to receive women into the Carmelite Order. The beguines of Ten Elsen were the first beneficiaries of the new link, but there were also several convents of sisters in Florence and northern Italy who were taken into the Carmelite family. More women would follow them. Up to this time, there were quite a few Italian houses for women not affiliated with any Order. Like the beguines, they tended to be virtuous, but not especially demanding, especially with regard to the formal enclosure. Sisters had a surprising amount of contact with outsiders in the busy towns, and all possible distractions, to the detriment of a disciplined life of prayer. The friars of the Mantuan Congregation were quick to help in the reorganization and spiritual direction of the convents in Italy, just as Soreth was doing north of the Alps. Some of these Italian convents even promoted regular formal meditation as a community activity, long before it became commonly accepted elsewhere. In time, the authorization of *Cum Nulla* would extend to both cloistered communities, properly known as the "Second Order" and convents of uncloistered working sisters, or "Third Order."

As John continued his travels in the lower Rhineland and Low Countries districts, he authorized several new communities of women. Within a very short period, convents were established at Nieukerk, Dinant, Liège, Huy and Namur in the late 1450s. Soreth composed a modified version of the Carmelite constitutions for these sisters, paying special attention to their rules of enclosure and to their spiritual directors. That legislation proved to be so successful that it would be copied over and over by other convents.

Affiliation was also extended to a unique group in France that had been founded by a noblewoman, Frances d'Amboise. Wealthy and powerful because of her position as Duchess of Brittany, Frances was also a deeply spiritual woman who tried to live as simply as an influential aristocrat could. It is likely that Frances inspired her husband's brief rule to be a generous and evenhanded one for the common people. She supported several communities of women who cared for the sick and the poor. After the death of her husband in 1457, she resisted all proposals (including the king's) that she marry again. On the contrary, she continued an intense prayer life, and used her wealth to help others. John Soreth met her during one of his visits to Brittany, and he was greatly impressed with both Frances and her work.

When she decided to found a Carmelite convent at Bondon in 1463, John brought several reformed nuns from Liège to help. He also agreed to write a special set of constitutions for the house, which were patterned on those already working in the Netherlands. In 1468, Frances decided to join the community herself, and John personally received her into the Carmelite family. Frances insisted that her noble birthright should not be a dividing factor within her house, but the other nuns insisted that she lead them as prioress. Even after transferring the house to Nantes in 1480, the quality of the prayer life in community remained very high indeed. At the time of her death in 1485, Frances was generally regarded to be the foundress of Carmelite nuns in France.

There is a similar story of Joan Scopelli in Italy. Joan was born to a middle class family in Reggio Emilia in 1428. Although she continued to reside in her parents' house, she received the Carmelite habit and lived the life of a semi-religious solitary called a "mantellate" because of her white mantel. After her parents' death, she took over spiritual guidance of a devout widow and her two daughters who were seeking a religious house to join. Joan's strong Marian devotion colored her spirituality and the attractiveness of her way of life. By 1485, she was able to establish a house of her own at Reggio, which eventually comprised 20 nuns. Spiritual care for the sisters was supplied by reformed friars from the Mantua congregation.

Archangela Girlani was another noteworthy foundress in the same region. She was born in the mid-15th century at Trino, in north-west Italy. She entered a local monastery, but found its closeness to her family to be a distraction. So in 1477, she transferred to the Carmel at Parma, newly established under the direction of the Mantuan friars, and was elected prioress shortly afterward. Within a few years, her house adopted a newer set of strict constitutions, based on John Soreth's legislation and standards. When the ruling Gonzaga dynasty of Mantua decided in 1492 that their capital city needed a Carmel, Archangela was designated to recruit nuns from her community in Parma and lead them to Mantua as prioress of the new foundation. She only had a few more years to live in her new home, but she made the most of her last days. She succeeded in creating a strong spiritual movement in her house, focused on the love of the Trinity. She died in 1495.

It was about this same time that the first convents for women were also established in Spain. There may have been about ten of them. John Soreth did not personally supervise their statutes, and there was a great variety in the degree of discipline and austerity. At least one convent, probably the one in Valencia, had a serious commitment to pray the Office in choir and a strict enclosure, but most of the others did not. The Incarnation at Avila was founded in 1479 and grew very large, but without strict statutes. This wide diversity of religious practice allowed the growth of an unhealthy sloppiness, which would lead to a crisis of conscience for Teresa in the following century. The good news is that since the Carmelite sisterhood was established so late in history, the long-standing abuses of some of the male communities never had a chance to take root in their convents. Even allowing for their many genuine problems, the women's communities were generally serious about their obligations, and free from outright immorality.

Carmel Among Lay People

One final contribution which John Soreth made to Carmelite outreach was the opening to participation by lay men and women in the Order's prayer and ministry. The secular version of the Third Order embraced lay people who continued to live in the working world, but took vows to follow the Carmelite Rule insofar as it applied to them. As early as 1284, there had been an informal association of lay people with the Carmelites at the church of San Donato in Lucca. There is evidence of other affiliations in cities like Bologna and Florence, in which lay people promised to follow a stricter and more dedicated way of life, based on Carmelite prayer and spiritual attitudes. Those who professed this dramatic step were sometimes called either *conversi* (people who have "converted" or turned their lives around) or *manumissi* (slaves freed from their bondage.)

Frequently, these lay men and women were able to become peripheral members of an existing First Order community. More commonly, they formed associations among themselves for prayer, ministry, and community under the spiritual guidance of a friar or a diocesan priest. Confraternities or associations of lay people were already a very well established tradition, especially in Italy. Sometimes a confraternity would adopt a specific social ministry, such as caring for the elderly poor, unwed mothers, hungry pilgrims, or condemned prisoners.

Throughout the 15th century, there were many examples of legislation for these lay associations, including charters by Bartholomew Fanti and other friars of the Mantuan reform. John Soreth's contribution to this development began with the papal document *Cum Nulla* (1452), which granted permission to receive women into the Carmelite family, including women who lived at home or outside of established community houses. Men were also included by 1476, when another document gave the Carmelite Third Order equal status with the tertiaries of the Franciscans and Dominicans. More systematic legislation followed, once the authorization of lay communities saw daylight.

Carmelite Joan Scopelli captured in a painting. Originally living as a semi-religious solitary in her parents' house, by 1485 Joan established her own house which eventually comprised 20 nuns. Joan's strong Marian devotion colored her spirituality and the attractiveness of her way of life. This painting hangs in the Carmelite monastery in Straubing, Germany *(Photo courtesy of Carmelite Media)*

There seemed to be no end of ordinary people who found the need to express their religious fervor in practical terms. Carmelite traditions and presence in so many towns often encouraged those manifestations, and opened the way to membership in associations related to the Order. The story of Ludovico Morbioli is a case in point. He was born to a wealthy family in Bologna, but squandered his riches on dissolute living. A serious illness in 1462 triggered a dramatic personal conversion, and he became a public penitent in the streets of Bologna for the rest of his life. Although he probably was not actually a Carmelite tertiary, he adopted a habit similar to the one worn by the Mantuan congregation, and preached to sinners with a cross in his hand. Baptist of Mantua wrote of his holiness and his success at helping others turn away from sin.

Spiritual Growth

One of the most influential promoters of piety among ordinary people was a Belgian friar, Arnold Bostius (1445-99). Arnold lived most of his Carmelite life in Ghent, where he was a respected scholar, humanist, and elegant Latin stylist. His massive correspondence with other luminaries of his age included conversations with not only Baptist of Mantua, but also such giants as Erasmus and Trithemius. Along with his admiration of antiquity came an interest in the spiritual roots of his Order. He studied the traditions of Carmelite dedication to Mary as sister, mother, and patroness. He also promoted devotion to Mary's parents, Joachim and Anne. When Bostius was asked to contribute to the ongoing deliberation about Mary's Immaculate Conception, he insisted that Carmelites should defend her purity. In 1479, he produced his masterwork, the *Patronatu*, in which he framed Mary's entire relationship to the Order of Carmel. He saw the scapular as a symbol and reminder of a simple exchange of favors: The Carmelites offer love and loyal service to Mary; she in return lavishes love and protection on them. His concentration on the scapular as the outward symbol of this commitment made it a direct and trouble-free emblem for lay people. Countless numbers of common people adopted it as an affiliation with the Carmelite way of prayer.

Blessed John Soreth who worked tirelessly as Prior General to reform the Order and expanded the Order to include female communities and lay people. Sketch is from the book by Carmelite historian Marianus Ventimiglia, printed in 1773.

The increasing attractiveness of the scapular devotion profited both from the inclusion of lay people in Carmelite life, and from the continuing popularity of Mary as role model and patroness. The idea of "patronage" as a spiritual affiliation had roots over a thousand years old. With the disintegration of the Roman Empire, most of Europe became a chaotic and dangerous place. Ordinary people had to assure their personal safety by finding a powerful patron who could protect them. Sometimes they showed this connection by wearing some sign or "livery" of their patron, so that they would not be mistreated by other lawless or dangerous people. In more civilized times, items of clothing, like small scapulars, were sometimes used to show a "belonging" to Mary as gratitude for her love and protection from temptation. The appropriate sign of gratitude to a patron was loyal service, which usually meant imitation in the religious context.

By the late 14th century, Carmelites were giving small scapulars to lay people who expressed interest in following a Marian spirituality. These people wore the scapular under their ordinary clothes as a material reminder of their dedication to turn away from sin and be faithful to the sort of life Mary lived. There was no need to clarify the symbolism of a loving parent clothing a devoted child. Members of this "scapular confraternity" went about their ordinary lives with a sense of connectedness to Mary and partnership with the Carmelites. Common expressions of this link were a greater dedication to prayer and a growth in virtue. Mary's openness to God's will inspired others to care for the needs of those who were less fortunate than themselves. It was during this period of growing devotion that the story of Simon Stock and his allegiance to Jesus and Mary took on a renewed life. In many parts of Italy, Spain, and France, wearing the scapular was almost universal.

In much of Sicily, Soreth's reform principles had only limited success, but individual houses at Messina, Catania, Randazzo, and Palermo adopted a stricter reformed observance. Aloysius Rabatà, the prior of Randazzo, was a devoted religious and a popular friend of the poor. Contemporaries describe him as living as a true hermit in reflective silence. Among his duties as prior was the distasteful need to reprove other friars living immoral lives. In 1490, Aloysius was seriously wounded by an arrow while begging for alms. Although others thought that his assailant was the brother of one of those he had disciplined, Aloysius never revealed his killer's name before he died.

Blessed John Soreth ruled the Carmelites wisely and devoutly until his death in 1471. He left the Order far better than he found it. But after his death, the overall leadership was disappointing and lackluster at just the time in history when the Church was entering a period of crisis. The next 40 years represented an interlude during which Soreth's solid improvements began to languish, and the momentum of reform was unquestionably interrupted. Old abuses had not been entirely uprooted, and began to flourish again in some places. On the other hand, there were still outstanding examples of holy and diligent men and women who continued to follow the narrow path of virtue and sanctity, despite the obstacles.

The Congregation of Albi

The story of the Congregation of Albi reads like a good novel. The city of Albi lies in south-central France, firmly in the heartland of the French Carmelites. The local bishop, Louis d'Amboise, was a successful reformer in his own right, and had already encouraged the improvement of the communities of Franciscans and Dominicans in his diocese. When he suggested a stricter observance to his local Carmelites, they gave him the impression that they were not interested in changing their easy-going ways, and just wanted to be left alone. So the bishop asked the Mantuan congregation for some reformed friars to start a new community in their place. Two Belgians were assigned to him. One of them died en route, but the other, Eligius Denis, arrived at Albi in 1499. He was given charge of 22 students recruited from one of the theology schools in Paris for the bishop's project. Eligius gave them a month's instruction in Carmelite life and traditions, and then he and the provincial of Aquitaine clothed them in the Carmelite habit in the bishop's private chapel.

Bishop Louis then invited the members of the local Carmelite community to a banquet at his palace. While their house was vacant, Eligius and his young colleagues seized the building and barred the door against its former inhabitants. When the revelers returned home, they were given the choice of joining their new reform, or asking for an assignment to some other house. Most of them opted to stay and join the new community. From this highly irregular start, friars of the Albi reform did surprisingly well at maintaining an admirable level of religious life and discipline. Although their congregation never embraced large numbers of houses, they promoted a higher degree of discipline throughout central France because of their moral influence.

In 1502, the community at Melun, in the province of Francia, asked to be affiliated with the Albi regime, and the two communities requested a special status, like the Mantuan congregation. Their wishes were granted by Cardinal George d'Amboise (brother of Bishop Louis), and Albi, like Mantua, was placed un-

Bl. Baptist Spagnoli of Mantua, the most important literary figure of the Order during the Renaissance, also served as vicar general for six terms. He was elected prior general in 1513 but accomplished little because of his age and health.

der a vicar general, whose position made him directly accountable to the prior general. One of the most dynamic leaders of the new Albi movement was Louis de Lire, who undertook the thorough renewal of the house of studies at Place Maubert in Paris. Because of the great prestige of this *studium generale*, students from many provinces lived happily in the well-regulated, spiritual environment, and returned to their native lands inclined toward a life of restraint and prayerful reflection. Years later, in 1517, the same Louis de Lire undertook a similar reform of the important southern *studium* of Toulouse. On the eve of the Reformation, it is fortunate that Carmel in France counted large numbers of holy and well-educated members.

Yet another reform effort consisted of a single house. The hermitage of Monte Oliveto was established in 1516 just outside Genoa. The founder and moving force was Ugo Marengo, of the Lombard province. He wanted at least one priory in Italy where the unmitigated, eremitical rule could be followed without the complications of the modern world. He attempted to join the reform of Mantua, but was refused, since the stark, eremitical life he proposed was already too austere for that group. So Monte Oliveto remained a single house of prayer within the province of Lombardy, or, after 1565, directly under the prior general. It seemed almost like a throwback to the wadi on Carmel, perched as it was on a hill high above the Mediterranean, where each friar had a separate cell with a garden, and an inspiring view of the sea and the sky.

On the Eve of the Reformation

In 1513, there was one more interesting scenario of an attempted renewal which failed. The Order's cardinal protector, Sigismondo Gonzaga, wanted to assure the election of another reforming general. The Gonzaga dynasty was the premier family of Mantua, so Sigismondo naturally thought that his old teacher Baptist Spagnoli would be an ideal leader in a time of troubles. He also felt that electing a member of the Mantuan reform congregation would be a practical way to reunite the disparate branches of the Order behind a highly motivated leader with an agenda of restoring the old virtues. A general chapter was already scheduled to meet in Barcelona, but Cardinal Gonzaga used his influence to get it transferred to Rome. Once the delegates were there under his control, he carefully manipulated the votes to guarantee Baptist's election.

Baptist had never been anything but a holy and obedient religious, so he accepted the office much against his better judgment. Perhaps if he had been twenty years younger, the Mantuan might have done a better job. But by 1513, he was too elderly and sick to do more than provide good example. Baptist promoted unity and regular observance within all branches of the Carmelite family, but little else. He was never really able to engage in the pressing issues of the time, or to restart Soreth's vigorous efforts at reforming communities. He resigned because of illness in 1516. It is genuinely distressing that he accomplished so little as general of the Order.

But by that stage, other events in Germany had taken on a life of their own. The upheaval of the Reformation would profoundly change the destiny of the Carmelites, and the entire Christian world.

+   +   +

Chapter 5
The Reformation Earthquake

Franconia: 1530. The young friar stared at the ground as he shuffled through the trash in the busy market square. Many printed leaflets intermingled with the usual scraps and straw. Pamphlets and flyers had become as common as autumn leaves. They made the friar uneasy because so many of them questioned the details of his chosen way of life. Is God really pleased with my prayer, my scholarship, my preaching? How could I improve the daily life of my community to be more faithful? So many opinions! Where to find the truth?

The immense upheaval known as the Protestant Reformation was a long time in the making. When Martin Luther posted his 95 theses in 1517, it was merely the spark which ignited mountains of inflammable issues, built up over at least two centuries. The increasing corruption of so many bishops and even members of the Papal court had sapped ordinary people's faith in the holiness of their leaders. The ravages of the Black Death had not only shaken their belief that God took care of ordinary, good people. It had also opened broad gaps in the ranks of the best clergy, which were then filled with less worthy substitutes. The scandal of the Western Schism and the glittering wealth of the Renaissance had served to sweep undeserving prelates into spiritual offices, which they could never serve properly. And among even the religious who were supposed to be closest to the working poor, so many had fallen away from their earlier simplicity and found comfortable ways to pamper themselves. Sadly, the Carmelites also shared in that appalling weakness.

Nicholas Audet

During the early years of the Reformation, the Carmelites were under the indifferent leadership of Bernardino Landucci, who was prior general from Baptist of Mantua's death in 1516 until 1523. John Soreth's work at renewing the Carmelite spirit was still incomplete, and needed to be strengthened. But Landucci's time as general was spent on concerns over jurisdiction, finances, and taking care of his family. There was precious little which he did to actually inspire his Carmelite sisters and brothers, or to enrich the quality of their religious life.

Providentially, Landucci's successor was the extraordinary Nicholas Audet, a fervent religious, and worthy successor of John Soreth. Nicholas was born on Cyprus, and entered the Carmelites as a member of the Holy Land province, which by this time consisted of Famagusta, Nicosia, and a few other Cypriot cities. His family was French in origin, but his noble ancestors had stayed on Cyprus after the crusades. His initial studies were at Nicosia, but he took advantage of the Venetian control of Cyprus to transfer to the Venetian province, and continue his learning at the superb University of Padua. He eventually earned a doctorate at Parma, and made some very useful friendships with good Carmelites in northern Italy. His own province elected him provincial in 1514. When Landucci died, Nicholas was nominated vicar general of the Order by the reform-minded Pope Adrian VI. A general chapter the following year (1524) confirmed him as prior general, and he remained in that office until his death in 1562.

During his year as vicar general, he devised a fast-track program of reform for the whole Order called the *Isagogicon*. It is interesting to note that Nicholas had no expectations of retaining high office, and looked upon his single year as vicar general as a tiny window to communicate his vision of a renewed Carmelite life. His status as a member of the Holy Land province reminded him of the Order's spiritual and institutional roots, but his experience in Europe also highlighted how far the White Friars had drifted from their original ideals. So the *Isagogicon* bears the frantic energy of one who hopes to make a one-time entreaty to return to the nourishing springs of Carmel.

Audet saw the sordid condition of many houses, together with the menace of the Protestant movement, as the urgent signals for speedy improvement. He bluntly states that many of the sons of Carmel had seemingly forgotten the motives for their vows and their commitment to religious life. They cannot cast simply aside the Rule and Constitutions any more than a believing Christian can disregard the commandments. He highlights the matter of religious poverty as a key issue, and calls upon each friar to immediately correct any illusion or conviction that he might actually own something.

He spells out in detail the formation studies that are essential for each level of responsibility. Studies which are missing must be made up, not waived or dispensed. Academic degrees and positions of authority are not for sale, and should only be attained in the normal manner. Provincials are responsible to see to it that their subjects are properly trained in theology, and aware of their responsibilities. The Carmelite Rule should be read and explained every week, as an essential element of this continuing personal commitment on the part of each individual.

He speaks harshly of those living outside their communities without very serious reasons. Unless they return immediately, they are to be punished. There is absolutely no justification for the sale or purchase of permissions to remain outside of a community setting. A community is the natural environment for the religious, since all the helps of community life will allow him to act according to the commitment of his vows. Audet spends a great deal of energy discussing the details of community life. Religious services and common prayer, dress and comportment, sermons, conferences, and meetings, education of new candidates, meals and recreation, all came under his scrutiny, and guidelines were laid down for each category.

Nicholas grounded his program on several assumptions. One

Nicholas Audet (1481-1562) appointed vicar of the Carmelites by Pope Adrian VI in 1523. He wrote *Isagogicon*, a detailed plan for reform of the Order. Audet remained in office 39 years until his death. This etching is from the book *Chronological History of the Priors General of the Carmelite Order* by Marianus Ventimiglia, himself a prior general and historian of the Order in the 18th century.

was that a religious family either had to strive for evangelical perfection, in imitation of Jesus, or it should not exist at all. Another was that time was short; since turmoil within the Church did not allow for leisurely reform. Still another was that no one would be allowed to oppose legitimate reform. Those who would not struggle to become virtuous should depart forever, and stop pretending to be serious religious.

The general chapter of 1524 at Venice confirmed not only Audet's election, but his program as well. Nicholas set out on his ambitious agenda, and one of the longest terms of any prior general in history. With the mandate of the chapter behind him, Nicholas consolidated his principles into a more detailed blueprint for reform called the *Caput Unicum* (single head). Copies of this and other documents were printed and sent to every house in the Order to stimulate discussion and action. Attention to common prayer in each monastery was the foundation stone of his plan. Exemptions from chapel might be allowed in some cases, but only for genuine needs, not mere convenience. Another essential element was the need for larger communities to promote studies and intellectual vigor among the friars. To

speed the development along, he also published a revised version of John Soreth's constitutions, then quickly and vigorously began to implement the details.

Visits to the Provinces

Beginning in 1524, Audet spent several years visiting communities throughout Italy. His results were mixed for a variety of reasons, including war and political turmoil. Some houses, especially in the north, welcomed his visits as a chance to restore their lives to a fervent imitation of Elijah's zeal. Others were so firmly entrenched in lethargy and institutionalized laxity that they wanted nothing that might upset their counterfeit piety. In parts of central Italy, he found so few dedicated friars that he had to recruit others from more faithful houses to flesh out the ranks of moribund communities. A handful of large houses, like Florence and Naples, actively resisted his reform efforts and refused to measure up to his demands. They continued to give mute testimony to the difficulty of turning hearts and minds against human frailty.

One important feature of Audet's reform was the understanding that each individual religious belonged to the Order at large, and not to any specific house. A provincial who transfers his men frequently between houses helps to build the sense of belonging to a larger group. There were examples of insubordinate friars who paid very little attention to their professed duties. Instead, they built up a clientele of lay people who paid them for services like blacksmithing and breeding of livestock. Periodic transfers would make such behavior less likely. In one northern Italian province, the brethren became so convinced that frequent change was good that they all exchanged houses…everyone moved within a month.

In 1528, Nicholas moved north of the Alps and began to visit the provinces in France, starting with the *studium* at Place Maubert in Paris. Like John Soreth before him, he reaped good results from personal contact with the various communities, and was able to exert a powerful incentive toward renewal wherever he went. He also visited some of the nuns' convents in France and Belgium with good results, including the enrichment of some helpful legislation. Most of the French provinces responded well to his urgings, but his progress was agonizingly slow. Some of the larger priories, like Toulouse, required more of his time than he had anticipated, so Nicholas asked other capable friars to visit parts of the Order which he might not be able to reach himself.

He sent one delegation to Scotland without much visible effect. Another delegation, two French friars, visited the Iberian peninsula, and promoted Audet's measures for revitalization. They raised the province of Castile to a high state of discipline, and supported the reforms already in progress in both Catalonia and Aragon. However, the province of Andalusia was wracked with factional disputes, and resisted all efforts to root out some very serious abuses. The visitators probably did not go to Portugal, but reports to them indicated that the restoration of good discipline there was already in good hands, thanks to the provincial Balthasar Limpo, a native of Moura.

Nicholas dearly wanted to visit the province of Lower Germany, one of John Soreth's great triumphs. But the slowness of his progress in France prevented him from getting there until 1531. Yet even before that moment, he had corresponded with the provincial there, Theodoric van Gouda, asking him for advice, as well as for the loan of good friars to help bolster his efforts to form solid communities. He described his ideal of reform to Theodoric as, "the introduction of a way of living according to the Rule, the complete elimination of private ownership, the betterment of morals, and the appointment of reformed superiors." His trust in Theodoric was so complete that he deputed him to visit the eastern provinces of Saxony, Denmark, and Bohemia. The visits were successful, but unfortunately those doomed provinces had only a few more years before they were engulfed in a powerful tidal wave of confiscation and expulsion.

Continuing Efforts

After 1531, Nicholas Audet suspended his travels for the general chapter at Padua the following year. He was able to report both successes and failures in his program, including his inability to reach every corner of the Order in person. Much of Germany and central Europe had become too dangerous for safe travel and communication, and the sheer size of the Carmelite world made it doubtful that any one person could visit every house. He reported on the status of education and scholarship of each province, which was good in many cases, but not as high as would be ideal. He also had to admit that some provinces had been weakened numerically by the loss of many friars who refused to accept his tighter discipline. In the long run however that reality might actually have fortified Carmelite resilience to prepare for difficult times. In short, the Carmelite family had increased its fervor during Audet's first term, but many depopulated communities faced the continuing storm of the Protestant Reformation with a sense of apprehension.

Audet attempted to carry on his travels as long as he was able, staunchly appealing to the lofty ideals of the Rule. Although the results of his efforts continued to be uneven, the number of houses in parts of southern Europe actually increased during this period of great unrest. Nicholas and his reforms received enthusiastic support from the chapters of 1532 (Padua), 1539 (Vicenza), and 1548 (Venice). Scholars revised the Order's liturgical books and disseminated the new editions widely, hoping for greater fervor at prayer.

Most of the Reformation's damage to the Order took place in northern Europe. Martin Luther, himself an Augustinian religious, came to the conclusion that religious vows had no power to help save a person's soul. So in the Lutheran world, there was simply no place for communities of friars, nuns, or monks, whatever their theology might be. The Carmelite provinces of Upper and

Carmelite church and monastery in Straubing, Germany in an idealized drawing. Founded in 1368, the Straubing kloster is the oldest house in the Order in continuous use. Two Carmelites from this house travelled to Louisville, Kentucky to establish the Order in what would eventually become the Most Pure Heart of Mary Province. A brewery was attached to the monastery. Now privately owned, the company continues to produce Karmeliten Bier. *(Photo courtesy of Carmelite Media)*

Lower Germany were severely damaged by the implications of Luther's condemnation, but managed to survive. The provinces of Saxony and Denmark did not fare as well. Some of the newer houses in Poland and Bohemia managed to carry on in spite of severe pressure, and some outright violence. The four newly founded houses in Hungary were all swept away entirely, but in this case by the advance of the Ottoman Turks, and not by the Reformation. The Turks also captured Cyprus in 1571, putting an end to the Holy Land province forever.

Henry VIII's nationalization of the English Church also annihilated the largest Carmelite province. The province of Ireland theoretically vanished as well when Tudor administrators seized control of the Irish houses. But the astute Irish friars managed to maintain a sort of clandestine presence in the countryside, completely bereft of their property. The province of Scotland disappeared without a trace, once John Knox's Presbyterian reform took hold there. Many of those dispossessed friars joined the ranks of the secular clergy. Others simply returned to civilian life. Still others fled to other parts of Europe as refugees, or tried to carry on secretly wherever they had been living. In any case, the destruction of the infrastructure usually meant the death of any lasting Carmelite presence.

Upper Germany

One of the most dramatic struggles took place in the Upper German province. The survival of anything at all was largely due to the tenacity and zeal of the provincial, Andreas Stoss. He was the eldest son of Veit Stoss, one of the finest religious artists and woodcarvers of his age. Andreas was born at Nürnberg and grew up in Krakow, as his father moved around to find work. He joined the Carmelites in Nürnberg, studied in Krakow and Vienna, and completed a doctorate in canon law at Ingolstadt in 1517. By 1529 he was provincial of Upper Germany.

But even in his early years, as prior of Nürnberg, Stoss began to involve himself in the vigorous debates which characterized the Reformation in Germany. He found many opportunities to dispute points of doctrine with other preachers, but also had to keep an eye on the rapacious civic authorities. Nürnberg was an imperial city in which the municipal council claimed sweeping authority to regulate religious communities. In this case, the councilors saw Lutheran criticism of the friars as all the justification they needed to impound their churches and houses. Stoss responded with good theology, good preaching, and good administration. Even his adversaries admitted that he was a praiseworthy opponent.

In 1523, the provincial asked Andreas to visit the priory of St. Anne at Augsburg. The prior there was one Johann Frosch, a personal friend of Martin Luther, who also shared many of his ideas. Luther had stayed at the Carmelite church five years earlier, when he came to Augsburg to present his principles to Cardinal Cajetan. Stoss gently tried to encourage the Augsburg community to remain faithful to the Order's commitments and traditions, and especially to its unique liturgy. In spite of his best efforts, Frosch resigned and left the Carmelites, together with many members of his community. The Augsburg house and church were definitively lost to the Order within about 10 years.

This episode forced Stoss to take a closer look at Lutheran theology and to evaluate the details of religious life as he found it in his province. The influence of John Soreth in Germany had greatly enhanced the quality of many Carmelite communities. But there remained many areas where observance of the Rule and constitutions still needed improvement, particularly on the issues of prayer and poverty. On one hand, there might be good things to learn from the Lutherans about the use of Scripture, the elimination of superstitious piety, and the personal need for God's grace. But on the other hand, there was no place for Carmelites or any other religious community in Luther's theology. He had objected strongly to celibacy and religious vows, to the veneration of Mary and other saints, and to the elaborate Latin liturgy, among other practices and beliefs. That left little hope that any variation of Albert's Rule whatever could be followed in the context of a Lutheran-influenced church.

Such distinctions may be clear to us centuries later, but it must have been very confusing for people living at the time to sort out the conflicting opinions and principles (to say nothing of the name calling and insults) as they were shouted back and forth in the public forum. Stoss threw himself into these debates with such vigor that he quickly became a spokesman for the Catholic faction in Nürnberg. Despite his best efforts, he was finally exiled from his native town when the Protestants gained the upper hand. He fled to Straubing, then later to Bamberg, but never gave up his struggle.

Stoss was elected provincial of Upper Germany in 1529. He visited the surviving houses of his province in order to motivate the friars to remain faithful to their vows, and to encourage them to strengthen their prayer and community duties. Straubing managed to survive with a small but faithful remnant of the community. Another city where Stoss did well was Bamberg, where he advised the local bishop, Weigand von Redwitz, on ways to reform his diocese and improve the religious climate there. The bishop had been inclining toward Lutheran dogmas as the best viable means of spiritual renewal, until Stoss showed him otherwise. The anarchy caused by the Peasants' War had given the bishop second thoughts about a general breakdown of authority. Andreas emphasized the factor that the Church's long legacy of constancy was grounded in the authority of millions of faithful people, motivated by the Holy Spirit. Stoss attended the Diet of Augsburg in 1530 as a consultant to Bishop von Redwitz, and took an active part in that meeting between the Emperor and the reformers. When Pope Paul III announced the opening of a council at Mantua in 1537, the bishop sent him to represent the diocese of Bamberg. That council never actually met, but Stoss managed to travel as far as Austria before he heard of the cancelation, and then returned home.

Most of his remaining time as provincial was consumed by a frantic struggle to hold his province together. The Lutherans were not his only problem. Predatory princes and municipalities continued to covet the land and buildings of his priories. Defections and death among his friars depleted the ranks of those who could lead communities, or provide quality preaching in the Order's churches. The increasing turmoil, in turn, had discouraged vocations among young men, and reduced earnings and donations so badly that some houses had to be abandoned for reasons of abject destitution. In spite of his best efforts, 14 out of 26 priories were lost, including those in Nürnberg, Augsburg, and Nördlingen. By some accounts, there were only the remnants of about 40 friars left, out of a total of what may have been hundreds. But these men did represent the remains of a province which could grow and develop again. Stoss died in 1540, still provincial, and still not yielding one step in his tenacious conflict.

Lower Germany

In the province of Lower Germany, the same forces were at work, threatening to put an end to its existence. As in Upper Germany, there were secular authorities waiting to seize monastic lands or buildings. Substantial numbers of friars kept deserting to work in parishes, as diocesan bishops pleaded for help. Others defected because of the appeal of the reformers and became Protestants, or

The Karmelitenkloster in Frankfurt, Germany, a late Gothic structure from 1460-1520, is noted for its murals by Jörg Ratgebs in the cloister. They are the largest known paintings north of the Alps from the period. Today the building houses the Institute for Municipal History, the Archaeological Museum and "Die Schmiere," a local theater group offering satirical performances. *(Photo courtesy of Carmelite Media)*

simply went back to their families out of deep discouragement. One additional factor was the intermittent warfare between shifting alliances of cities, princes, and Holy Roman Emperor, Charles V. Just as in Upper Germany, good leadership enabled many of the communities to survive, in spite of some bitter struggles.

The steadfastness of Andreas Stoss in the south inspired several provincials in the north, including his contemporary Theodoric van Gouda, and later Martin Cuyper, and Eberhard Billick. The large northern province had 36 priories, grouped into 4 regional subdivisions for convenience. The important subdivision of Brabant was not as badly mauled as the German-speaking houses, and served as a reservoir of good friars who provided strength for the others. The province's most important foundation was at the holy city of Cologne, which was also a center of studies. So it is no surprise that the quality of scholarship, scripture study, and preaching reflected the engagement of these Carmelites with the new movements.

Eberhard Billick, in particular, played a major part in helping the Rhinelanders clarify their religious principles. He was probably born in Cologne about 1499 or 1500, entered the Order there as a young man, and received his doctor-

Carmelite Church of the Annunciation near the center of Krakow, Poland, dates back to the 11th century with the Italian-Baroque interior dating from about 1675. The famous Our Lady of Piasek, the 15th century fresco of Mary allegedly with features of Poland's Queen-Saint Jadwiga is in one of the church's chapels. A large Carmelite monastery adjoins the church. *(Photo courtesy of Carmelite Media)*

ate from the University. Even before he was one of his province's leaders, Eberhard promoted good scholarship and careful reasoning as tools of reform. Like Erasmus, he did not hesitate to criticize the countless abuses among local churchmen, as he called for improvement. A favorite and recurring theme of his was that badly educated priests caused untold evil in the Church; but that good theology and strict living could transform them into worthy servants. He was prior of the Cologne house by 1536, and was elected provincial in 1542.

By that time, many of his houses had already lost so many friars that they were unable to function normally. By 1530, the big community in Frankfurt was calling for help because they had only seven healthy priests left to carry on their many religious commitments. Other priories at Speyer, Mainz, Worms, Strasbourg, and elsewhere were even harder pressed. Like Stoss in Bamberg, Billick also had to deal with a crisis of conscience with his own bishop. In the case of Cologne, Archbishop Herman von Wied was one of the most important religious and political leaders in Germany. He was an easy-living prelate, who belatedly became aware of his need to improve or be replaced. He had summoned Alsatian reformer Martin Bucer from Strasbourg to restructure his diocese, a step which met with intense opposition from the university, the cathedral chapter, and many civil magistrates.

Billick wrote a sharply reasoned essay which called Bucer to debate points of theology. His provocation succeeded so well that he faced not only Bucer, but Philip Melancthon and John Olendorp as well. In fact he caused enough commotion in the years between 1536 and 1546 so that most educated people in Cologne began to discuss religious issues seriously among themselves. The trend of public opinion began to turn against the archbishop's plans to institute a Protestant reform. When von Wied tried to proceed with his measures anyhow, the local leaders prepared a rebuttal against him with Billick's help, and finally appealed to the emperor and the pope. Archbishop von Wied was finally excommunicated and deposed, with Billick making a dramatic dash across military lines to deliver the relevant documents.

The new archbishop, Adolf von Schauenburg, kept Billick close to him as a friend and advisor, especially on issues of church reform. Together they attended a conference at Regensburg (1546), the Diet of Augsburg (1547), and the Peace Conference of Augsburg (1555) which finally established a sort of truce between Lutherans and Catholics. Von Schauenburg appreciated Eberhard's talents so much that he named him as coadjutor bishop in 1556. Before Billick could be ordained, however, he died in January of 1557. He was still provincial of a wounded province, but one which survived in great part thanks to him.

Other Northern Provinces

The Carmelite province of Saxony, located in Luther's home territory, was newer than the other German provinces. Audet had called it a good province, but it never seems to have been very strong. Most of the surviving records are incomplete, since all the houses were lost. Thus it is difficult to know the details of exactly what happened to most of the communities there. It is likely that a substantial number of friars converted to Lutheranism, others fled to Catholic areas and tried to carry on, and still others were absorbed into the dwindling ranks of the diocesan clergy. There is mention of one redheaded friar, Valentine of Magdeburg, who engaged in a spirited dispute with a local Lutheran preacher. A satirical poem describes the end of the encounter, as a mob of onlookers threw Valentine in jail. We have no certain information about his fate, or indeed that of most of the province. We do know that the big priory at Magdeburg was torn down in 1550 to make way for new fortifications. Most other houses were taken over by municipal governments and demolished or turned over to private use. In any case, the entire province of Saxony disappeared, with nothing left.

The province of Denmark also ended its short but truly glorious history. The original Danish houses were part of the Saxon province, and probably separated from them about 1462. There seem to have been no more than nine houses, including a small territory in what is today southern Sweden. But even though their numbers were small, the Danes achieved a very high standard of intellectual and religious scholarship. In their first year as a province, John Soreth gave the Danish houses his highest rating for observance and religious fervor.

In the late 15th century, a time of increasing friction between partisans of humanism and theology, it seems that the Danish Carmelites colored their theology with a strong Christian humanism, reconciling the two trends. Some older style systematic theologians disliked their approach so much that they sometimes screamed "heresy," when in fact no heresy was found. Most Danish friars based their scholarship on scripture, the early Church Fathers, and their own intensive studies of spirituality. Indeed, some of them were the very best academics in their kingdom. They tended to oppose the impenetrable rationalizations of late scholasticism, and the excessively shallow piety and superstition found in many places in Germany and other northern countries. On the contrary, they did their utmost to make Jesus and Paul come alive in their preaching.

Good leadership was the principal reason why the Carmelites represented some of the most learned and zealous people in pre-Reformation Denmark. One provincial in particular stands out, Paulus Helie (probably Pavl Helgeson). As the first regent of studies in his province, Helie was unrelenting in his criticism of the abuses in the Danish Church, and actively promoted the intellectual vigor which his fellows modeled so well. After 1522, during his time as provincial, many of his best and brightest students abandoned both the Order and the Catholic Church, some of them to become the first Danish Lutheran bishops. This defection was a source of great anguish to Helie, but he never abandoned his vigorous assault on Lutheran theology and those who followed it. Some contemporaries described him as "the only real Catholic left in Denmark." But Protestantism prevailed in Denmark simply because King Frederick I had decided that it would do so. No matter how good Paul's arguments were, he began to realize that he could not succeed. By the time of his death, he had become a symbol of fighting the good fight, even though he had come to expect no victory in this life.

In Poland and Bohemia, the Reformation made great advances in its early years. Many of the communities were hard pressed, especially Prague and the other Bohemian houses. But others survived because there were enough friars who tenaciously held onto their professed way of life. In Krakow, for example, there have been Carmelites living continuously since 1397, even though their large house has been destroyed more than once. Gdansk, Bydgoszcz, and four other Polish houses were still making a heroic effort to survive as late as 1562. The Turkish advances in the Balkans caused the loss of Lwów. Other smaller houses vanished without clear reasons why.

Britain and Ireland

In the British Isles, the Reformation succeeded with much less violence, even though in the end, the extinction of the Carmelite provinces was complete. King Henry VIII saw no point in the destruction of the English Church, if he could gain control of it as a compliant "state church" which would do his bidding. The efficient transition which he produced by the Act of Supremacy

Etching of John Bale, a Carmelite who embraced Lutheranism but became a major source for information about the English Carmelites of that time period.

(1534) allowed a changeover so subtle that many people were unaware that their Church had changed. But the religious orders played no part in Henry's plans, now that he controlled the bishops. The Mendicant orders were simply suppressed in 1538, and their property in England, Wales, and Ireland was sequestered by the crown for whatever use he might wish.

The English province was one of the largest in the Order, with about 39 houses, and over 300 friars. But the reforming vigor of John Soreth and Nicholas Audet seems not to have made much impact in Britain. Only a handful of English Carmelites fought against the royal policy with the same zeal as their brothers on the continent. The last provincial, John Bird bent over backwards to collaborate with the King's guidelines, and twisted to every change in the political wind. We have the names of a few bold friars, like Lawrence Cook, prior of Doncaster, who was in Newgate prison for supporting a noble rebellion against Henry. He was condemned to death, but it is uncertain if he was actually executed. William Gibson and John Pecock were charged with insurrection at Norwich and condemned to perpetual imprisonment. Robert Austin, another Carmelite, was charged with preaching Catholicism, but again, we are not sure of the final outcome of his case.

One other English Carmelite who made himself well known by his passionate writing was John Bale. He went further into the Protestant camp than many of his fellows by embracing Lutheranism by 1534. In spite of his vitriolic disapproval, John was a true scholar and a writer of considerable skill. He criticizes his former Order bitterly, and at the same time argued for a more dramatic reform in the Church of England. He was condemned and banished several times, but continued his aggressive polemic writing. It is ironic that much of the detail we have on the Carmelites in England comes from the hand of one who had decided to condemn them.

In theory, Ireland was also subject to English law, at least in the eastern counties. But the slowness of enforcement always added an element of uncertainty to the Church's destruction. Henry's Act of Suppression was issued in 1538, but many Irish communities seem to have lingered on, some even until the end of the century. The Irish may have had as many as 30 houses originally, a few of them rather large. Dublin was suppressed in 1539 and most other houses during the 1540s. The records of the friars and their movements are very sparse, which may have been part of an intentional stratagem on the part of the Irish themselves. Written records make it easier for the authorities to find those who prefer to hide. As late as the general chapter of 1575, Ireland was represented by its provincial, Mahon McSweeney. Even with no formal houses, Irish friars continued to be professed and educated during the 17th century in France, particularly in the Touraine province. Then they were sent back to Ireland to live a shadowy existence and keep the old faith alive. The Irish province was finally restored legally in the 18th century.

In Scotland, the dissolution of the Carmelite province took place somewhat later, after the Presbyterian Church had become the state religion. Scottish Carmelites continued to attend the general chapters of 1539 and 1548. The last known provincial was John Christeson, who ruled until 1565, at least in theory. The destruction of perhaps a dozen houses began about 1558, with the disturbances fomented by John Knox in Perth, which was one of the oldest Carmelite foundations. By 1567, Knox and his supporters among the nobility had completed their conquest of power in Scotland, and no one was able to stand against him.

The Council of Trent

Carmelites were very significant at the Council of Trent, which met intermittently between 1545 and 1563, and finalized many of the reforms which should have been carried out long before. There were only five general superiors who attended the first session in 1545, but Nicholas Audet was one of them. Together with only four archbishops and about twenty bishops, they represented a pathetically modest beginning for a universal council which would have global impact. But they did indeed begin. The length of the council was aggravated by disagreement about what was most urgent. Prelates from the north wanted to discuss doctrinal issues which were under assault by the Lutherans, while the southerners felt they should address the moral and disciplinary reforms that had been neglected for so long. In the end, both subjects were dealt with in great detail, but the clarification of doctrine had to come first.

Audet was most active in the earliest sessions, before his health began to deteriorate. His contributions were marked with great clarity of thought and the precision of non-technical language which betrayed his long experience as a reformer and pastor. His theological positions generally supported the moderate ideas of the English Cardinal Reginald Pole, who served as one of the early presidents. Audet himself contributed a rather important document on Sacred Scripture, concerning the distinction between canonical and deutero-canonical books. He also offered valuable insights about the place of religious in the Church, as well as on subjects such as preaching, original sin, justification, and the sacraments, especially baptism and marriage. Even after Audet was too sick and feeble to participate actively in the council, he named Giovanni Stefano Facino as vicar to represent him. He continued to send written opinions from

Rome on subjects like the need for bishops to reside in their dioceses.

Keeping company with Audet, there would be several Carmelite bishops, who also had the right to vote on proposals. One particularly active and important participant was Balthasar Limpo, former provincial of Portugal, and a tough reformer in his own right. By the time the council convened, he had been named bishop of Oporto, and eventually became archbishop of Braga and primate of Portugal. He was the first Portuguese to arrive, and one who would remain until the very end. Although he was well respected by the king, he did not act as the official envoy of his country. But unlike most bishops at the council, Limpo was also a fine theologian, and made valuable contributions to the spirited debates. Among the other Carmelites at Trent, there were over 40 theologians and experts, including members of the Mantuan congregation. These others did not vote, but served as consultants and helpers to the prelates who actually did vote on the proposed legislation. Taken as a whole, the council comprised 25 distinct sessions, and Carmelites were present to contribute to 24 of them.

Trent put powerful tools into the hands of any reforming religious superior. After so many years of arduous reform within the Carmelite family, a prior general could finally take advantage of strong church legislation which supported the efforts of reformers. After Trent, no one could claim that strict observance was merely an option, or that fidelity to the spirit of the Rule was a trifling alternative. But as always, rules and legislation were only pieces of paper until they were taken into the hearts and minds of those who were expected to obey them. The hard work of implementation was only beginning when the council adjourned. The renewal of Carmelite spirituality and moral values was still a matter for the future.

+ + +

Chapter 6
Teresa's Renewal

Castile: 1570. The dark-eyed nun smiled gently as she contemplated the sunlight's dazzle in the spray of the small fountain. After so long, after so much delay, she now saw a chance to simplify her quest for the face of God. For the first time in her life, she had now embraced a community where silence was truly unhurried and rich in its possibilities. She fingered the simple wooden cross and asked God to strengthen the reformers in their resolve...they still had much to endure.

Giovanni Battista Rossi succeeded Nicholas Audet as prior general in 1562, and certainly knew that he had some very large shoes to fill. Yet Rossi (called "Rubeo" by the Spaniards) was an excellent religious and a determined reformer in his own right. At the outset, he asked for God's blessing on his undertakings, and called for support from all Carmelites for his ambitious program of revitalization. In his favor, at least for a while, was the spirit of freshness and optimism following the Council of Trent, which promised renewed energy in making all of the Church's undertakings into signs of God's grace. Trent had legislated in meticulous detail how religious had to observe their regulations on prayer, poverty, enclosure, and formation of candidates. Rossi also had the rock-solid support of Pius IV, the reform-minded pope who appointed him after Audet's death. The general chapter of 1564 in Rome confirmed that choice, and promised collaboration in every way.

Values into Action

Even before he received the chapter's endorsement, Rossi had visited some of the Italian provinces, urging the continued tightening of Audet's disciplinary principles. He had tentatively given permission for a select handful of friars to establish stricter hermitage or desert houses, where prayerful solitude and silence were the accepted norm. He had also assimilated some of Audet's reform standards, honed by 40 years of trial and error. He had learned, for example, that proposing high standards or ideals was always good, but that expecting to attain them quickly was not likely to succeed. He had also come to understand that insisting on severe legislation that not everyone could accept was unlikely to bring on successful change, but rather a division into angry factions. One particularly sensitive issue, for example, was just how much control an individual had over money which he or she had earned in the name of the community. Perfection would not come overnight.

Rossi's most urgent task was the communication of a huge mass of new legislation to the rank and file of the Order. So many new reforming regulations had become mandates during the council, that some previous customs, traditions, and conventions now had the force of law. There were also specific new statutes governing prayer and liturgy, simplicity of dress and footwear, and placing money in a common cash box. Nearly every community, every province, no matter how good it might already be, could benefit from the tightening of self-control regarding material belongings, strictness of enclosure, and a greater fidelity to the spirit of prayer which made the Carmelite ethos so unique. The exciting new legislation of Trent made it possible to unify the Order both in law and in practice, without undue rigidity.

Rossi understood better than many of his contemporaries that the Carmelites were more than just another group of mendicants. Even the finest works of ministry did not outweigh the prayerful link with the living presence of God. He stated that the original hermits from the slopes of Carmel followed an ideal which drove them to unite all their human powers with God's will. That day and night, they must actively work to be one with God by prayer, contemplation, and constant love. Everything else was chaff. Centuries earlier, Nicholas of Narbonne had proclaimed the same mantra, which had now taken on the force of law.

Sadly, the Achilles' heel of this otherwise noble ideal was the difficulty of implementation. Thousands of men and women had already taken vows to obey Albert's Rule under a great variety of understandings. They had become the existing fabric of Carmelite life for a broad spectrum of splendid and banal motives. If the energized fervor which Rossi foresaw were ever to become a reality, then it needed to find a dwelling place within those same living Carmelites, even before it inspired new candidates. For Rossi, that meant the necessity for him to travel, in the pattern of Soreth and Audet before him. He accurately saw that he needed to pass on his hopes to communities and individuals in person. The quicker he could get started, the better.

The Visitation of Spain

Spain quickly became the most urgent place for official travel. No prior general

John Baptist Rossi, prior general, who traveled extensively to promote reform of the Order. He was the first prior general to visit Spain where he met Teresa of Avila and encouraged her reforms.

had ever visited there. By 1500, there were four Spanish provinces, Catalonia, Aragon, Castile, and Andalusia, together with one in Portugal.[1] Reports about the condition of religious life on the Iberian Peninsula did not agree, since there was apparently a wide disparity between the best and the worst levels of observance. Rossi certainly intended to visit Spain as soon as he could, but one factor accelerated his timetable. The King of Spain, Philip II, had his own plan for the Carmelites.

Philip saw the Spanish Church as the strongest buttress of his regime in its "Golden Age." In particular, he felt that Spain should go far beyond the disciplinary rules of Trent, which he considered half-hearted. This same monarch, who promoted use of the Inquisition so energetically, also vowed that religious orders in Spain had to be stricter and more militant than those elsewhere. He envisioned the Spanish Catholics as the shock troops of a new crusade against Protestantism, as well as the bulwark of Christianity against the incursions of the Turks. The Ottoman Sultans had long since occupied Greece and the Balkans, had destroyed the Hungarian monarchy, and had almost captured Vienna in 1529. In effect, King Philip believed that he was a better religious reformer than the Council of Trent for Spain and all its far-flung possessions.

Philip wanted every major religious order to appoint a special vicar general for Spain, a sort of super-provincial who could coordinate disciplinary improvements with the utmost energy, in harmony with the monarch. Rossi correctly saw this ploy as an attempt on the King's part to interfere with his responsibility as chief reformer of the Carmelites. He politely told Madrid that he would see to everything that was needed, but Philip was not convinced. He had probably heard that a special reform congregation, like Mantua or Albi, already had a special vicar general charged with upgrading religious observance. It is possible that the king got his information from Miguel de Carranza, provincial of Aragon, who may have imagined himself as vicar general for Spain. So when the King pressed for more immediate action, Rossi had to promise that he would visit

---

1. Contemporary records indicate that Andalusia was the biggest province with 16 houses and about 250 friars, Castile had 9 houses with a few more than 100 friars, Aragon had ten houses with 112 men, and Catalonia had 13 houses with 85 men. There were also twelve nuns' convents with a great variety of customs and regulations. The Incarnation at Avila was the largest convent with 180 nuns. During this same period, Portugal had nine houses of men, and three of women.

Spain personally within two years. If he failed to do so, then he would agree to name a vicar general and let Philip implement his plan.

Trouble in the South

Because of the crush of paperwork in Rome, and other pressing issues, Rossi had difficulty meeting his own deadline, but finally crossed the Spanish frontier in the spring of 1566, just in the nick of time. He made a courtesy call at the royal palace to receive the needed approbation for his visits, and then got about visiting the houses of each province. The communities in Castile had already been visited by Nicholas Audet's reformers. Castile was depleted by many departures, but otherwise in very good condition. He would also find Portugal to be in a high state of fervor. The provinces of Aragon and Catalonia were still only partially reformed, but in the process of building themselves up to a more perfect status. The biggest headache was in Andalusia, where a faction led by the three Nieto brothers had control of the provincial finances and the priors of the most important houses. The brothers, named Gaspar, Melchior, and Balthasar, had placed their friends in positions of authority, and turned a very large province into a highly corrupt regime. They lived opulent lives themselves, while the ordinary members of the province languished in poverty and a state of near-servitude, sometimes with only the most trifling allowances for even food and clothing.

When Rossi arrived in Seville, it did not take him long to understand the depth of the crisis. He deposed Gaspar from his office of provincial, and replaced him with a better candidate. He ordered Melchior to be arrested for violent crimes, and eventually expelled him from the Order. Balthasar was given severe punishment, but was allowed to remain in the province. Most other Andalusian friars applauded his measures, and resolved to regain control of their province. Rossi made a sincere effort to show mercy, and reconcile the evildoers with the rest of the friars. But compassion toward the Nietos turned out to be a tactical mistake. Not long after the general resumed his travels, the Nieto faction began to stir up rumors and calumny against him among their powerful and well connected friends at the royal court.

The antics of this criminal family were to have far-reaching consequences, not only for their own Andalusian province, but for Rossi's entire reform program in Spain. Well-meaning prelates from the hierarchy and inept political bunglers from the royal entourage were drawn into a hopeless jurisdictional tangle, made even worse by officials in Rome, all at the mercy of a very risky postal system. The vigorous reform of the Order by its own prior general should never have triggered a crisis of any sort. But these other factors created a toxic environment for the otherwise brilliant revolution of Teresa of Avila.

Teresa's Vision

Teresa de Ahumada y Cepeda was born in Avila to a respected family of "new nobility." She entered the convent of the Incarnation in 1535, at a time when it was one of the largest houses in Spain. The community consisted of about 180 nuns, who had entered for a variety of motives. Surprisingly, there was little or no outright immorality there, but discipline was sloppy at best. The predisposition toward laxity was made much worse by the poverty of such a large community. There was no enclosure at the Incarnation, simply because no one had ever insisted that the nuns needed to have one. As a result, the house was a very busy place, with men and women coming and going at all hours. A surprising number of the sisters were there simply because their families had despaired of ever finding husbands for them. The families had effectively "dumped" them into the convent, sometimes providing lavish donations for their upkeep. Some of these aristocratic daughters had never stopped being noble ladies with their own cooks, servants, and suites of rooms, where they entertained friends. Such behavior was tolerated in part because it was common in other convents, too. Of course the extra income to a poor community tended to dull the instincts of a vocation director.

Although Teresa accurately observed that her convent could have been better governed, she lived rather contentedly at the Incarnation for about twenty years, following Albert's formula of life and steeping herself in Carmelite traditions and other spiritual literature. But after a personal spiritual crisis in 1554, she experienced a "conversion" to strive more intensely toward spiritual excellence. The religious revival of Trent prompted her desire to live the Carmelite vocation more perfectly. She envisioned a new sort of convent which would be small enough to make the sisters a true religious family, and strict enough to really protect them from all the distractions which might keep them from seeking the face of God. In the fall of 1560, she formulated a more detailed plan with a circle of like-minded friends.

She asked for, and received, permission from the provincial of Castile to design such an observant house. Teresa planned to follow the original simplicity of the Rule after the first mitigation (1247), thus restoring the meatless diet and strict enclosure. Her nuns would wear a greatly simplified habit, and sandals instead of shoes. (This feature is the origin of the reform's being called "Discalced" or barefoot.) Family names were to be abandoned in favor of religious names, so Teresa herself now became Teresa of Jesus. Early in the reform, each house would have no more than 13 members. Community activities, including housework and recreation, were designed to truly build a sense of community, which would sustain each individual through the rigors of her spiritual discipline. Although her followers were to be not just nuns, but solitaries, Teresa still wanted a true religious family. When she opened her convent of St. Joseph in 1562, Teresa happily began the most productive phase of her life.

Rossi and Teresa

Prior general Rossi visited Teresa in 1567 and was very impressed with the woman herself and with the quality of her reformed house. He promised her that she could found as many houses as she wished, as long as she could find

Monastery of the Incarnation, Avila, Spain - Teresa of Jesus lived here for 20 years before the monastery accepted the enclosure. After a spiritual crisis in 1554 Teresa decided to establish monasteries according to the "primitive Rule" which was actually the mitigated Rule of 1247.

sisters to live in them. Over the next twenty years, she would make over a dozen reformed foundations. Spain's superheated religious climate was encouraging to vocations, and Teresa's enthusiasm drew some outstanding women to join her in her renewal of religious life. She stated repeatedly that the Catholic answer to Protestantism was not to be found in diplomacy or warfare, but in the witness of holy religious. Although Teresa maintained that she only intended to "restore" the life of the primitive rule, she was in fact building a unique and powerful model for prayer and contemplation which had never existed before her time. Her inspiration may have been in the tales of Elijah and the wadi community, but the closeness of her communities and her emphasis on the hermit's intensive meeting with God were unique to Carmelite tradition.

It is difficult to imagine how such an active woman ever found time to write anything. But Teresa's principal writings trace her life and busy activities, as well as her teachings on the spiritual journey. Her *Autobiography* sometimes known as the *Book of her Life* (1562-5) is a straightforward narrative of her passage from desultory convent routine to the fervent life which became her trademark. The *Way of Perfection* (1566-7) is in effect a textbook for those who seek closer union with God. Her lively and charming book of *Foundations* (1574-82) traces the capsule history of each of her houses, with items of practical advice spliced into the chronology. The masterpiece of her *Interior Castle* (1577) illustrates the stages of advancement in the spiritual life through a series of seven "mansions." The massive impact of Teresa's writing continues to influence countless people today, from the lofty to the most humble.

Within a short time, the regimen of life which worked so well for women began to attract the attention of men, too. The convents had an obvious need for chaplains and spiritual directors who understood what was going on in Teresa's houses. So in 1568, a house was established at Duruelo where friars from the Castilian province could pledge themselves to live according to Teresa's stricter constitutions. One of the first volunteers for this community was Antonio de Heredia, who became Anthony of Jesus. He in turn brought in another young friar, John of St. Matthias (later John of the Cross) who became novice master. Despite the difference in their ages, Teresa and John formed a strong and beneficial friendship. A year later, a second house was established at Pastrana which also accepted volunteers from Andalusia. One of the newcomers was Balthasar Nieto, of the now disgraced faction of that Andalusian province.

Rossi was especially concerned about the spread of communities of Discalced friars, not only because they followed a different observance from the other houses he wanted to reform, but also because he feared the emergence of another semi-independent congregation. For the time being, he hoped to contain the male reform within the observant Castilian province, and to protect it from turbulent Andalusia. But he was not aware of Nieto's transferal from the Andalusian jurisdiction. Although Rossi had originally authorized only two houses of men, a third priory was founded at the university town of Alcalá in 1570, and he allowed it to remain.

Threats to the Reform

Sadly, members of the Nieto faction complicated the perfectly legitimate reform by attempting to regain their supremacy in the south. Rossi had been merciful to them before he left Spain in 1567, but they betrayed his trust. Using well connected friends in the royal government, they lodged complaints and shocking accusations against Rossi and the new superiors in the Andalusian province, hoping to regain their power in the resulting confusion. Their protests even reached the ears of Pope Pius V, a former Dominican inquisitor and a strict reformer. Neither the king nor the pope wanted to ignore allegations of corruption and political dishonesty in high places. Since King Philip had a fundamental distrust of Italians, he was already inclined to believe the slander, and assumed that Rossi had only tried to hide the abuses.

So Philip II once again pressed his proposal to reform the Carmelites himself with the help of the Spanish bishops and the pope authorized him to go ahead. Philip's chosen agents were drawn from the hierarchy and diocesan clergy, most of whom were well intentioned, but understood very little about nuns or friars. Since there was a different visitator for each religious house, there was almost no consistency in their results, and certainly no clearly charted path toward the perfect religious community. Rossi's visit had generally inspired most of the friars to press their renewal according to the Order's own recent legislation. But the king's reform efforts poisoned the atmosphere of the houses and confused the friars with divided authority and continuous tinkering. Their most common response was not compliance, but anger, resistance, and even violence.

The Dominican Visitators

In January of 1570, Pius V tried to remedy the organizational pandemonium by appointing three Dominicans as special visitators to the Spanish provinces. These powerful officials were given authority to name or depose superiors, found or suppress houses, and even override decrees of the prior general himself. Unfortunately, the pope's communication with prior general Rossi and King Philip was very poor. The resulting chaos was the product of too many good people attempting to do good things. When the local Carmelite superiors wrote to Rossi, asking for instructions on how to proceed, he helplessly told them to obey the pope's visitators, but to defend the rights of the Order whenever they could.

The Dominican visitator for Castile was Pedro Fernandez, who carried out his duties with great thoroughness. He found the friars' communities in fairly good order. He was also quite impressed with Teresa and John, and gave them complete freedom to continue their reforming activity. He reported to Rome that the trouble seemed overblown to him. Miguel Hebrera served as visitator for Aragon and Catalonia with similar success. But the visitator of Andalusia, Francisco Vargas, made very little progress against the wild protests of the Nieto faction, and the unyielding obstinacy of their foes. He also noted that a shocking number of friars continued to engage in immoral behavior, largely because genuine religious discipline had been so rare in recent years, and had not yet been restored.

Vargas had certainly been assigned the most troublesome province, but he greatly complicated his task by exercising less attention and prudence than his colleagues. He tried to visit some of the houses, but then quickly backed away from the passionate wrangling which he discovered. He decided instead to bring in reformed friars from Teresa's Castilian houses to staff three communities, even though it contradicted Rossi's plan. But his worst mistake was naming Balthasar Nieto in 1573 as his own personal delegate for the reform of the entire province. This decision nearly touched off an open revolt when the southern friars were faced with the return of one of their oppressors. Vargas caught his mistake after only 4 months, and replaced Nieto with Jerome Gracian, a gentle, sincere, and charming friar, who courageously accepted the daunting task. Teresa found Gracian to be a captivating and highly principled man, and took a motherly interest in his welfare. Her trust in him seemed boundless, although she acknowledged his lapses of judgment, passing them off as youthful indiscretions. A growing number of reformed friars did not share her enthusiasm.

Jerome Gracian

Gracian was only 28 at the time, highly motivated and richly talented, but fresh from the novitiate and still lacking experience. His skills as a preacher and a spiritual director drew high praise from Teresa. Although Vargas gave him the task of governing friars of both observances, Gracian's primary interest was promoting Teresa's reform, whatever the cost. By way of contrast, the friars in the older houses were afraid that Gracian would impose the Discalced statutes on them by force, even though they had taken their vows to observe an entirely different way of life. In the midst of all this turmoil, it is astonishing that no one informed the prior general of these dramatic events.

Vargas had also overstepped his authority by moving people from one jurisdiction to another. In June of 1574, he also appointed Gracian vicar provincial of Andalusia, without removing the existing superior, Augustine Suarez. Countless appeals and legal challenges followed, making the situation even murkier. A large number of the friars outside of Teresa's houses became so angry that they protested against the Discalced reform itself, and the confusion it had unleashed. Their fury went so far as to launch unfounded personal attacks against Gracian and even Teresa herself.

The new pope, Gregory XIII, tried to help simplify the confusion in August, 1574 by withdrawing the authority of the Dominicans Fernandez, Hebrera, and Vargas. He favored a direct renewal by the prior general and his representatives. That dramatic step should have solved the jurisdictional problem once and for all. But the highly respected Papal Nuncio for Spain, Nicola Ormaneto, decided to use his own authority to complete the reform in Andalusia. Gracian had met with both Ormaneto and the king during the previous year, and had pleaded for help. Ormaneto, for his part, saw Teresa's reform as something that had to be defended at all costs, and had already become personally involved in the struggle.

The Chapter of 1575

From Rome, Rossi desperately tried to follow the unfolding confusion. He wrote to Teresa pleading for information. He asked what had gone wrong, and how could he support the good reforms they had planned, as well as restore harmony to the quarreling communities. One letter mailed in October, 1574 and another of January, 1575 never reached Teresa until June. Despite his favorable estimation of Teresa, Rossi began to have second thoughts about what he may have unleashed. In the meanwhile, a general chapter met in Piacenza during May, and Rossi was unable to answer any of the questions about whether Teresa's reform might be causing Spain to disintegrate. No Discalced friars had arrived at the chapter who might have explained their actions. The chapter delegates heard only one side of the story, complaints springing from genuine frustration, as well as some outright lies and slander.

The chapter delegates grew angry enough to pass a resolution that all unauthorized foundations would be suppressed, and that anyone who had acted against the will of the general should be deprived of office. No one criticized Teresa by name, but Rossi advised her to stop traveling and maintain a low profile until the trouble had passed. He also appointed a respected Carmelite, Jerome Tostado, as his special representative to sort out the mess, once and for all. But once again, the king intervened and the royal council blocked Tostado from doing anything.

To make things even more confusing, Papal Nuncio Ormaneto anticipated the decrees from Piacenza and acted first. He appointed Gracian to help him as "provincial superior" for Andalusia, and special visitor, a job which Rossi had already assigned to Tostado. Gracian, for his part, followed the generally sensible methods of visiting and reforming the southern houses, but he seemed to ignore the good legislation at his disposal from the chapter of 1575. And despite Teresa's repeated urging, Gracian neglected any form of communication with Rossi, who might otherwise have become his ally and sponsor.

Gracian's Defense

From his point of view, Gracian felt that the entire Teresian Reform was under attack, and decided to protect it from all other Carmelite authorities. On his own initiative, he used Ormaneto's authority to cluster all houses of Discalced nuns and friars together into a single, special "reformed province" in August, 1576. He confirmed all new foundations, and summoned the superiors of all reformed houses of friars to a special chapter. When the chapter met, they elected councilors, but no provincial, since Gracian himself was obviously in charge already. Even though she was not involved in this action, Teresa had probably reconciled herself to a separate Discalced province by this time. She could see that any further effort to co-exist would be too painful for both sides. Gracian's primary motive was defending what he knew to be good and virtuous, even if matters of jurisdiction had to be ignored. Unfortunately, jurisdiction was the primary consideration to nearly everyone else in the arena.

Rossi, on the other hand, wanted to prevent any sort of separatism, since it might lead to the segregation of his most reformed friars from the others who badly needed their example. Good ideas tend to catch on more easily in a peaceful atmosphere. Rossi continued to hope that the Discalced houses of men would remain attached to the stable province of Castile, and have nothing to do with Andalusia, where their presence might act like oil thrown onto a fire.

Ormaneto the Nuncio died in January, 1577. His replacement, Filippo Sega, felt that Ormaneto's activism had been a mistake, and that the Carmelites should be allowed to reform themselves. Sega reversed the royal prohibition on Jerome Tostado's power as Rossi's trouble shooter. Tostado, in his turn, was frustrated and annoyed at what he considered legalistic obstructionism against the prior general's authority. He was in an extremely angry mood when he launched an investigation of Gratian, based largely on Balthasar Nieto's bitter denunciation. He suspended Gracian's authority and disbanded his interim province. Sega, the Nuncio, supported Tostado by naming a special vicar general for the Discalced houses in 1579. The choice was Angel de Salazar, provincial of Castile, who seemed to be acceptable to most of the principal players.

Tostado then moved to begin his visitation of the Discalced houses. At Teresa's old convent of the Incarnation, he found John of the Cross and Germain of St.

Mathias, whom Fernandez had named chaplains and confessors to the nuns. In Tostado's judgment, Fernandez' appointment was illegal, so he ordered both friars arrested and locked up. It was during this period that John was incarcerated at the large priory at Toledo for eight and a half months, with meager food and regular punishment. Living in an airless and silent storage room, he managed to compose the first 30 stanzas of his *Spiritual Canticle* and considerable work on the *Dark Night of the Soul* and other poems. During this entire ordeal, he never deviated from his dedication to simple and devout living in God's presence. He was finally able to escape in spite of his weakened condition, and he fled to a Discalced house. From Teresa's point of view, John's treatment was inexcusable, and a sign that her entire reform was in danger of increased violence if there was not some legal protection.

MATER TERESA DE IESVS FVNDATRIX CARMELITARVM EXCALCEATARVM.
OBIIT A̯.° CHRISTI DOMINI 1582. ÆTATIS SVÆ 68.

Engraving of St. Teresa of Avila (1515-1582) by Jerome Wierix based on the famous painting by Br. Juan de la Miseria. His portrait, done in 1576 when Teresa was 61 years old, is the only portrait of the saint.

A Discalced Province

Rossi had died in 1578, and the new general, Giovanni Battista Caffardo, was eager to put an end to the extreme animosity between the factions in Spain. Sega, the nuncio, favored a separate province for the Discalced, since there was no longer much hope of blending two groups with such different observances of the Rule. With the support of Teresa, the Discalced friars asked for a separate province for all the reformed houses. The pope granted the request, and it was confirmed by the general chapter of 1580. Teresa exerted a great deal of her personal influence to have Gracian elected the first provincial, but then only by a narrow margin. Special constitutions were then drawn up to codify the principles of Teresa's more disciplined formula: simplicity of life, solitude, mental prayer, devout liturgical worship, and strong bonds within the community.

Teresa was finally content that she had achieved a measure of safety for her reformed houses. Her health had deteriorated considerably, but she bravely resumed her work of founding still more convents. On her return trip from Burgos in the late summer of 1582, she became too ill to continue. She died peacefully on October 4, knowing that she had indeed created something beautiful for the God who loved her so dearly. During her final years, she had traveled with her devoted companion and "guardian angel, Anne of St. Bartholomew.

Profession of St. John of the Cross - painting from the 18th century in the chapel of St. John of the Cross in Medina del Campo. The artist is unknown. *(Photo courtesy of the Discalced Carmelite Province of Castille)*

Anne was a lay sister, who had entered Teresa's very first community with little education, and the prospect of doing no more than simple manual labor. But she demonstrated her outstanding personal traits by her loving and constant care of Teresa. In time, she would contribute substantial energy to the establishment of Discalced sisters in France and the Low Countries.

It was during these same years that the writing of John of the Cross reached its zenith. John had always been a skilled confessor and director. In his earlier years, his competence as a preacher made him reluctant to write, but the enforced solitude of his prison may have set free his poetic soul. John's writing is remarkable insofar as it began with intense poetry, to which he added commentary on the verses he had already composed, and then revised and retouched the same works extensively. His most wide-ranging and systematic work is the *Ascent of Mount Carmel*, composed 1579-84. It is a description of the soul's journey toward union with God, based on his own sketch design of the spiritual mountain of Carmel. Between 1582 and 1585, he worked simultaneously on his *Dark Night of the Soul* and the *Spiritual Canticle*, both of which he revised meticulously. At the end of this same period, he completed most of his *Living Flame of Love* in less than a month of blazing creativity. These and his other works comprise a unique treasury of spiritual literature which has never been equaled.

After the death of its energetic foundress, the reform experienced a spectacular period of growth. By 1595, there were 1400 Discalced religious living in 58 houses of friars, and 34 of nuns. Gracian's term as provincial was marked with apostolic zeal for preaching, works of spiritual renewal, and missionary activity in Spain's flourishing empire. Beginning in 1582, Gracian launched several attempts to establish a mission in central Africa, but with disappointing results. A much more successful effort in 1585 launched a mission to Mexico which flourished from its very beginning. Despite many hardships and setbacks, the Mexican mission took root and grew into a self-sustaining province. But for all his outward success, Gracian's visionary leadership came under the criticism of a number of friars, led by the observance-minded Nicholas of Jesus Doria.

Doria and Independence

Nicholas Doria, of the Genoese banking family, entered the Discalced reform in 1577. He was a talented administrator, who had already won well-placed friends, thanks to his skill at sorting out financial chaos in high places. Once he took his vows as a reformed friar, he followed the details of Teresa's formula of life to the minutest detail. His religious fervor was genuine, but his dedication expressed itself in formalism and legalism. Doria's discipline and austerity frightened some, but impressed others by imprinting his community with a high quality of observance, no questions asked. The Gracian-Doria controversy in many ways represents the classic showdown between dynamic ministry and prayerful adherence to a formula of life. Gracian would argue that Teresa had tightened the rules of religious life to enable God's grace to shine more brightly, and not to be hidden under a basket. Doria then countered that Gracian's activism would dissipate the fruits of the reform by his wild projects, especially because Jerome did not observe Teresa's regulations very meticulously in his own life.

Gracian's inexperience and lack of political sophistication may have led him to underestimate Doria's ability. Doria in turn continued to impress other friars with his single-mindedness, and was easily elected provincial at the chapter of 1585. He lost no time reorganizing the central administration to enforce a stricter regimen in each community. Missions and other external ministries were to be curtailed, and the relative autonomy of the nuns was dismantled in favor of tight supervision by the friars. Doria was also the primary force behind the complete independence of the Teresian reform, first as an autonomous congregation in 1587, then a totally sovereign order by 1593.

The New Regime

Jerome Gracian was sent to Lisbon to preside over Portugal, which Philip II had annexed in 1580. (It was not until 1640 that Portugal and its empire regained full independence.) Gracian refrained from open criticism for the time being, but kept his eye on Doria's tightly-disciplined administration. It was largely Doria's new policy of governing the nuns that caused renewed friction between the two men. The new regime wanted to control not only the women's finances, but naming superiors and chaplains as well, which of course meant that Teresa's well-respected constitutions would have to be changed. The first loud objection came from Anne of Jesus, one of Teresa's earliest followers, who was now prioress in Madrid.

Anne set out to defend the old constitutions, using some very important political friendships, as well as her own stature as one of Teresa's closest collaborators. She managed to obtain documents from both the nuncio and from Pope Sixtus V, endorsing the quality of Teresa's legislation. Jerome Gracian and John of the Cross also joined their voices to support her position. Doria was both angered and embarrassed by these attacks against his plan, and resolved to strike back.

In 1591, he ordered Anne of Jesus deposed from her office as prioress, and confined in seclusion in her own convent. Then he petitioned for and received a reversal of the papal brief, leaving him free to act. Finally, Doria had Gracian detained for interrogation at Madrid. John of the Cross had already been somewhat marginalized, and kept on the periphery of the province. John did not object to this, largely because he had little interest in politics or administration. On the contrary, he had kept himself very single-minded in his reflection and writing. Doria ordered him to join the mission in Mexico, but he died on December 14 before he could leave Spain, not yet 50 years old. It is ironic that John, who craved only solitude and reflective quiet, spent most of his days in such fruitful apostolic activity. His only real periods of stillness were his period in prison, and the final weeks before his death.

Throughout Doria's years as provincial, Gracian had been a constant thorn in his side because he felt that he had to oppose an excessively rigid asceticism which contradicted Teresa's joyful service of the Lord. Doria, on the other hand, saw Gracian's flamboyant activism as a threat to the reform. Jerome honored the ideal of the primitive Rule in principle, but often evaded such details as solitude, simple living, and abstinence from meat, pleading reasons of health or ministry. After all, if Gracian or anyone else could reason away strict observance for any apparently good motive, then how could anyone safely defend the ideal? Doria found Gracian to be a rebellious and hopeless spoiler, and wanted him out of the Order. More and more reformed friars began to agree, seeing Gracian as a threat to the solitude and contemplation which Teresa had promised them. Jerome was expelled from the reform in 1592, and for a time wandered as an outcast. He found his way at last to the Carmelite house in Brussels, where he continued living the primitive Rule in a non-Discalced house. His final years were marked by dynamic writing and preaching, as well as extensive help in the establishment of Discalced foundations in the Low Countries. But he never stopped being a tragic figure, rejected by the people to whom he had devoted his life. He died there in 1614, wondering if his life had been a miserable failure.

Nicholas Doria emerged supreme from the mêlée, but did not long survive. At a time when Gracian's flamboyant view of the Carmelite charism could have spun the new reform into a whirl of activism, Doria held steady to a more sober life. His decade of leadership had definitively driven home the absolute need for strict living and fidelity to the primitive ideals of silence, solitude, and interior prayer. Those standards retained their high position long after him, although the rigidity of his system was quickly relaxed by his successors. Doria died in 1594, and was succeeded by the peaceable and kindly Elijah of St. Martin.

Carmel after the Reformation

On his way home from Spain in 1566, prior general Rossi had hoped to visit the French provinces as well, spreading his gospel of reform. After all, France was still the virtual heartland of the Order. He had traveled from Narbonne to Montpellier, giving advice and encouragement, but was not able to proceed toward Paris, and its all-important house of studies. Warfare had broken out because of the increasingly unstable relationship between religious and political factions.

Lutherans had never made much of an impact in France, due largely to the efforts of King François I. But John Calvin's more militant reformed church, operating from nearby Geneva, exerted a broad religious influence in the French-speaking world, no matter what the royal government decided. The primary appeal of the Calvinists was in the south and west, which were the areas of strongest concentration of Carmelite houses as well. And most of the Calvinist Huguenot preachers operated with a dynamism which made their impact far greater than their limited numbers might suggest. Although no more than 10% of the French population converted to Calvinism, their numbers included some very important aristocrats, including members of the royal family, and as many as half of the lesser nobility. Significantly, there were also many noteworthy merchants and tradesmen in just the sort of commercial towns and cities which had welcomed the early Carmelites.

Beginning in the 1560's, a three-cornered struggle known as the French Wars of Religion brought the entire country to its knees. The Huguenots were the most radical faction, sharply opposed by an equally bigoted bloc of Catholic rigorists, and also by moderate Royalists who wanted a peaceful reconciliation. However, the two militant factions were far stronger than the Royalists, and quickly touched off a savage civil war which spanned the reigns of four kings, and ravaged nearly every part of France. Until the final settlement of 1598, violent bands of marauders could gather suddenly and often devastated entire communities.

When Rossi learned that he might be in physical danger if he attempted to visit any of the French provinces, he determined to reach out instead by his written word, at least. He appointed several respected French superiors as his vicars for reform and renewal, but they generally had indifferent success amid the growing atmosphere of chaos. He scheduled the next general chapter for 1572

Carmine in Venice - On the left side of the church is the building housing the famous *Scuola Grande dei Carmini*. The *scuola* (or confraternity), founded as a lay devotional group in 1593, is still active today. The church was populated in the 17th and 18th centuries with paintings of Carmelite saints and events of the Order's history, but otherwise structurally unaltered since the 14th century.

in Paris, as an affirmation of Carmel's importance in France. He and his companions had actually started out for that chapter when they learned of the death of Pope Pius V, who had endorsed their travel. The chapter never took place, and it may be doubtful that anything within Rossi's power could have helped to delay the gathering tempest.

The southern provinces of Narbonne, Provence, Aquitaine, Gascony, and Toulouse suffered most severely. Most houses suffered some damage, and many were utterly destroyed. A shocking number of friars were killed, some with appalling tortures. Estimates of the casualties include over 5000 priests killed, including 677 who were Carmelites, Dominicans, or Augustinians. Even for the individuals and communities which were not physically harmed, the devastation and depopulation of the countryside nearly brought an end to the vocations and support they needed from the civilian population. In most areas, an orderly, stable religious life became virtually impossible for the next generation or two.

The devastation was too much for the Congregation of Albi. Nicholas Audet had declared the congregation to be in good condition in 1531, but the fervor of the members had declined rapidly, especially in the houses of study. The Congregation's houses and friars were so severely injured by the ceaseless fighting that the distinct entity of Albi was abolished in 1584, and the remnants taken over by other provinces.

In the Low Countries, the Dutch-speaking northern provinces largely adopted

Calvinist teachings, as they fought to win their independence from Spain. All Carmelite houses in the north were lost during the 1570's, including Haarlem and Utrecht. The French and Flemish-speaking provinces of the south remained Catholic, and generally loyal to Spain. Carmelite communities there also suffered serious disruption from the constant fighting. Rossi sent the impressive Peter Wolf to visit and strengthen the spiritual fervor of those houses. He succeeded to a remarkable degree, especially at Antwerp, Mechelen, and Brussels. Wolf himself died heroically in the fighting at Mechelen in 1580. Similar visits to Upper Germany helped to hearten the badly weakened communities which had survived the ravages of the Reformation. Rossi spent the remainder of his life in Italy, unable to travel, but always promoting prayerful reflection and the common life.

The general chapter of 1575 at Piacenza, which had such dire results for the Discalced communities, actually helped the reform efforts in the rest of the Order. The chapter produced a great deal of legislation, which made stricter observance of the Rule into the ordinary state of affairs, not just an interesting option. Relations with the Congregation of Mantua were improved. The Mantuans felt more closely connected with other Carmelites, as the quality of religious practice improved in the Order at large. Since the Turks had captured Cyprus in 1570-1, Famagusta, Nicosia, and the rest of the Holy Land province had been lost. Plans to revive it with foundations on Crete came to nothing. It was increasingly obvious that the growth of Carmel would have to be in the future, since the past was firmly closed.

+   +   +

Chapter 7
Reaching Outward

Genoa, 1640. The lean, balding friar clutched his mission cross apprehensively as the ship's weathered bow nosed out of the harbor. "Well, we're in God's hands now!" he thought to himself. "It's either preaching Jesus' love to thousands of his children on other shores, or torture and martyrdom at the hands of unbelievers." He glanced back at his companions, as they leaned against the rail. They seemed confident and unafraid. Being in God's hands was really a very good place to be.

At the dawn of the 17th century, the Carmelite world faced daunting challenges everywhere. The northern provinces had been either damaged or extinguished by the Reformation. The Wars of Religion in France had inflicted extensive damage on those important provinces, as well as the urban communities which supported them. Belgian and Dutch houses faced a similar loss of their ability to function. Turkish military advances had totally eradicated the Carmelite presence in Cyprus and Hungary. The Discalced Carmelites, newly independent with the vigor of renewal, were just beginning their breathtaking growth outside of Spain, but faced the same daunting problems as the rest of Europe when it came to finding support and vocations.

Spiritual Growth

One powerful element in the success of the Discalced reform was the restoration of the ancient custom of the "desert" house, or hermitage. It was Thomas of Jesus who first conceived the idea of a formal house where individuals could live the primitive eremitical life which had first inspired Albert's Rule. He began in 1592 at Bolarque, near Pastrana in Spain, where his experimental community devoted itself totally to solitude and contemplation. Silence was to be absolute, and there would be no active ministry. He proposed a staff of four permanent members, who would welcome other friars who could volunteer for one year at a time. The original configuration of the *wadi* provided the model for the hermitage: a central chapel, surrounded by solitary dwellings separated from one another. The hermits would come together only for prayer and meals. In his vision, each province was to have a desert house to act as its spiritual core, and a sort of "leaven in the loaf" for the many other hard-working communities. It was particularly useful for preachers, scholars, or missionaries to spend time in such a house, as they connected their work with an intense personal experience of God.

Following the secession of the Discalced, the remaining Spanish houses of the Ancient Observance remained depopulated, discouraged and, of course, still unreformed. It is providential that the reform of the women's houses proceeded faster than those of the friars. The general chapter of 1586 stipulated for the first time that Carmelite friars had a special mission to care for the nuns. Periods of formal meditation and spiritual reading were phased into the practice of each convent, and the liturgy was somewhat simplified to allow more time for personal prayer, as Teresa had wished. Beginning in 1595, there were official constitutions for the nuns in Spain, which aimed at tightening the practices which had touched off the need for reform.

So vigorous was the growth in the numbers of Discalced friars in Spain, that the mission-minded Pope Clement VIII forced a crisis of sorts. Nicholas Doria had established only one foundation outside of Spain, at his own home city of Genoa in northern Italy. Doria subsequently rejected all wider expansion, including the complicated task of sending out and maintaining foreign missionaries. But the pope had other ideas, and would not take no for an answer.

The Genoa community comprised several particularly dynamic Spaniards, like Peter of the Mother of God, as well as other newcomers from many countries. Pope Clement offered the church of La Scala in Rome to Peter and the Carmelites, but Doria's successor refused to take on any other duties outside of Spain. So the pope placed the houses in Genoa and Rome directly under his own jurisdiction, and set the stage for a juridical division of the Discalced Carmelites. In 1600, Clement VIII set up an Italian Congregation, with its own general and administration. The new group would be free to make foundations anywhere except Spain, Portugal, and their empires. The Spanish Congregation was not unhappy with this arrangement, and the division lasted until 1875. During that long period, most of the superb Discalced missions were the work of the Italian Congregation.

Other Mission Initiatives

The Ancient Observance province of Portugal had already begun a successful missionary effort in 1579, when the Cardinal-Regent Enrique sent an expedition to Brazil. Four friars went with the first ships to Pernambuco, where their original foundation at Paraíba failed to materialize. But the same men tried again, and successfully established a house at Olinda. Other foundations followed, including Rio de Janeiro. By 1595, their efforts were so successful that the provincial chapter set up a vice-province of Brazil with four houses. Other Portuguese friars and locally recruited men joined the effort enthusiastically, and by 1635, there were eleven houses, with over 200 friars. In 1720, two free-standing Brazilian provinces were created for Rio in the south and Bahia-Pernambuco in the north-east. There was yet another Brazilian mission of Maranhão in the far north of the country. Uncooperative winds and ocean currents along the northern coast made it easier for people there to communicate directly with Lisbon than with the rest of Brazil. Friars along that difficult shoreline tended to think of themselves as part of the mother-province, rather than Brazilians. Even so, they established an inspiring history of prayer and ministry to colonists, slaves, and Amazonian natives alike.

Before Nicholas Doria became Discalced general, Jerome Gracian sent out several missionary expeditions, with Teresa's blessing. The foundations in Mexico proved to be the strongest and most durable, and were well supported by the Spanish Congregation. These missions would continue to flourish. But it was the Italian Congregation which literally helped "write the book" on the exhilarating mission campaigns of the 17th century. In particular, Peter of the Mother of God became the pope's special adviser on mission affairs, and contributed greatly to their success.

The personal friendship between Peter and Clement VIII led to the dispatch of a small team to Persia in 1607, which met with remarkable success. The great Persian Shah Abbas I welcomed the missionaries warmly, in great part because he wanted western political help against his enemies, the Ottoman Turks. The Carmelites, after many delays and hardships on the road, took full advantage of the Shah's kindness. They established a house at his capital of Isfahan, and attracted a surprising number of converts to their little community. With added support from both Orthodox and Uniate Christians, they were able to build a climate of tolerance and good will in that largely Muslim empire. Another Carmelite foundation at Hormuz enriched a mission effort, and generated yet other foundations, some of which still exist to this day.

Perhaps the most splendid symbol of the Discalced missions in the East was the return to Mount Carmel. Prosper of the Holy Spirit was one of the earliest missionaries to Persia. But he longed to return to the physical cradle of Carmelite life, and followed his dream in spite of discouragements. By 1631, he managed to buy land on the crest of Carmel, overlooking the bay of Haifa. The exhilaration of returning to the Holy Land was well received within the Order. The lovely Stella Maris monastery, which was begun in 1720, stands there today.

Pope Clement VIII also used his authority to transfer some of the most talented Spaniards to Italy, including Thomas of Jesus, and Dominic of Jesus and Mary. Thomas went on to write a pair of remarkable books about the organization and support of missions, studies of language, culture, and techniques

St. Mary Magdalene de'Pazzi, captured in a painting by Juan de Valdés Leal, in the retablo of the Carmelite church in Córdoba, Spain. *(Photo courtesy of Rafael Lieva, O. Carm.)*

of evangelization. Together with Peter, both Thomas and Dominic were so successful at managing and systematizing the missions that Pope Gregory XV made their work permanent in 1622 by founding the Congregation for the Propagation of the Faith.

Among the earliest Carmelite martyrs in the mission lands were Denis of the Nativity and Redemptus of the Cross. Denis (Pierre Berthelot) was originally a French navigator, and Redemptus (Tomas Rodriguez de Cunha) was a Portuguese soldier. Both entered Carmel at the Goa mission, where friars under the dynamic Philip of the Trinity were struggling to proclaim the Gospel in India. Both friars were murdered by hostile natives at Aceh in northern Sumatra when they refused to renounce their faith. Carmelite communities flourish today in that very same region.

During the same period, the Ancient Observance Carmelites were not generally allowed to send missionaries anywhere within the Spanish empire, because of their continuing differences with the government of Philip II. There were some who served as missionary bishops in Latin America, like Bernardo Serrada of Cuzco, but not as missionaries in the strict sense. Such individual friars as made it to the Americas were not generally able to establish proper Carmelite communities.

Antonio Vasquez de Espinoza is one notable author whose work is still respected. He was a member of the Andalusian province who entered the Order at Seville and taught theology there for several years, before joining a sailing expedition as chaplain. For the next ten years, he traveled throughout much of South America, taking good notes on everything he saw. When he returned home, he produced what was probably the best geography and travel book of his time, the *Compendium Description of the West Indies* (1623-30). In this comprehensive work, he testifies to the excellence and success of the work of the Discalced brothers in Mexico and elsewhere, and the great popularity which the scapular devotion and Carmelite spirituality enjoyed in the New World.

Mary Magdalene de'Pazzi

It is easy to neglect Mary Magdalene de'Pazzi, since she is a contemporary of both Teresa and John, and because she lived in Italy, where things were relatively quiet. Yet she is a first-rate mystic and spiritual author. Born in Florence (1566) to a noble family, Catarina de'Pazzi was strongly attracted to prayer and religious matters even as a child. As soon as she was able, she acted on her wish to live as a consecrated virgin, and entered the convent of Santa Maria degli Angeli in her native city. She lived there until her death in 1607, and served as sacristan, novice mistress, and sub-prioress.

Shortly after she professed her vows, Mary Magdalene experienced a period in which she was lost in ecstasy for hours at a time over a period of 40 days. Then she was subjected to frequent mystical raptures for about a year after that. During these periods, she was so totally lost in her contemplation of God that everything else in her life seemed to go into a sort of suspended state. After that period, she experienced a vision which lasted six days and six nights. This episode was followed by a time of great spiritual suffering because of the condition of the Church, lasting from about June 1585 until June 1590. She had to cope with doubt, temptation, and despair about her salvation. Once that ordeal had passed, her life seems to have settled into a very ordinary condition, in which she remained a model religious, with very few unusual experiences.

During those more intense periods of her life, she created some rather unique "works" of spiritual literature, which are not so much writings as they are descriptions of her experiences, while absorbed in her dramatic encounters with God. These spiritual "glimpses" were usually recorded by one of her sisters at the time, and usually included her words, as well as physical descriptions of her actions and facial expressions. These accounts fill four hand-written volumes, and do not resemble treatises or explanations of any sort. Rather, they are a sort of biography-by-experience, tracing the soul's walk with a loving God. They remind the reader of intense poetry, inspired by divine love.

Throughout most of her life, Mary Magdalene wrote a considerable number of letters to her family and friends, in which she discusses every conceivable topic, from health, to politics, to daily trivia. She was indeed a nun within a strict cloister, but very much aware of the outside world and its troubles. As part of her concern as one passionate Christian for others in need, she had a special interest in the reform of the Church. This correspondence was her "ministry" to the world outside the walls of her house. Especially during 1586, she also composed advisory letters to Pope Sixtus V, the Archbishop of Florence, cardinals of the Roman Curia, and other important people on a wide variety of spiritual and reform-oriented topics. However, many of those letters were intercepted by her superiors, and never reached their intended readers. But her reforming ideas were good. There are some who consider her spiritual insights to be as good as those of Catherine of Siena. She also exchanged letters with St. Catarina de'Ricci, and other religious contemporaries about a variety of spiritual matters.

One of her most interesting friends was Maria de'Medici, who regularly visited her convent before leaving to become Queen of France as wife of Henri IV.

By this time, all communities of women with solemn vows were declared by the Council of Trent to require strict enclosure. Loosely governed groups of women who had worked in the neighborhoods were no longer permitted, so any religious house of women was automatically cloistered. All others were forbidden to accept new vocations. Henceforth, the nuns' life focused on solitude, silence, and prayer centered on the liturgy. A recent addition was private, interiorized prayer, as promoted by Teresa. Their apostolic dimension was now intercessory prayer for embattled humanity.

The other works of mercy fell to lay women and men, many of whom maintained their link to Carmel by joining local chapters of Tertiaries. Usually under the direction of friars, they professed private, or simple, vows according to their state in life. They embraced regular prayer, fasts and abstinence, simplicity of life, silence, and countless acts of charity. Carmelites of both branches supported these lay organizations with great energy, like Miguel de la Fuente (1573-1625) who wrote a detailed rule for them. A white mantle was their distinctive symbol of the Carmelite habit. Only later did the brown scapular replace it as their badge of dedication.

Devotion to the scapular had been growing steadily, however, especially during the religious revival after Trent. The story of Simon Stock and his scapular commitment began to grow from the mid-14th century, and were greatly enhanced by the circulation of the so-called sabbatine privilege. Based on a supposed vision of Pope John XXII in 1322, those who wore the scapular, prayed the Office, and abstained from meat on Wednesdays and Saturdays, would be released by Mary from purgatory on the Saturday following their death. Despite the popularity of the story, actual papal documentation was missing, and there was no mention of the practice before 1430. Later popes spoke well of the pious practices, and agreed that the good actions would be rewarded, but cautioned Carmelites in 1613 not to preach the Saturday release from purgatory. Despite this limitation, the scapular grew into one of the Church's most popular devotions. Observers reported that vast areas of Italy, Portugal, and Spain, as well as their colonies, had almost universal acceptance of this dedication to Marian prayer. Cities like Cologne even had a special Wednesday fish market because so many people were abstaining from meat.

Discalced Beginnings in France

Although many Spanish friars were reluctant to allow the Discalced Reform to expand outside the Iberian peninsula, it was almost inevitable that it would do so. A young French priest, Jean de Brétigny, had befriended some of Teresa's nuns in Spain, and became a zealous advocate of a similar convent in France. At his request, Gracian proposed the idea to the Discalced chapter of 1585, where it was approved. But the same chapter also elected Nicholas Doria, who was reluctant to allow foundations in France, due in part to the sharp political rivalries between the French and Spanish kings at that time.

Frustrated and angry, Brétigny returned to France and collaborated instead in translating Teresa's works into French. His work bore fruit in a way that he could not have predicted. By the end of the century, Teresa had become a household name. The translations were very well received by French readers, and some of Teresa's more popular writings were even used for discussion at various salons, sponsored by wealthy ladies.

One of the most popular women in Parisian society was the beautiful and talented Barbe Acarie, a well-connected aristocrat, wife, and mother. She had recently experienced a spiritual conversion which made her abandon her role as a frivolous socialite. While never neglecting her beloved husband or children, Barbe dedicated more of her time to serious prayer, and devoted herself to charitable works in the streets of Paris. Her scholarly salon took on a more spiritual character, where some of the leading religious figures of her day were guests. It was a time of dynamic religious revival in France, driven by such giants as Francis de Sales, Vincent de Paul, and Barbe's own young cousin Pierre de Bérulle.

Jean de Brétigny visited Barbe's salon, too, with an eye toward promoting Teresa's ideas, and the excellence of her communities. Barbe was skeptical at first, since she did not immediately appreciate the depth of Teresa's message. But she gradually discovered the power of the woman behind the writing, and began to champion her works. When Brétigny pursued his dream of bringing Discalced nuns to France, Barbe joined Bérulle and Francis de Sales in support. Francis wrote directly to the Pope for permission, and received it. King Henri IV quickly agreed, to the surprise of many. Since there were no Discalced friars in France as yet, the nuns were to be supervised by diocesan priests, led by Bérulle.

Although he was still a relative unknown, the future Cardinal Bérulle would become one of the leading forces of an entire French school of spirituality. He was a brilliant thinker and an energetic builder, who would establish the Oratory in France, support the Sulpicians, and shape the spiritual formation of the French clergy for the next centuries. He already had plans for a women's order founded on the same principles, and considered the importation of Spanish nuns to be a shortcut to his goal. His cousin Barbe already had plans of her own to subsidize a convent, and knew several French women ready to join it. But she really wanted sisters who had actually known Teresa to impart some of their foundational fire.

The general of the Spanish congregation, Francis of the Mother of God, wanted nothing to do with releasing any of his nuns, and said so. But he was no match for Barbe's connections and Bérulle's initiative. Bérulle set out on a personal journey to choose the very best nuns he could find. Under pressure even of excommunication by Clement VIII, the frustrated general relented. With Brétigny's help, Bérulle selected six veteran sisters, including Anne of Jesus and Anne of Saint Bartholomew. They reached Paris in 1604, moving immediately into their unfinished convent on the rue Saint-Jacques. Barbe not only became a close friend of the newcomers, but vigorously directed vocations and donations to their new foundation. Within a year, there were enough women to found another convent. Just ten years later, there were eight houses in France and others in Belgium.

Following the death of her beloved husband, Barbe entered Carmel herself in 1614, with the name of Marie of the Incarnation. She had already given powerful help to the nuns at retaining the open, human spirituality of Teresa. Bérulle had been working steadily to substitute a very different sort of philosophy, based not on Teresa's writing, but on his program for priests. Instead of a simple and uncluttered love of God, Bérulle promoted a rather pietistic and mechanical series of devout practices and penances throughout the day. Barbe's success at forestalling his program assured a continuing flood of vocations in France and Belgium, even after her untimely death in 1618.

By this time, Anne of Jesus and Anne of Saint Bartholomew had founded several more convents in the Flemish and French-speaking provinces of the Low Countries. In 1619, a special house was added in Antwerp for English women who were refugees from the penal laws in their own country. That community, in turn, established two others at Lierre and Hoogstraten, from which the first nuns would be sent to America two centuries later. Anne of Jesus applied to the Italian congregation for friars to assist the Flemish houses. Now that his good ideas on hermitages and missions were already bearing fruit, the intrepid Thomas of Jesus led a small band to Brussels in 1610, where they soon attracted a large number of new vocations. These men signaled that a flourishing province of the Netherlands was not long in coming.

The first Discalced friars came to France at about the same time. Two pioneers from Spain began building a house and a church on the rue de Vaugirard in Paris, both of which remain to this day. One of the most celebrated members of that community would be Brother Lawrence of the Resurrection. Born Nicholas Herman in the borderland of Lorraine, he served as a soldier in a mercenary regiment, and experienced the horrors of the Thirty Years' War first hand. Death, violence, and suffering forced him to think deeply about the ultimate things in himself. A profound religious conversion changed his young life. He found his way to Carmel in his forties, and worked as a cook for most of his remaining days. His personal prayer life developed along the extremely practical lines of practicing the presence of God in his kitchen. Blessed with a clear and no-nonsense way of speaking, he wrote lucid advice to help others follow his method. After his death in 1691, his notes were published in book form, and remain a popular source of spiritual wisdom even today. By the end of the century, there were 35 Discalced houses in France, but care of the nuns remained in the hands of the diocesan clergy.

The broad appeal of the Discalced nuns drew vocations from some of the most unlikely sources. Louise de la Vallière (1645-1710) became the mistress of King Louis XIV as a young girl, and bore him three children. But like many royal mistresses, she was cast aside at the age of 24, and entered a period of deep self-searching. Within a few years, she entered the Carmel on the Rue Saint-Jacques, and spent the next 35 years there as an exemplary nun with the name of Louise of the Mercy.

Following the separation of the Discalced, the older branch of the Carmelites still faced the urgent need to complete a proper reform of the surviving houses in Spain, France, and elsewhere. During the period when Enrico Silvio was prior general (1598-1612), the Order generated a vigorous renewal in the style of John Soreth and Nicholas Audet. Like Rossi before him, Silvio had the organizational benefits of ecclesiastical legislation and papal reformers to strengthen his efforts. Pope Clement VIII had laid down uncompromising directives that no friar should be exempted from community prayer, and that systematic mental prayer twice daily should be introduced. Since this form of meditation had not been widely known before Teresa's time, there was a fresh demand for books and writings on the subject, which the Order's scholars hastened to produce.

Silvio also appreciated the need to travel, as Rossi had done before him. It was no small task to promote greater fidelity to Carmelite ideals, like evangelical poverty, prayerful union with God, and prophetic resistance to the values of the increasingly secular world. His journey led him through Italy, France, Spain, Belgium, Germany, and finally into Poland, where he was the first Carmelite general to visit. Everywhere, he encouraged and supported efforts to introduce local reforms. In many places, the basic elements of prayer, enclosure, and the common life were observed badly, and needed to be accentuated by someone in authority. In some extreme cases, he restructured entire provinces so that lasting improvements could take hold.

The Reform of Touraine

It was during one of those visits that he learned of the earliest efforts to improve religious life within the province of Touraine, in north-western France. The cradle of this movement was the large house at Rennes. Members of that community, led by Pierre Behourt and Philippe Thibault, had taken dramatic steps to return to a more ascetic life. They set aside much of the second mitigation, embracing almost permanent abstinence from meat, and agreed to renounce any private ownership of property. More dramatically, they made a serious commitment to give up advanced scholarship and the privileges that came with it. On one hand, this measure brought a certain reduction in intellectual accomplishments, but on the other hand, it brought about a true homogenization within the brotherhood of the community.

Beginning with the single observant house at Rennes, the proposal for a more spiritual life spread to a majority of the Touraine houses. From 1611 onward, the entire province decided to introduce stricter constitutions, based on the obvious success and happiness of the reformed communities. It is worth noting that Behourt was a pivotal figure in launching the reform, but that his personal strictness tended to intimidate those friars less inclined to reform their lives. It was Thibault who promoted a slower and more flexible policy, designed to win over the suspicious friars. By not forcing the reform on everyone too quickly, he achieved the remarkable result of an entire province which ultimately agreed on a stricter life, and was pleased with that final result. Silvio and his successors endorsed the excellence of the Touraine constitutions for the Order at large, and they became the foundation of a general intensification of discipline.

The Touraine reform also promoted a very high level of spirituality and prayer at all levels. But the renewal pursued a distinctly modern path. According to the Medieval approach, religious life had generally been seen as an organic whole, a sort of twenty-four hour "attitude" which covered everything, including formal prayer in choir, private spiritual reading, study, work, even eating and sleeping. Everything was done as a sort of unified life of devotion, which might (or might not) include apostolic ministry. That spiritual outlook was sincere enough, but not always very vigorous.

Beginning early in the 16th century, that very same unified outlook evolved toward a greater attention to the individual elements. The Jesuits, for one group, were committed to intense prayer, even though they were founded for apostolic work. But for them, prayer was compressed into certain times of the day by their ministerial needs. Especially in the works of Teresa and John of the Cross, "prayer" became identified with interior prayer, clearly divorced from distracting activity. By considering prayer and ministry as distinct entities, a Carmelite could work to improve the excellence of both.

Although the Touraine communities produced excellent preachers and effective missionaries, they also recognized the need for regular prayer in community as a way to compensate for time lost to performing works of mercy. Whenever possible, they returned to a more traditional structure for the Divine Office, celebrated as a community throughout the day, with careful attention to rubrics and rituals, including first rate music. They also established times in the community schedule for spiritual reading, prayerful retirement to the cells, and private work there. Even though one might be tempted to quibble about the "opposition" between prayer and activity, one result of this dialogue was the fixing of specific times of day for methodical mental prayer. During the 1590's, the Ancient Observance constitutions had adopted the Discalced practice of specific periods of formal mental prayer, twice a day.

This was also the stage at which Carmelites adopted the private examination of conscience, which might commonly be utilized just before a meal. The individual would silently review the previous few hours, in light of a shortcoming to

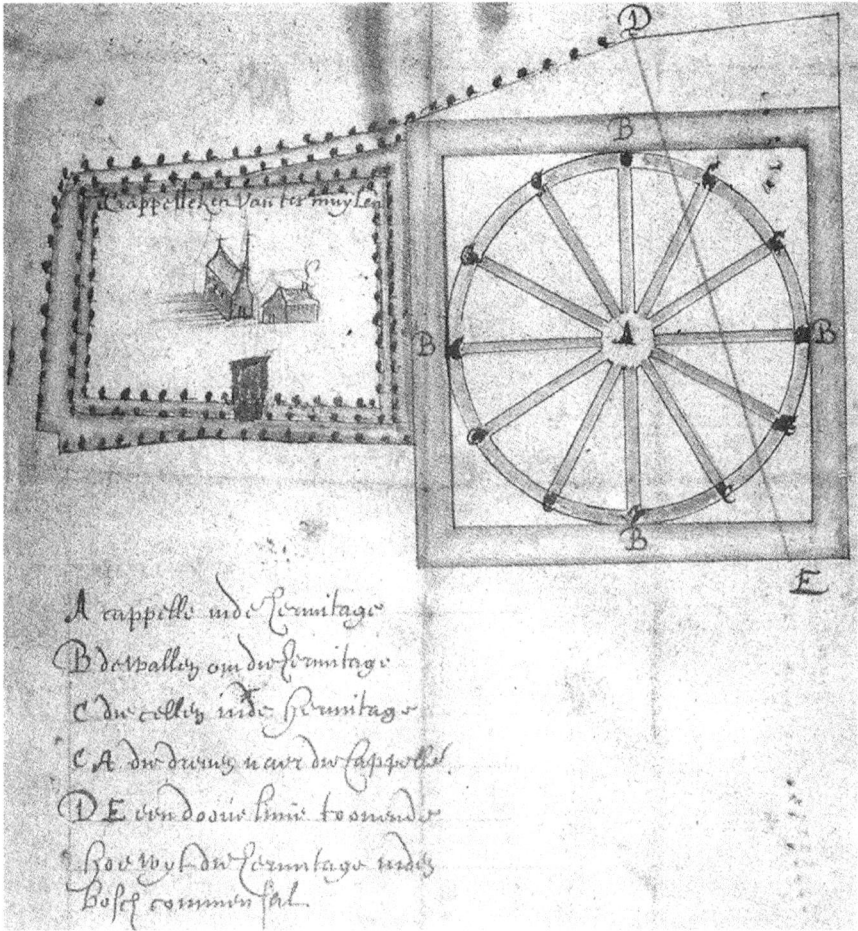

A house of the Touraine reform– the hermitage of Liedekerke of the Flemish Belgian Province, in Termuylen, Belgium. A = the chapel in the hermitage; B = the walls around the hermitage; C = the cells in the hermitage; CA = the walkways to the chapel; DE = a line showing how the hermitage will lead into the forest. *(Drawing courtesy of Joachim Smet, O. Carm.)*

be eliminated, or a particular virtue to be cultivated. There was also a renewed emphasis on aspirative prayer: short phrases or prayerful thoughts which were lifted up to God silently, as they occurred at any hour. No matter what other activity was in progress, working, walking, eating, washing dishes, or falling asleep, these tiny bursts of prayer could issue from the soul, like breath from the body. Finally, the practice of the presence of God became a favorite method for integrating activity into one's reflective life, and vice versa. It is an easy way for the individual to "carry the chapel along" when leaving the physical chapel for other commendable activity.

The Discalced communities had done pioneering work at integrating their valuable ministry into an intense spiritual life. Touraine now amalgamated many of

Sketch of John of Saint Samson, writer and reformer of the Touraine tradition. Blind from an early age, orphaned at ten, he entered the Order in 1606 as a brother.

those best ideas into the older traditions of the Order. There continued to be some division of opinion about the importance of ministry. Thibault still considered apostolic work to be quite an important element of Carmelite life. His co-reformer John of St. Samson preferred to relegate the apostolate to a fairly minor role.

Authors of the Touraine Reform

John of St. Samson may be the best known of the Touraine writers. He was born Jean Moulin (1571-1636) into a middle class family at Sens, near Paris. A severe bout with smallpox at the age of three left him blind for the remainder of his life. Orphaned at ten, he was raised by a devout uncle who read to him from spiritual books and taught him a love of prayer and reflection. The uncle also taught him music, uncovering a promising talent for playing nearly any kind of instrument. Later in his life, Jean was living in Paris not far from the *studium* at Place Maubert. He befriended the organist at the chapel there, and got to know more about Carmelite traditions of prayer. He entered the Order as a brother in 1606, where he contributed his talent as a musician, as well as a man of prayer.

John spent the next 30 years instructing novices in the spiritual life and methods of prayer. His conferences and mystical insights were taken down and organized by other writers, and eventually filled two huge *folio* volumes. He was a popular spiritual director at the novitiate, and a powerful influence on the Touraine reform. John developed a whole abstract school of mysticism, and refined it every year for his classes with the novices. His thinking tends to be somewhat abstract, as one might expect from a sightless person who compensates with other senses. John is very much a spiritual original in his own right.

One noted contemporary of John's at Rennes was Dominic of St. Albert (1595-1634). Dominic's writing was much more structured and methodical than John's. In his early years, he studied with the Jesuits, and then entered the Carmelites in 1612. He was in the same novitiate class with John of St. Samson, and likewise taught scholastic and mystical theology to students, and helped with the formation of novices. When Dominic was only 21, he wrote an excellent manuscript for novices and professed students on mystical theology and mental prayer. He was later named prior of the house in Nantes and vicar provincial. Although he shares many principles with John, Dominic's writings are highly ordered and betray his background in scholastic philosophy. But they are wonderfully clear and logical.

Another illustrious son of the reform is the formidable Leo of St. John (1600-71), remembered for his vigorous ministry. This disciple of John of St. Samson established a new house in Paris (Les Billettes) from which he spread the Stricter Observance to other parts of France and Germany. A renowned orator, he preached at Versailles and enrolled Louis XIII and Louis XIV in the scapular. He also delivered the funeral orations for Cardinals Richelieu and Mazarin, and was greatly admired by Vincent de Paul and Charles de Condren. From Paris he also founded a country refuge in the forest of Fontainebleau, which became a unique hermitage.

Although it took them a while to develop a hermitage community, members of the Touraine province did indeed follow the example of Thomas of Jesus in his desert houses. However, Touraine and the Stricter Observance built in one significant distinction between the Discalced hermitage and their own. Their new hermitage at Fontainebleau had to be a separate part of a working monastery, which would take care of the practical needs and act as a link with the outside world. Solitude, silence, and contemplation were strictly observed, of course, and no more than 12 hermits were allowed in one community. Outside preaching, ministry, and scholarship were not allowed. But the hermits would join the regular community on Sundays and feast days for meditation, office, Mass, and a chapter of faults, in harmony with the rule. Simple living in a restful setting was the ideal, in imitation of Elijah himself.

One more great accomplishment of the Touraine province was its mission activity, which set it apart from the other French provinces. About 1646, two of their friars accompanied an explorer to the West Indies, hoping to provide spiritual care for a proposed colony on Grenada. That settlement never worked out, so they landed instead on St. Christopher ("St. Kitts") where the governor general urged them to stay. He pointed to the desperate need of providing pastoral care for people of many nationalities. The two Carmelites established a small mission, after which one of them returned to France to bring others to help. He not only left a valuable account of his travels, but also motivated others to join the mission effort. Royal permission was slow in coming, but the reinforcements were sent out in 1650, and began a noble endeavor which continued until the extinction of the Touraine province during the French Revolution, over a century later.

Because of its lush tropical climate and its extensive range of exotic diseases and fevers, St. Kitts was always a gamble for mainland Frenchmen. Some friars died rather quickly after arrival, and in most cases were buried on the island. The history of the Antilles mission is a demoralizing rhythm of new arrivals, then sickness and death, followed by pleas for additional help, and then more new arrivals. But to the credit of the home province, there were always more brave volunteers to take the places of those who died or returned. After several years, they founded another mission on the island of Guadalupe, which also flourished and met the needs of many islanders. Most of those people were French settlers, of course, but there were also many African slaves and a few surviving Indians, in addition to the many non-Catholic Europeans, like English or Dutch colonists. Whenever there were at least six or more missionaries in the central houses, it was possible that some of them could travel up and down the chain of islands, caring for anyone in need. But these travels never resulted in any enduring foundations beyond the original two.

Lasting Benefits

The general chapter of 1645 was a landmark in the reform of the Ancient Observance. The obvious success of the reform of Touraine and the more observant communities north of the Alps had raised the possibility of a newly renewed Order from top to bottom. But even within the reformed sections, there was a bewildering hodgepodge of legislation. It almost seemed that no two communities were governed by exactly the same set of rules. So it was clearly time to streamline and simplify the legislative morass for the good of everyone. But many of the older communities, especially in Italy and Spain, were not yet ready to commit to the full rigor of the French reformers.

So there was a legislative compromise between the more skeptical communities and those of the "Stricter Observance." At the 1645 chapter, the reforming provinces did in fact unify their more rigorous programs by accepting the constitutions of the Touraine province (with a few changes) as the reform standard for the entire Order. A perfect common life and a contemplative spirit were established as the ideals for everyone. Unreformed provinces were granted additional time to reach those ideals, but it was clear that they were expected to do so. The streamlined legislation made the process of transformation appear clear and attainable.

The Reform of Monte Santo

During the 17th century, there were several more reform congregations founded in Italy, which somewhat replicated the work of Touraine. The most successful of these was the Monte Santo reform which began in 1619. Desiderio Placa, provincial of the St. Albert province of eastern Sicily, attended the general chapter in 1593, and met Discalced friars for the first time. He was inspired by their idea of a strict reform, and began to attract others to his side. The bishop of Catania gave them a new church and encouragement to continue their reform. Prayer in solitude was the primary concern. Midnight office and the other hours at proper times were enhanced by two hours of mental prayer each day. The reform grew rapidly into a parallel series of communities in all parts of the island.

The original foundations in Sicily were joined by a distinct foundation in Rome

(1639) which actually grew into a separate province within the reform. So there was an odd situation of a special congregation with its own vicar general, but two separate provinces under him, in Sicily and the Papal States. The flagship house in Rome was the lovely church of Santa Maria di Monte Santo, designed by Carlo Rainaldi and completed by Gian Lorenzo Bernini on the Piazza del Popolo. It was for that same oval-shaped church that the young Georg Friedrich Handel composed and performed his stunning "Carmelite Vespers" for the first time in 1707. That work was commissioned by Cardinal Colonna for the solemn vespers of Our Lady of Mount Carmel, July 16 of that year.

The Monte Santo reform also attempted to imitate the success of Discalced friars in the foreign missions. The house in Rome was actually envisioned as a college where missionaries could study foreign languages. They launched several missionary endeavors of their own, including a new house in the Holy Land, and another on Cyprus, both parts of the Ottoman Empire at that time. There was also an attempt to establish a house in Isfahan, Persia. It is unfortunate that none of these schemes ever came to fruition.

Other Congregations

Among the other reforms was the congregation of Santa Maria della Vita, in southern Italy. That effort grew out of several unsuccessful attempts to discipline the very large community of Carmine Maggiore in Naples. Those constant endeavors had produced a healthy response among some of the community members. Although they remained a minority, a group of 26 Neapolitan friars wanted to bind themselves to a stricter criterion of poverty and prayer. But instead of renovating the big, unwieldy community in the city, they asked for permission in 1631 to take over smaller country houses around the bay of Naples. They designated them as observant hermitages for their stricter life. These included Sorrento and Torre del Greco. By 1660 these houses were recognized as a distinct reformed province. Although this group had no special observances, their community life remained excellent, and produced many spiritual writers.

There was also a small local reform which began in 1633 in Piedmont, in northwestern Italy, promoted by two royal princesses. The community at Turin split from the Lombard province, vowing to observe strict poverty and regular mental prayer. Other existing houses joined in due time. One particular observance of theirs was abstinence from meat on Mondays. After a good start, it seems that the quality of the group's faithfulness began to falter, since the reform had to be restarted in 1686.

Much later, there was a second reform in Sicily from 1728 onward, called Santa Maria della Scala Paradisi. The saintly hermit Girolamo Terzo was the force behind the new movement, although he refused ordination to the priesthood. Beginning in Siracusa, this wave of austerity concentrated in the southeastern corner of the island. Their strict discipline was accompanied by imposing churches, as well as a thriving hermitage, which also served as novitiate.

Another interesting, if short-lived, French reform was the single desert house of La Graville. Its founder was a member of the province of Narbonne, André Blanchard, who asked for permission to establish a hermitage of the same type as Monte Oliveto, near Genoa. André had already discussed the possibility of a special house of prayer with John of St. Samson, as an outgrowth of the Touraine observance. Although his proposal was not generally accepted by his own Narbonne province, prior general Teodoro Straccio was enthusiastic. In 1639, a house was opened directly under Straccio's authority in a pretty wooded area of Gascony.

But then, after a decade of peaceful prayer, the house was thrown into turmoil by the bizarre mystic and self-appointed prophet, Jean de la Badie. There is no evidence that la Badie ever took vows as a Carmelite, but he used La Graville as a base for another project. He launched a scheme to reestablish his own version of primitive Christianity. The havoc which he brought upon the tiny community led to quarreling and physical violence. Eventually the disorders had to be put down by the local authorities in 1650. The hermitage never revived.

Carmel in Eastern Europe

Rebuilding the Order in Germany and the East was a daunting task after the ravages of the Reformation. But still more devastation would follow before peace was restored. At the beginning of the dreadful Thirty Years' War, Pope Paul V sent Dominic of Jesus and Mary, superior of the Italian Congregation, on a special diplomatic mission. Dominic had come to Rome with Thomas of Jesus in 1607, and now acted as the pope's envoy to King Louis XIII of France and Emperor Ferdinand II. Ferdinand's army was preparing to march against Protestant rebels in Bohemia, and he asked Dominic to be a chaplain for his troops.Dominic's vibrant fervor inspired the soldiers, and in 1620 they won a sweeping victory at White Mountain, near Prague. This event led to the joyful renaming of St. Paul, the newest Discalced church in Rome, as Santa Maria della Vittoria. Gian Lorenzo Bernini later contributed to that church's glory with his spectacular sculpture of St. Teresa in Ecstasy.

In 1623, Pope Urban VIII made Dominic of Jesus and Mary his permanent legate for diplomatic affairs. Emperor Ferdinand was so grateful to Dominic for his loyal service that he endowed a Discalced house in Vienna in 1622. This was quickly followed by others in Prague, Munich, Würzburg, and elsewhere in southern Germany. A German Discalced province was established in 1626. The first Polish foundation in Krakow (1605) was followed quickly by others in Poznan, Czarna, Vilna, and elsewhere. Anne of Jesus sent nuns to Poland from her Flemish houses, beginning in 1612. The Polish province came into existence with nuns' convents already well established.

As the ghastly carnage of the Thirty Years' War continued, these new foundations, like the older houses, had to endure more suffering. The new church in Prague was only one of many to be looted and badly damaged by unruly soldiers

Interior of San Gallus Carmelite Church in the Old Town of Prague, CZ. Several important reformers, including Jan Hus, preached here. Today the interior is decorated in the baroque style with many Carmelite figures and symbols. *(Photo courtesy of Carmelite Media)*

in the 1630's. A small, broken statue of the Infant Jesus was salvaged by Cyril of the Mother of God, and lovingly restored. As a symbol of God's constancy and protection, the Infant Jesus of Prague became a popular devotion in many parts of the Catholic world. The phrase "The more you honor me, the more I will bless you" expresses the simple, direct theology of Jesus' loving humility.

The late 1600's also saw a burst of expansion among the Ancient Observance houses in Poland. From Krakow, priories in Poznan and Gdansk were re-founded to replace those lost in the Reformation and new ones were established. The Polish province of St. Joseph eventually had 16 houses, including Krakow, with 216 friars. Reforms in both branches of the Order spurred a remarkable burst of energy. The Corpus Christi reformed province of Poland had 11 houses and 162 members. A group of White Russian houses separated from Poland in 1687 (others in 1755) with an eventual total of 15 houses and one residence, plus two convents of nuns. The Lithuanian province of St. George had ten houses and a residence.

With the three partitions of Poland in the late 18th century, these eastern houses would be suddenly thrown into a new existence as part of the Russian, Austrian or Prussian empires. Those who found themselves inside of Austria were certainly the most fortunate, since Austria had a strong Catholic majority, and certainly knew all about religious orders and their value. Neither Prussia

The ruins of the Carmo church in Lisbon, built through the generosity of Carmelite St. Nuno Álvares Pereira, stands today as just a shell following the Lisbon earthquake of 1755.

nor Russia was a Catholic country, but both suddenly found themselves with numbers of new Polish and Lithuanian Catholic subjects. Frederick the Great's Prussia had a healthy respect for religious communities with social ministries, like schools and aid to the poor, but saw no practical use for contemplative friars or cloistered nuns. The Tsars of Russia shared that viewpoint, and added a strong desire to transform other nationalities into good Russian Orthodox subjects by a cultural "Russification."

The Lisbon Earthquake

Probably the biggest shock to the Portuguese province and its missions was the great 9.0 Lisbon earthquake of 1755. The ground shook for six minutes, and was followed by a cataclysmic tsunami. As many as 40,000 lives were snuffed out in a very short time. Of the twelve houses in the province, all but two were damaged, including the main house in Lisbon. The massive Carmo church, endowed by Nuno, was filled with worshipers on All Saints' Day when the roof fell in, killing many of them. The adjoining priory collapsed and then burned, killing 14 friars, and destroying the large library of 5000 books and the archive housed there. Most of the priceless records of the Portuguese province went up in smoke. Today, the roofless shell of the church stands as a silent but elegant monument to those who died there.

Three other Portuguese houses were totally destroyed, and four more were damaged beyond repair. The student house at Coimbra was damaged, but later repaired well enough to be inhabited. The provincial at the time was a Brazilian, an accomplished author who had been working on a history of the province at the time. After the emergency, he set about with great energy trying to rebuild, but the task was too great. Although the province struggled on, most of the entire country of Portugal had been devastated. There were simply no realistic sources of help to restore the old energy.

For people of the 18th century, the cataclysm in Portugal seemed like the most horrible event they could imagine. It retrospect, it may be seen as a portent of the last days of Europe's *Ancien Régime,* because there was an even more serious crisis looming on the horizon. The French Revolution and its ensuing wars would cost 25 years of fighting and turmoil. The outward tranquility and harmony of that exquisite world of the eighteenth century would shortly be swept away. Nothing would ever be the same again.

+ + +

Chapter 8
The War Against Religion

Lyon: 1790. "But how could it ever come to this?" shouted the elderly priest, his voice trembling with rage. "Here in France, which we call the eldest daughter of the Church!" He thought of those who had already left the monastery with pathetic bundles of things. It might be more courageous to stay in the house on principle, to show the "God-haters" that some things were worth suffering for. He could already name some who had been deported, or shot, or were waiting for the guillotine. Yes, they were heroes, but now who would take care of their people? Who would encourage the helpless in these difficult times? "Someone has to be more astute than the tyrants! Has the age of catacombs returned?"

Throughout the early years of the 18th century, Carmelite communities grew and flourished in quiet solitude. Very few spectacular events broke the march as one year followed upon another. Church leadership from most of the popes and bishops was restrained, and sometimes actually boring, especially after the Jansenist controversy died down. The vigorous Church of the Baroque age settled into a comfortable but uninspiring routine of maintaining institutions and customary practices. For even the most zealous religious communities, the lethargy of peace was a strong temptation to settle into a cozy withdrawal from their reforming vigor.

Many houses or provinces experienced a slowing of vocations that left isolated monasteries depopulated or actually abandoned. Community life and prayerful zeal relaxed into mechanical practices, unless superiors or enthusiasts were able to energize the rank and file of their brothers or sisters. And yet, as always, even in times of slowing fervor, there was always a handful of outstanding Carmelites who showed their love for God and neighbor in the most unlikely places.

Streams of Sanctity

In the working-class neighborhoods of Rome, the poor found a friend and protector in Angelo Paoli (1642-1720). Although Angelo was a Tuscan by origin, the prior general sent him to Rome to inspire the community at San Martino with his prayerfulness and charity. He quickly set to work caring for the city's many sick and the homeless. Some days there were as many as 300 people who came to be fed, and no one was ever turned away. As some people recalled a parallel to Jesus and his loaves and fish, Angelo merely pointed out that he had managed to motivate many rich and powerful cardinals, princes, and ambassadors to join his efforts. His devotion to Jesus' suffering included placing a large wooden cross in the coliseum in memory of the martyrs who died there.

On the other end of the social spectrum, Madame Louise de France (1737-87) shocked her father, King Louis XV, when she announced that she planned to enter the very strict Carmel at Saint Denis. The free-living monarch consented, since he stated that he could not oppose the will of God. The determined young princess took the religious name of Thérèse of St. Augustine, and refused to accept any special food, clothing, or consideration because of her royal status. Whenever the king visited his daughter, she always insisted that he sit on her straw mattress, and accompany her to prayers in the chapel, perhaps a spiritual nudge to atone for his sins. A generation later, another courageous French sister would take the same religious name to honor the devout princess.

In Florence, young Anna Maria Redi entered Carmel with the religious name of Teresa Margaret of the Sacred Heart (1747-70). Even as a child of six, her family had considered her a little contemplative. Her short life in the convent seemed unremarkable at first, except for the fact that she carried out every task and detail with perfection. Her central motivation was to imitate the loving heart of Jesus, as a human reflection of the Trinity, in everything she did. In her capacity as infirmarian, she had to care for a hysterical old nun who heaped verbal abuse on her at every turn, and yet Teresa Margaret remained serene and concerned only with her welfare. Her loving embrace of the world served as a stark contrast to the secularist ideals of her era.

The Age of Reason

That same eighteenth century saw the beginnings of a movement known as the Enlightenment, or the Age of Reason. The Enlightenment was largely a cultural trend that had extreme respect for the intellect, but not a great deal for emotion, or for any sort of heartfelt sentiment, including spiritual fervor. The philosophers of the Enlightenment included such luminaries as the great Isaac Newton, John Locke, the French philosopher Voltaire, Baron Charles de Montesquieu, and Jean Jacques Rousseau. These thinkers, most of them English or French, were Deists in their religious approach. The Deists acknowledged a God as a creator, or at least a supreme intellectual force in the universe: someone who created the intricate mechanism of the cosmos and set it into motion. But then

Blessed Angelo Paoli, a member of the Carmelite community of San Martino ai Monti in Rome, ministered to the poor and the sick with methods used today, such as rehabilitation centers, and managed to involve the wealthy and politically powerful of the town in his efforts. He was beatified in Rome in April 2010.

God (or this great creative force) lost any personal interest in the universe and its people. It is as though God were what some people called the "divine watchmaker," who set the machinery of the universe into motion like a very intricate toy or diversion, but then put it on the shelf and lost all further interest in the day-to-day affairs of human beings.

On one hand, the Enlightenment was a very optimistic and hopeful period, when every problem was seen to have a rational solution. Since human beings saw themselves as the new custodians, the caretakers of the universe that God had created and then abandoned, it was their world to exploit. They seemed to be truly free: mini-gods in their own right! God, the harsh celestial taskmaster, did not really exist. Original sin was a useless myth. They no longer saw a personal God who cared about them or listened to their prayers, who responded to their hopes, their fears, or their aspirations. God had no further interest in their mundane concerns. So if God doesn't care, the universe is ours now, one way or another. And if the universe is now in human hands, then we do well or badly strictly on our own merits. There's no one else to answer to.

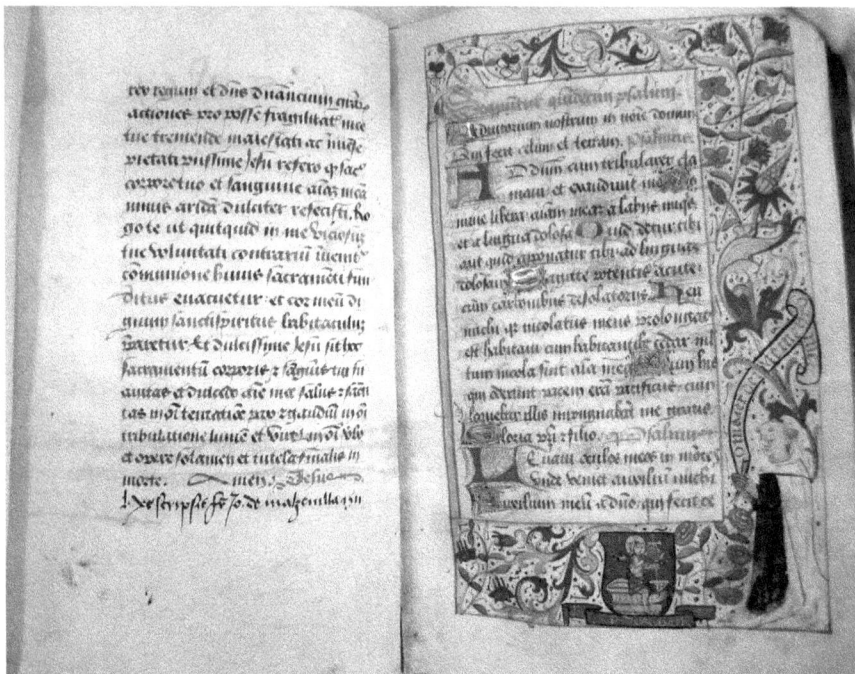

Carmelite Book of Hours, perhaps copied in Eastern France in the first quarter of the 16th century, was taken from the Carmelite monastery in Baccaret, France. The decorations indicate the book belonged to Frére Pandargent, the prior. They also indicate that the scribe was Johannes de Malzevilla, a Carmelite from Baccaret.

On the other hand, seen from the viewpoint of the Church, the philosophers of the Enlightenment were overly focused on human intellect in a secular world. The response from the Church hierarchy and intellectuals was largely confined to condemnation, but very little dialogue or engagement. During the entire eighteenth century there may have only been two or three popes who truly understood the challenge of this excessively intellectual position. Most of the attention of the hierarchy and the theologians had been drawn to the fight against Jansenism early in the century. The Jansenists were extreme rigorists on the other end of the political and religious spectrum. They criticized the Church hierarchy, and particularly the mendicant orders and the Jesuits, for supposed laxity in their moral theology. They saved special scorn for confessors who were tolerant of those sinners who confessed serious offenses and then asked for God's forgiveness. The Jansenists were heavily influenced by Calvinist theology, and French Calvinists had a way of being very unforgiving. Most of the Church's intellectual leaders had successfully responded to the Jansenists, and reduced much of their influence in some areas, particularly in the Netherlands and in northern France.

But after the fight with Jansenism in the early eighteenth century, the subsequent conflict with the Enlightenment seems to have taken the hierarchy by surprise. The efforts of secularizers to remove all religious influence, whether intellectual or political, were met with no effective response from the intellectuals, the theologians, the spiritual writers, and above all the hierarchy. Indeed most well-educated bishops, themselves mainly from noble families, had very little day-to-day contact with the cares of peasants and working class people, who of course made up the vast majority of the population. By way of contrast, most of the lower clergy and religious (including friars, cloistered nuns, and working sisters) continued their prayer and ministry with the Church's ordinary people quite effectively and sincerely. But that day-to-day impact was not at all in the same realm with the hostile intellectual forces. That engagement would have to come from the Church's intellectuals, who were conspicuously absent.

Perhaps the biggest failure of Church leadership can be seen in the all-out assault on the religious orders by many of Europe's crowned heads in the second half of the century. Nearly all of the major Catholic monarchs seemed to want to reduce the influence of the Church in society. A docile "state church" would no longer function as a social conscience, but meekly bless the monarch to rule as an absolute despot. Kings and queens generally tended to feel that they could easily manipulate the hierarchy, since bishops were largely from the same class and mentality as the nobility. But religious orders could still be stubborn and problematic. Even with a compliant national hierarchy, the rank and file of the religious orders owed their allegiance directly to the pope, and not to the local bishops. So any modern eighteenth century monarch might feel that he or she needed to reduce the power of those whose primary loyalty was to the international Church, symbolized by Rome. A secularizing monarch could even appear to be a patriotic custodian of national pride against a meddlesome foreign prince, the pope.

Losses in France

In France, King Louis XV instituted a government committee known as the Commission of Regulars. (The term "regular" in this sense denotes a member of a religious order, someone who follows a *regula* or monastic rule.) The Commission first met in 1768 under the leadership of Étienne Loménie de Brienne, the Archbishop of Toulouse. Loménie was a fine administrator and a brilliant financial mind, one of the most intelligent men in France. However, he shared the quality of many of his fellow French bishops in being a rationalist and an agnostic. Like so many of those same aristocratic bishops, he saw his duty primarily as an administrator, one who created jobs within an institution. A bishop existed to help manage the lower classes as a kind humanitarian, but not necessarily to be a saint, a theologian, or a role model. An Enlightenment bishop was certainly not expected to lead his people to heartfelt worship of a God who loved them and cared about their every action.

According to the rationalist way of thinking, any sort of worship, especially emotional or devotional veneration, seemed uncomfortably close to the superstition and ignorance of the Dark Ages. Ignorance of any sort was the great bane of the Enlightenment. Human reason, completely unaided by any divine revelation, had to be the norm. Since intellect, reason, and learning were seen as the solutions to all possible human problems, it is no surprise that the Commission of Regulars saw a need to control the baser sentiments, the superstition, and the benighted ignorance of the lower classes. They noted with distaste that such prayerful emotionalism was often fueled by the members of religious orders with their devotions, their novenas, and their pursuit of a God who might actually care about humble people and love them.

To the mind of an Enlightenment thinker, the spiritual life of someone like a cloistered nun was incomprehensible. The thought that an able-bodied, intelligent woman could seal herself up behind the grille of a convent, behind closed doors, and spend her days in prayer, was a denial of the scientific spirit. Enlightenment critics might concede the good done by friars or sisters who worked in schools or hospitals or who helped to ease the sufferings of the poor. But cloistered convents did no constructive work. Understanding this mentality helps to explain why, during the French Revolution, there was such violence and hatred directed toward cloistered sisters of a community like Compiègne!

The French Commission of Regulars eventually legislated that all religious orders needed to restrict the admission of new candidates to the novitiate and accept only young men and women who had reached the ages of 21 and 18, respectively. Another directive stated that only one house per town or city was allowed for any religious community, and that each house needed to have a minimum number of community members who lived there regularly. The law stipulated that all religious orders had to meet within a very few years to draw up special statutes for their French provinces under the direction of government officials. This special legislation became a requirement for religious orders who wanted to continue to function in France. Any houses which did not meet these standards had to be sold or suppressed. All religious had to be consolidated into communities that were large enough to support community life.

Some of these regulations were helpful in reducing the proliferation of small or vacant houses. Encouragement of true community life was long overdue in some cases. But the basis of the reforms was hardly friendly to the Church in general or the religious orders in particular. By the time the French Revolution actually broke out, the Carmelite communities in France had seen a substantial drop in their numbers.

The Commission's first legislation addressed restrictions on the age of novices in 1768. It was a sure formula to dry up vocations. At that time, the Carmelites of the Ancient Observance had 1199 men in their eight French provinces with 129 houses. By 1790, these numbers had been reduced to 721 friars, a reduction of approximately one-third. The last general chapter before the Revolution took place in 1788 when 45 provinces were listed for the entire order. Among the Discalced Carmelites in France, there were six provinces of friars, living in 75 houses. In addition, there were 65 convents of cloistered nuns. The Discalced family worldwide included ten provinces of friars in the Spanish congregation, with 113 convents of nuns. The Italian congregation had 24 provinces of friars, and 169 convents of nuns. The vast majority of those communities did not survive the French revolution in any form.

Josephism in Austria

A similar process began by 1781 in the large and important Austrian empire, most of whose subjects were Catholic. This campaign to control of the religious orders in Austria was called Josephism, after the Emperor Joseph II. His mother, the Empress Maria Teresa, had been a very devout Catholic herself and one much beloved by her people. She had been active in Church affairs, but largely with an eye toward guiding and protecting the religious activities of her beloved subjects. Joseph worked hard at being a good emperor, but he never succeeded in capturing the love and devotion of his people the way that his mother had. His efforts to manipulate the Austrian church became almost laughable. He involved himself in matters like the salaries of priests, or the minutest details of new church construction. He tried to legislate things as small and petty as how many Masses should be allowed in a country church, or the number of candles which could be used for each service. Many of the common people derisively called him "the sacristan," since what he intended as good reforms were mainly seen as ridiculous and absurd. But it was no laughing matter when he formally suppressed most religious communities in 1781. His only exception was a handful of communities who ministered to school children, the poor, or the sick.

The Enlightenment monarchs probably enjoyed their greatest triumph in the suppression of the Jesuit order. Beginning in 1759 with a dispute over mission policy in Portugal, the ban on Jesuit houses spread to Spain, France, Naples, the Austrian empire, and many of the minor kingdoms of Europe. The final outrage came in 1773, when Pope Clement XIV meekly yielded to political pressure, and globally suppressed the Jesuits throughout the church. This war against the Jesuits deprived the pope of some of his most dedicated thinkers and defenders among the religious orders. Voltaire and many of the secularizers celebrated, hoping that the suppression of the Jesuits would herald the beginning of the end for the institutional church. It is ironic that Jesuit institutions managed to survive in such non-Catholic empires as Prussia under Frederick the Great, and the Russia of Catherine the Great. Fortunately, Pope Pius VII brought back the Jesuits in 1814, although they only survived by the skin of their teeth. But they rebounded strongly in the post-revolutionary world, wherever there was need for good leadership within the Catholic family.

Revolution

The dramatic events of the French Revolution began in May 1789, when King Louis XVI called the Estates General to help him resolve a desperate financial crisis. Within about two months, he had lost administrative control of his country to the self-proclaimed National Assembly. This new body set itself the goal of turning France into an enlightened, constitutional monarchy, free of what they considered outdated privileges and exemptions for the clergy and the nobility. The exemption from taxes for both clerics and ecclesiastical property had grown out of their very close partnership with the state. The Church oversaw many social functions, including the principal recording of vital statistics, schools, care of the sick, social ministry to the poor, even care of travelers in rural monasteries. The Church also acted as the social conscience and moral watchdog over French society. More than a few Enlightenment thinkers felt that these functions belonged better to the State than to the Church.

The National Assembly undertook a breathtaking series of reforms, many of them very good and long overdue. Other restructuring, however, reflected the rationalists' prejudice against organized religion in any serious form. The principal measure adopted to bail France out of its bankruptcy was the wholesale confiscation of all Church property, which was then sold to raise money to pay off the national debt. That idea was advanced by the bishop of Autun, Charles-Maurice de Talleyrand, another agnostic prelate who was more aristocrat than churchman. That suggestion, in turn, led to a series of other regulatory measures, based on Enlightenment principles, which were designed to reduce the enormous ecclesiastical establishment to a sort of religious ministry of the state.

At the stroke of a pen, all lands and buildings owned by the bishops, the diocesan clergy, or any religious community in France were put at the disposal of the state. It was a quick fix, which created almost as many problems as it solved. To facilitate the dismantling of so much real estate, the government issued various denominations of redemption certificates called "assignats." These certificates were then sold to investors and speculators, who could later trade them in for former church property. The loss of so much ecclesiastical land, together with the income that it generated, eliminated the many social services which the French Church had hitherto maintained so efficiently. All that remained to the Church was the purely spiritual function, which the rationalists considered utterly useless, in any case. The measures which followed surprised no one.

Readers today sometimes find it puzzling that such extreme measures could be legislated in a country where the vast majority of the people were Catholics, many of them very devout. Many of those Frenchmen might admittedly feel irritated by the all-encompassing influence of the Church in society, but most could not imagine that such a dramatic or even violent outcome would follow. How could such a bloodbath occur? The simple answer is that the atheists and rabid anticlericals were indeed a minority, but that they were very dedicated to removing all mention of religion from their society. During the early stages of the Revolution, they were better organized than members of other factions. Later, as their power grew, they felt that was in their interest to exterminate the most influential religious leaders, the clergy and religious, before the level-headed majority could recover the initiative.

Anticlerical Measures

Two principal items of anticlerical legislation were adopted in 1790, one act in February, the other in July. For members of the religious orders, the February legislation was far more significant, since it undermined the justification of a spiritual community. Although most history books say little about it, the February 13 law declared that religious vows were null and void, and that religious communities were therefore dissolved and nonexistent. At one stroke, religious life in France came to an end. All religious men and women were invited to avail themselves of the "freedom" which was now bestowed upon them by the benevolent state. The implication, of course, is that anyone in a convent or monastery was an unwilling prisoner, held in bondage by evil superiors. Why else should anyone lock themselves voluntarily behind stone walls or iron grilles?

The July law, the Civil Constitution of the Clergy, is better known. It essentially secularized and nationalized the French Church, transforming it into a department of the national government. From then on, all bishops and parish priests were to be elected by voters, and were essentially turned into government employees. A somewhat more positive element of this law was the realignment of French diocesan boundaries to match the new civil "departments." The number of diocesan bishops was thus reduced from 136 to 83, and the area of responsibility for each was more uniform. Since members of the clergy were now considered to be employees of the state, they were also put on the government payroll, since landholdings no longer paid for their livelihood.

But this entanglement also led to the requirement of an oath of loyalty to the new national regime. Many secularizers applauded the oath, since they felt that it would disconnect the priests from their loyalty to Rome. For the same reason, many otherwise patriotic priests and bishops faced the agonizing dilemma of a choice between loyalty to the Church and allegiance to France. Nearly half of the French priests went through the motions of swearing fidelity to the new government, while the other half (including most of the bishops) refused to do so. Henceforth, the "non-juring" clergy (those who refused the oath) were seen by many people as disloyal or even traitorous to the reform movement.

Eviction of the Religious

In the course of 1790, all monastic properties were to be taken over by state administrators and liquidated to help pay off the national debt. The religious were to be sent away with a small pension, and urged to find constructive work in the economic sector. In practice, this decree from the Assembly was to be followed up with a systematic visit to each religious house in France by representatives of the government. They were to interview each religious man or woman to explain that the vows they had taken did not further bind them any longer, and that they now had to leave their houses. It was better to accept the pension and go quietly, since they would be evicted in any case. For those who might prove too stubborn, there would be a few generic monasteries where they were to be put into storage until they died, without regard to their particular order or monastic rule. The primary issue was that they were no longer free to remain together as a community, wear their habits, pray in common, and carry on their former life as though nothing had happened.

Faced with this rather awful dilemma, most religious in France were expelled from their houses and told to look for jobs. In practice, this edict was sometimes put into operation by fairly humane functionaries, who found ways to delay or soften its rigors, at least for the time being. But sooner or later, the law had to be enforced. So thousands of vowed men and women in all parts of France, many of them elderly or sick, had to choose between dreadful alternatives. One fundamental choice was whether to accept the new order of things, or to resist it. Resistance to this law was a severe ordeal to members of any religious order. Most of them had successfully lived their days by going along with rules and regulations, and not by opposing them. So for most, this moral dilemma was a brand new issue.

Those friars or sisters who chose to be released from their vows were not necessarily giving up on religious life. Some of them correctly judged that they might have a better chance of living a spiritual way of life in private. The composite communities designated for warehousing the most obstinate men or women had no appeal whatever. For any Carmelite who wanted to continue living according to Albert's Rule, the fundamental alternative was whether to do it alone, or with the remaining members of a community. Some dedicated people chose one option, others the alternative.

By way of example, the large Discalced house on the rue de Vaugirard had 64 friars when the 1790 laws came into effect. After the visit of the government representatives, only eight decided to accept release from their vows. The other 56 remained steadfast, and were not bothered at first. They were generally popular in their neighborhood, since they had favored many of the moderate reforms of the early revolution. Even so, their church was closed and they were not allowed to function as priests. But they were not actually evicted from their house until August of 1792.

A few Carmelite churches managed to survive as parish churches, usually with other diocesan pastors. Monasteries were sometimes taken over by municipalities for use as public buildings, or turned into private dwellings. Many were torn down to vacate the land, or so that the building materials could be used on other projects. Books, furnishings, and works of art were sometimes saved in local museums or libraries, but more often found their way into private collections. Far too many compilations of priceless records, manuscripts, and spiritual books went into bonfires. The governing principle for the disposition of religious property was to raise the greatest quantity of money for the state.

Male religious who were also priests had the option of placing themselves under the jurisdiction of a bishop in order to continue working in a parish. But since the vast majority of Carmelites were not engaged in parish ministry, they were not even asked to take the oath of loyalty, which might afford some legal protection. Other men or women who had experience with any social ministry might continue to work with the young, the elderly, the poor, or the sick, but probably not in any church-related institution, since the state had already taken over the schools in December of 1789. In the minds of the religious, this impasse of bad alternatives sometimes hinged on how they could best serve God and neighbor. Do I oppose an unjust institution, and make myself a martyr to principle? Or do I collaborate with the new regime, and endeavor to pull some good out of a bad situation? Most sisters and friars now had to choose one or the other.

There were also those who attempted to go underground and carry on their community activities in secret as best they could. Others fled as refugees to other countries where the law did not apply. Since many Carmelites lived in the south, they were able to make their way to Spain or Italy. Those who lived further north might find Belgium or Germany more suitable. Some found Protestant countries like Britain and the Netherlands surprisingly welcoming. Unfortunately for many of those refugees, the next few years would see a quick advance of French revolutionary armies, which overran their places of sanctuary yet again. Events which no one could control would upend their lives as fewer and fewer places of safety remained.

The standoff between the clergy who espoused the Civil Constitution, and those who did not, also served to polarize the lay people of France. In common parlance, the "black clergy" supported the pope and the idea of a universal Church community; the "red clergy" favored a national Catholic Church, based on French patriotism and egalitarian principles. In some western provinces like the Vendée and Brittany, substantial numbers of citizens eventually took up arms against their own government to defend their religion against what they called the "triumph of Atheism." The central government responded with harsh measures to safeguard the revolution against the "black clergy" or anyone else who might be counter-revolutionaries and traitors.

In August of 1792, a second, more moderate, oath was substituted for the first, in the hopes that more priests would pledge their support to the beleaguered government. It simply stated that "I swear to maintain liberty and equality with all my strength, or to die defending them." From that moment onward, the oath was mandatory for all priests, not just those in parishes. The testimony of any six citizens against a non-juring priest could condemn him to the penalty of deportation. But the political situation began to deteriorate the following month with the fall of the monarchy. The hapless Louis XVI was eventually put on trial and executed by his own people. From that point onward, the most militant of the atheists pushed the Revolution into its most radical phase.

Terror in France

The bloodbath known as the Reign of Terror actually began with a shocking episode called the September Massacres. After the Discalced friars had been evicted from their monastery on the rue de Vaugirard, the building was pressed into service as a holding prison for diocesan priests from Paris who refused to swear loyalty to the state. Inflamed by panic at the battlefield losses of the French revolutionary army, a violent mob broke into the ex-priory on September 2, 1792, and slaughtered 115 helpless clerics. Together with the victims in other prisons, there were over 1100 fatalities, including at least three bishops and 250 priests. These horrid murders unleashed a period of bloodthirsty lawlessness which lasted almost two years.

It is unlikely that any one leader really controlled the Parisian mob, but members of the radical Jacobin party certainly encouraged the violence, and attempted to benefit from the chaotic situation. The Jacobins saw stark fear as one method to coerce or frighten the population into supporting their militant policies of building a secular, egalitarian community, which was otherwise an impossible hope. Historians estimate that 40,000 men, women, and children died in the Terror, most of them harmless victims of hatred and bigotry. It was only in July of 1794 that the Terror ended with the execution of Maximillian Robespierre, the driving force behind the bloodbath. It may be significant that he was sent to the guillotine less than two weeks after the 16 heroic nuns of Compiègne.

The epic story of these women has been immortalized in the screen-play *Dialogues of the Carmelites* by Georges Bernanos, and by Francis Poulenc's powerful opera of the same name. Although the scripted dialogue and some of the characters are fictitious, the fundamental story is very real. Compiègne is about 50 miles northeast of Paris. The Carmelite convent there was founded in 1641, and held 20 nuns when the Revolution began. There seemed to be nothing unusual about these women, whose ages spanned 50 years, and who represented every social class. Their prioress was Thérèse of St. Augustine, elected at the age of 35. She had selected the religious name taken by Madame Louise de France, her fellow Carmelite from the previous generation. Like her namesake a century later, Thérèse had a deep sense of trust in God's goodness.

Following the legislation of 1790 against religious orders, an official visited the convent in August, and was surprised that each member of the community refused the "ridiculous freedom" which he offered. But the municipality did not require the nuns to leave their house until September 14, 1792, when all of them were evicted, including two who were elderly and sick. The date seemed symbolic, since it is the Feast of the Holy Cross, when Carmelites begin their long period of fasting to prepare for Easter, celebrating the Resurrection of the Lord.

Mother Thérèse and the community had taken advantage of the two previous years to prepare themselves for their ordeal. Although they were very ordinary women in many ways, they seemed to grow in strength as their tribulation grew,

Venerable Martinien Pannetier, with the Lay Carmelites, Anna Rosa Bernard and Thérèse Thiac who had harbored Martinien, going to the guillotine during the French Revolution. They are three of at least 34 members of the Order known to have suffered death or imprisonment during the Revolution. Giuseppe Gonna painted this scene in 1928 at the request of Gabriel Wessels, postulator general of the Order. The painting hangs in Collegio Internazionale di Sant'Alberto in Rome. *(Photo courtesy of Carmelite Media)*

and they appealed to God for help. They made a conscious decision to offer themselves as victims, if God wished such a sacrifice, as they prayed for peace between France and their Church. They resolved to follow the Lamb of God, Jesus crucified and resurrected. According to their previous plans, they now split into groups of four, adopted secular dress, and lived in separate houses, where they continued their simple and prayerful life. Mother Thérèse urged them to renew their dedication every day for the next two years.

As the Reign of Terror drew toward its bloodthirsty climax, 16 of the sisters were denounced and arrested for living the religious life in violation of the constitution, and supporting the memory of the king. After a two-day trip to Paris, they were presented to the revolutionary tribunal and accused of being religious fanatics and supporters of the King. The outcome was not much of a surprise, and all of the nuns were condemned to die on July 17th. Before they arrived at the guillotine, they managed to use pieces of cloth they had brought with them to add black veils and white mantles to their brown dresses. Imagine the shock of the jaded population of Paris when they saw women dressed as Carmelite nuns singing and riding joyfully to their death at the scaffold. Thérèse of St. Augustine asked to be the last to die, so that she could encourage her sisters. Contemporary accounts tell of the remarkable silence of so many people in the square, as the heavy blade fell and rose again, time after time. It was becoming increasingly obvious to the mob that these gentle women were not a threat to public safety, and that the violence against them was pointless. By the end of that same month, the Terror had ended.

Other Victims

Another less noted victim of the guillotine was Martinien Pannetier, former Carmelite prior and novice master of Bordeaux. He taught theology at the University, and had written two popular books: a manual for the Third Order, and a life of St. Simon Stock. When challenged to accept release from their vows, 24 of the 25 members of the Bordeaux community refused, electing to remain in religious life. Nevertheless, they were turned out of their large priory on April 27, 1790, and told to live elsewhere.

Martinien convinced the youngest member of his community, Dominique Soupré, to join him in a "holy burglary." They gained access to the church by means of their former house, and removed the chest containing the relics of Simon Stock. At a time when many tombs were being profaned by rampaging mobs, they felt that they had to hide the remains of the great Carmelite in a safe place.

Martinien was arrested with two secular priests in 1792 for trying to continue their ministry. A rabidly anticlerical mob murdered his two friends, while Martinien escaped in the confusion. He was hidden first by a Jewish merchant, then by his cousin Thérèse Thiac. All the while he carried on his care of faithful Catholics as best he could. Since he remained so active, he was not able to disappear entirely from public view, but still managed to survive for another two years without being denounced to the police. He was finally arrested in 1794 and sent to the guillotine, just four days after his heroic sisters of Compiègne.

After Martinien's narrow escape from the mob, his young friend Dominique Soupré decided to leave France with two other Carmelites. They hiked over the Pyrenees to Spain where they found refuge with the Carmelites in Pamplona and Zaragoza. While he was there, Cardinal Lorenzana of Toledo found a position for Dominique as tutor to the Prince of the Asturias, later King Ferdinand VII. But when the situation in France stabilized in 1801, Dominique returned to Bordeaux, where he worked as a parish priest for the rest of his long life. He maintained contact with other Carmelites, but it was never possible for them to re-found a proper religious community. Together with one of his parishioners, Dominique founded the congregation of Sisters of Christian Doctrine to do social work. He also revisited the site of his former "theft" when he recovered the remains of Simon Stock, and consigned them safely to the cathedral in Bordeaux.

Several of the other Carmelites who were arrested were sentenced to be deported with hundreds of other non-juring clergy. Ex-slave ships were designated to collect priests and religious at two ports of embarkation, Bordeaux and Rochefort, and then transport them to the unhealthy coasts of either French Guiana or West Africa. But as things worked out, the ships were not able to leave port because the British navy controlled the seas. Hundreds of clerical prisoners were sent out to the disease-infested ships which never sailed, and many of them died in the teeming holds. Most of those unfortunates who died of heat, bad food, horrid sanitation, and outright mistreatment were buried on the islands of Aix, Madame, Oléron, and Ré off of France's western coast.

One noted Carmelite who became a victim of these insidious deportations was Jacques Retouret, a native of Limoges. He was noted for his natural talent as a preacher and teacher, distinguished himself as a first-rate spiritual director, and always lived as a prayerful friar. His Lenten sermons were especially memorable because of his zeal, finesse, and authenticity. As a compassionate confessor, he helped many humble people struggle to live moral lives. Although Jacques tried to find common ground with the revolutionary authorities, he was condemned to the prison ships. There his health broke down entirely and he died August 25, 1794. Another Carmelite from the same community, Isidore Dupont, was also condemned to deportation, but managed to survive the revolution. In all, we know the names of over 60 male and female Carmelites who endured death or imprisonment during the French Revolution. But how many others suffered and died, and yet are not identifiable by name? Most of the more ordinary victims of the Revolution remain unknown.

With the death of Robespierre and the end of the Terror, France became somewhat safer. The succeeding regime, called the Directory, was still militantly anti-royalist and anti-clerical, if less bloodthirsty. The new policy toward the wounded Church was one of neglect. It would be allowed to wither and die, but was not as actively persecuted. But there was a growing consciousness among even dedicated atheists that an accommodation was needed between themselves and the more religious segment of society. There were too many observant Catholics to ignore, especially at a time when national unity was becoming vital because of the war against the major powers of Europe. The only alternative was to allow the other states to overturn the Revolution completely, while the French were hopelessly divided among themselves.

Napoleon

By 1799, France had descended into a morass of chaos and corruption. Although the tattered revolutionary armies had managed to hold their own in the continuing war against nearly all of Europe, the French people were badly in need of inspired leadership. A young Corsican officer, Napoleon Bonaparte, provided the crucial connection between military genius and political know-how, as he efficiently engineered a seizure of power. Napoleon brought exceptional talent to France and Europe at a pivotal time. He had been schooled in the ideas of the Enlightenment, and ruled as an enlightened despot. But he was no friend of the Church, and had no use for religious orders. Napoleon accepted the usefulness of religion in society, but hoped that he would always be able to manipulate it for reasons of state. In the last analysis, he assured the survival of some revolutionary principles by stripping away the traces of terror and instability which had damaged the early reforms.

Napoleon went to work with his customary energy on a massive reorganization of the French state. He signed a Concordat (church-state treaty) with Pope Pius VII in 1801 which allowed the Church relative freedom to act within his empire. He restored the hierarchy, but planned to keep it always under his powerful influence. For the surviving religious, it was now safe to return home and resume their religious practices, but they were not yet authorized to form communities. Napoleon also set up a Council of State to streamline the administration of France, especially when he might be personally absent on some distant battlefield. He completely revised the legal system and the banking structure of France. He restructured the educational system, now effectively removed from all control or influence from the Church. At no point did he contemplate a restoration of the religious orders, since he viewed them as sources of foreign power and influence (the pope's) which would not be under his direction.

Napoleon inherited a France which had already conquered Belgium and the left bank of the Rhine. Over the next decade, he would add most of Italy, Spain, and Central Europe to his possessions. Everywhere that the French armies marched, French laws were applied, including the suppression of religious communities and the seizure of ecclesiastical property. His most dramatic transformation may have been in Germany, where he dismantled the intricate fabric of local governments and mini-states, especially the free cities, ecclesiastical territories, and the estates of imperial knights. He abolished these small enclaves because he wanted to govern them directly. But he also hoped to buy the loyalty of the displaced rulers, and compensated them with former monasteries and church properties. He capped the consolidation in 1806 by formally abolishing the Holy Roman Empire, which had lasted over a thousand years. By a few strokes of the pen, hundreds, even thousands, of men's and women's religious houses passed into nothingness.

Enforcement of these decrees was uneven, and various convents or hermitages managed to survive here and there. But the overall effect was devastating. Entire Carmelite provinces disappeared with only a few remnants. Twenty years of nearly continuous warfare added to the overall disruption of religious and civil life. Former religious were conscripted into the French and other armies, and died on battlefields far from home. In Spain, a vicious guerilla war erupted when French administrators and troops moved too quickly to close Spanish monasteries and despoil the churches. The French occupation of Malta ended suddenly when a throng of Maltese citizens rallied to defend the Carmelite church in Mdina. They killed the commanding officer, and then pleaded for help from the British fleet, resulting in a British colonial regime on Malta until the 1970's.

But by the time of the final defeat of Napoleonic France in 1815, vast harm had been done to the Carmelites and other orders. The only areas of Europe which were left untouched were Britain and Ireland, as well as Sicily, Sardinia, and offshore islands where Napoleon's armies could not march. If there were to be any recovery at all, it would require time and trouble, as well as God's blessing. But still more bleak days were to follow.

+ + +

Chapter 9

Back from the Brink

Lisbon: 1834. The haggard brother trudged out through the city gate with an arm-load of heavy choir books. "It's just so unfair!" he grumbled. He and his community had just been turned out of their house by the new justice minister who claimed that they were useless parasites. "We pray, we study, we care for the poor," he added. "Where did we go wrong? What could we have done better?"

Essentially, the French Revolution wiped out the presence of the Carmelites in France, and most other parts of occupied Europe. Although Carmelites of the Ancient Observance did not return to France until 1989, the Discalced Carmelites were blessed by an extraordinary act of heroism.

A wealthy young woman, Camille de Soyecourt, had entered the Carmel on the rue de Grenell in Paris in 1784, taking the religious name Camille of the Infant Jesus. She was imprisoned in 1793 when her convent was suppressed, and was only released when the political situation stabilized. Although the Reign of Terror had claimed her brother and both of her parents, most of their substantial wealth was invested outside of France, and now Camille found herself exclaustrated, but a very wealthy woman. Acting through agents, she managed to buy the now abandoned monastery of the friars on the rue de Vaugirard.

It was not yet safe to re-establish a religious community openly, but Camille moved into the large house in 1797 with a few other Carmelite nuns, and they managed to carry on a clandestine community behind the walls of what seemed like a derelict property. It is ironic that the confiscation of so many religious houses in France created a surplus of them on the market, and lowered the prices. Camille cautiously took advantage of these conditions to buy back several other Carmels in the provinces over the next 10 years. She acquired the old convent at Tours in 1798, Amiens in 1799, Montauban in 1801, Bourges in 1803, and Agen in 1807. Simultaneously, she supported other nuns in their efforts to re-establish quiet communities without habits or proper authorization. Quick action in re-establishing communities was easier while many of the expelled religious were still alive. This valiant woman, worthy to stand with the saints of the catacombs, provided the fragile link in a chain of survival. Carmel in France had been severely injured, but managed to stay alive.

The Restoration

Following the final defeat of Napoleon in 1815, the leaders of Europe tried to reestablish some semblance of the political and social equilibrium which had preceded the French Revolution. This period is sometimes called "the Restoration" by historians, since it represented the return to a balance of several conservative monarchies, each with an established church, and a system of traditional institutions. But to call it "turning back the clock" is ridiculous, since too many things had changed. From now on, nearly every state had some form of written constitution, a legislative body which was at least partially elected by voters, and some enduring protections for the rights of each citizen. France and other countries did indeed "restore" the Church's hierarchy and parish structures, but the religious orders were not a part of what was restored.

Yet the Church of the early 19th century was also shorn of its wealth and landholdings, and therefore somewhat "purified" of its entanglements with corrupt monarchs. The new bishops were more likely to be men of prayer and austere habits, dedicated to the spread of the Gospel, rather than to administration of an institutional empire. But these commendable prelates had to struggle along without religious men or women to help them rebuild a Church worthy of the Good Shepherd. So much of the "richness" of the pre-revolution Church was measured in the spirituality and evangelical values of Carmelites and other religious. And although the survivors of that devastation were willing enough to carry on and rebuild, they frequently had lost their houses, churches, novitiates, and libraries, as well as the important traditions which had flourished among so many of their brothers and sisters. They certainly had the will to rebuild, but the means would be lacking for a very long time.

One bright spot in the 19th century was the dramatic growth of women's congregations dedicated to many varieties of ministry. The newly respectable image of sisters laboring at teaching, nursing, and social outreach made these new groups of working religious both popular and effective in extending the practical outreach of the Church. It was no longer assumed that women's communities needed to be strictly cloistered. As a result of this "golden age of sisters," many congregations would soon request affiliation with the Carmelites, following the Third Order rule. As the 19th century unfolded, there would also be countless new missionary efforts. These initiatives would attract Carmelites, both women and men, to put a charitable and zealous component onto the otherwise ruthless colonial rush to the far corners of the globe.

One zealous example of heroic virtue was Joachina de Vedruna de Mas (1783-1854), a Catalan noblewoman caught in the Napoleonic maelstrom. While her husband was away with the Spanish army, she raised their nine children amid great privation, and managed to nurse the sick and wounded as well. After her husband died, and her children were grown, she assembled a handful of friends in 1826. With the local bishop's blessing, she founded the Carmelites of Charity to carry on the ministries she knew best, teaching and nursing. She established a hospital at Tárrega which looked after victims of the bloody Carlist Wars without distinction of which faction they supported. The great charity of her sisters assured a period of astonishing growth in the years that followed.

Embers in the Ashes

The friars of the Ancient Observance had convened their last general chapter in 1788, only one year before the revolution began. There were 45 provinces listed at that time, but only 26 were able to send representatives, so 19 were missing for various reasons. But for the next 101 years, only two general chapters were possible, either because of war and turmoil in Europe, or simply because the Order was too weak and poor to be able to send people to meetings. Generals were either appointed by the pope, or selected by some governing committee, or elected by mail. The chapter of 1838 had only nine provinces attending, with mention of three other provinces and a vicariate not present. The other chapter, in 1856, listed only 11 provinces attending, and three missing. At that same chapter, it was specifically stated that the Order no longer had any provinces in France, Germany, or Portugal.

Between 1863 and 1889, there was no formal prior general, only a vicar general appointed by the pope. But this man, Angelo Savini, was an extraordinary religious who promoted strict fidelity to the Rule, and a vigorous community life whenever it was possible in such adverse conditions. Even during the suppression of the Order in Italy, Angelo refused to accept defeat, and urged the survivors to hold fast, waiting for the chance to revive at a better moment. The state of religious observance had gotten so poor that Pope Pius IX found it necessary to urge the introduction of the common life, at least in the novitiate. Most of the surviving provinces were now in Ireland, Poland, and Brazil, as well as in Italy and its surrounding islands.

The Discalced friars were similarly decimated. The numerous houses in Spain had suffered badly, but were in the best shape of any surviving communities. Some of the foundations, like the desert at Las Palmas, were too poor and remote to appeal to any of the land-grabbing "reformers" and were left alone. The spiritual resilience of the hermits living there was an incalculable godsend to others whose strength would be tested. The priory of Loano, near Genoa, survived because the powerful Doria family actually held the deed to the property, and refused to yield any of their private lands to confiscation. In Belgium, the friars of Bruges, Ghent, and Ypres managed to hold out, as did the nuns at Liège. Communities at Würzburg in Germany and Czarna in Poland stayed stubbornly active throughout the century with great difficulty. Although the Carmelite missions were seriously hurt by the devastation of their sponsoring provinces, several of them managed to carry on, particularly the Stella Maris house in Palestine, and some of the foundations in Mexico.

Throughout the remainder of the 19th century, local wars and hostile governments would continue to make it difficult to re-found stable religious communities. The Carlist Wars in Spain pitted clerical and anticlerical forces against one another. Revolts and wars leading to the unification of both Italy and Germany made peaceful growth nearly impossible between 1848 and 1870. During Garibaldi's defense of the Roman Republic in 1849, some of the sharpest fighting took place at the Porta San Pancrazio, near to where the *Teresianum*, the wonderful Discalced school of spirituality, would eventually be founded in 1926. Whenever an anti-clerical government came to power in a given country, the suppression of religious orders was often among the first items of legislation. Religious houses were suppressed in Portugal in 1834, Spain in 1835, and Italy in 1866. Once again, some religious were murdered in scattered incidents reminiscent of the Reign of Terror. Some of those communities were able to recover within a few years, but so many others did not.

One especially stubborn friar was Francisco Palau y Quer (1811-72). He entered the Discalced Carmelites in 1832, just shortly before the formal suppression of the Order in Spain forced him into exile. He returned to Barcelona in 1851, where he established an effective catechetical method called the "School of Virtue." Once again, he was arrested and exiled in the Balearic Islands, where he founded both the Carmelite Missionary Sisters and the Teresian Carmelite Missionaries who continue to minister in schools and carry on social work today. For the remainder of his life, Francisco practiced and preached his deep spirituality in every possible manner.

During the first half of the century, most central European states did not allow the surviving religious to accept new members. Monasteries called "dying-out houses" were designated where the existing friars could live out their last days together, but then that would be the end of them. One of these sad houses at Straubing, in Bavaria, had only one friar, Peter Heitzer, by 1841. He was the last German Carmelite of the Ancient Observance. But in that year, the law changed, allowing new candidates to join. Twenty years later, Straubing sent the first two friars to the United States, with very successful consequences. A similar house at Boxmeer in the Netherlands held only two priests and one brother. By this time, Boxmeer was the last surviving house observing the Touraine reform constitutions. They too were permitted to accept novices in 1840, and within 15 years, they had enough men to open another priory in Zenderen. Those three houses joined in 1879 to form a province of northern Europe. The process of rebuilding was under way, but agonizingly slow.

Following the unification of the German states in 1870, Otto von Bismarck

The Curia and *Studium Generale* of the Carmelite Order stand to the right of Santa Maria in Traspontina Church in this photo before the destruction of the curia and *studium generale* building. Following the general suppression of the Order in Italy in 1866, Traspontina itself was seized in 1873. Late in 1893 the curia building was turned over for use as an army barracks while the church and a few rooms remained in the hands of the Order. *(Photo courtesy of the General Archives of the Carmelite Order)*

launched a personal crusade to reduce Catholic influence in his new Germany. This "War for Civilization" or *Kulturkampf* was a thinly veiled campaign of bigotry which also included the now familiar ban on religious communities. In this case, even Bismarck's genius could not defeat the stubborn German Catholics, who had learned how to protect their institutions and worship by concerted political action, and by actively supporting their nuns and friars. After a decade of struggle, Bismarck abandoned his fight, partially because he now needed Catholic support against the powerful Socialists in parliament. Some Carmelite houses had to be relocated, others were lost for a while, but Carmel in Germany had become victorious, militant, and well-supported by hundreds of fervent lay people.

In more than a few places, a Carmelite presence was maintained by lay tertiaries in spite of government suppression. Third Order Carmelites had a lower profile than habited religious, and almost always survived, even when their beloved local monasteries and convents were confiscated by civil authorities.

Countless faithful associates of suppressed Carmels carried on their prayer and heroic ministry, even under rabidly anticlerical regimes. One valiant tertiary, Librada Ferarrons (1803-42), endured grinding poverty and the loss of the Carmelite friends in her town of Olot, in Catalonia. Yet she went on to maintain a devout life as a loom operator and supervisor in a textile factory. She transformed her workplace into a joyful oasis of prayer, along with a large number of her workmates. Another Catalan, Carmen de Sojo (1856-90), proved to be a saintly wife and mother in a bourgeois family, despite the hardships of the Carlist Wars and her own delicate health.

Peter Heitzer, the last remaining Carmelite in the monastery at Straubing in 1841, captured in a painting. *(Photo courtesy of Rainer Fielenbach, O. Carm.)*

Heroic Rebuilding

The timely courage of Camille of the Infant Jesus had already set the stage for the rebound of Carmelite foundations in France. Camille resumed active community life in the rambling Vaugirard building, but moved her nuns to a better site in 1845. Technically, the convents which were re-established with her help were illegal, but the support of ordinary people nearby sustained and protected them from harm. French law eventually permitted the establishment of women's communities, but only with official permission. The venerable house at Compiègne was restored in 1865. The popularity of these nuns is evident in the fact that there were 113 Carmels in France by 1880, but that only 18 of them were "legal." One of those small convents was at Lisieux, founded in 1838 by the Poitiers Carmel. In time, the former friars' house on the rue de Vaugirard passed from hand to hand until it became one of the anchors of the restored Catholic University in Paris in 1875, which it remains to this day.

The Discalced friars had a much more difficult time in their attempts to return to France. Several promising ventures were swept away by recurring waves of anticlericalism. It remained for a Spanish refugee, Dominic of St. Joseph, to restore a durable presence in France. Dominic fled the suppression of his own community in Navarre, and finally set up a small house in the wild mountainscape near Bordeaux. With the help of other Spanish friars, he attracted a surprising number of young Frenchmen, and kept right on founding other successful communities. By 1853, he was chosen provincial of a reconstituted French province.

But the zeal that Dominic showed in the rebuilding did not let him rest. By

1865, he had established 15 French houses, and then was elected general of the Italian congregation. By 1868, he was able to support the rebuilding in Spain. Undaunted by many setbacks, the Spanish Discalced friars built or reclaimed 38 houses in five provinces by 1914. By the end of the same year, there were 108 restored and new convents of nuns in Spain. At the conclusion of his life, Dominic of St. Joseph also participated in the First Vatican Council of 1870.

A great part of the sudden popularity of the Carmelites in France resulted directly from the spiritual journey of a talented German Jew. Hermann Cohen was born in Hamburg to a devout family in 1820. As a very young man, he came to Paris to study music under Franz Liszt. He became an overnight sensation, and threw himself into the fast-paced artistic world, with all its dangers to his moral and religious upbringing. After a dramatic religious conversion at the age of 27, he was baptized a Catholic and adopted a very simple and austere style of life. He discovered the Carmelites and began to read St. Teresa's works, which drove him into a remarkable decision to join her religious family. He received the habit from Dominic of St. Joseph, and professed his vows in 1850, with the name of Augustine of the Blessed Sacrament. To his talent as a musician, he added a reputation as an eloquent preacher and a popular spiritual adviser. His fame was so great that he raised the profile of the French Carmelites among the general population, and paved the way for their return to Paris in 1864.

But there was still more noble work for Augustine of the Blessed Sacrament. Cardinal Nicholas Wiseman met him in Rome, and was so impressed with his talent that he asked Pope Pius IX to send him to restore the Carmelite presence in England. Augustine reluctantly left France for London, but immediately threw himself into the new venture with his characteristic energy and optimism. He gave concerts and recitals to draw the attention of sympathizers, while he perfected his use of English for his dramatic style of preaching. He rapidly became a celebrated figure, and his original foundation at Kensington led to many others, as vocations redoubled. He returned to France just before the Franco-Prussian War of 1870. Because of his German origins, he had to leave France by way of Switzerland and ended his days ministering to French prisoners in Berlin. Although his remarkable life reads like a good novel, Augustine wanted no more than to live and die quietly in the service of God and neighbor.

A very similar story developed in Poland. A man from Vilna in his 40's, Josef Kalinowski, asked for admission to the Carmelites. He had been a soldier in the Polish army, and participated in the revolution of 1863 against the Russian occupation. He spent ten years as a prisoner in Siberia, where he passed through his own dark night of suffering and spiritual renewal. After he was released in 1874, he resolved to turn around his past unfaithfulness, and dedicate his life to softening the hatred in his world. He was professed with the name Raphael of St. Joseph, and was ordained a priest. As prior of Czarna, he worked ceaselessly for the reconciliation of Polish Catholics with Orthodox Russians and others. His dedication to the Gospel value of repaying evil with good was enhanced by his own robust spirituality. And his obvious patriotic fervor enhanced the excellence of his preaching and counseling. Many young men were attracted to join the Carmelite family simply because they wanted to be like Raphael.

The devastating losses which the Carmelites suffered during the 19th century impelled the faithful remnant to clarify and purify their motives, as they attempted to return to their spiritual roots. Issues which had seemed vital in previous times might pale quickly for those faced with outright extinction. Especially in Italy, the violent process of national unification had disrupted the confident sense of stability in what once had seemed to be the unshakable heart of the Church. With the wholesale confiscation of ecclesiastical property, the lion's share of Carmelite priories and convents were at least temporarily lost to the Order. One hidden blessing was that losing abandoned or sparsely populated houses forced the surviving religious to consolidate into the more viable communities. The sense of desperation forced a closer cooperation among the faithful remnant that was determined to carry on. By 1914, the Discalced Friars had restructured their 32 Italian houses into five provinces. Friars of the Ancient Observance also retained many of their ancient foundations, but the old structure had been severely mauled.

Given the hostile attitude of so many European governments, it became obvious that hope for the Church and the Carmelites might be much brighter in mission lands. This issue of missionary expansion drove the Spanish Discalced congregation to abandon its long-held reluctance to send men overseas. After much soul searching, they dispatched missionaries to several countries in Latin America, beginning in 1880. Missionaries from France, Italy, and elsewhere continued to set out for distant lands, as they had already done so well for many years. Of special note is the continuing mission effort in the Middle East, particularly Oman and the Persian Gulf, together with the Ottoman provinces which would become Syria, Lebanon, and Iraq. Already in 1875, Pope Pius IX had approved the reunion of the Spanish and Italian congregations under one general and a single administration. The resulting unity of purpose could not fail to help the revival.

Carmel in America

Another tiny opening toward renewed growth had already been made before the French Revolution really got under way. A little band of four Discalced nuns left the Hoogstraten Carmel for America in 1790. For nearly two centuries, there had already been three English-speaking houses in Flanders, thanks to Anne of Jesus. Beginning in 1619, she had opened Carmelite spirituality to Catholic refugees from England, since they were not legally permitted to found convents at home. By 1794, all three Flemish communities would have to flee to England ahead of the advancing French armies, an ironic reversal of history. (By 1960, there were 40 convents of nuns in Britain.) But the Hoogstraten community now resolved, together with the convents in Antwerp and Lierre, to found and support daughter houses in the English-speaking world, and specifically the newly independent United States.

The Mount Carmel Monastery in Port Tobacco, Maryland: a sketch from Bishop C.W.
Currier's "Carmel in America." The monastery was founded in 1790, after the American
Revolution, by Carmelite nuns from Belgium, three of whom were originally from southern
Maryland. After years of labor and prayer on the site, the eight or more buildings on the
property fell into disrepair and the nuns were living under conditions of extreme hardship.
Archbishop James Whitfield transferred the 24 Carmelites to the City of Baltimore in 1831.
(Photo courtesy of the Archives of the Carmelite Monastery, Baltimore, MD)

The intrepid group, one Englishwoman and three Americans, braved the
two-month crossing of the Atlantic in a sailing ship, and made their way to
Chesapeake Bay. Their original invitation had come from Bishop John Carroll
of Baltimore, where most American Catholics were concentrated at that time.
The first foundation was established at Port Tobacco, led by Bernadina of
St. Joseph, who was herself from one of Maryland's old Catholic families.
The new Carmel was successful, but it took a long time before it was entirely trouble-free. Vocations were promising, but Maryland had yet to build
a strong tradition of exactly how to support a contemplative convent. As a
result, economic and political troubles continued to plague the nuns. Their
foundation was the first women's convent of any kind to be established under
the American flag. (Technically, the French Ursulines in New Orleans dated
from 1727, but Louisiana was not yet part of the United States.) By 1831, the
community left Port Tobacco for Baltimore, a much more promising location.
Within the next century, the Baltimore Carmel founded energetic houses in St.
Louis, New Orleans, and Boston, from which many others would flow. The
vast majority of American Carmelite nuns trace their heritage to that heroic
venture of 1790.

Despite the travels of some fascinating Carmelite explorers and missionaries,
there was no permanent presence of friars in North America until the time of
the American Civil War. It was then that Angelo Savini, vicar general of the

Carmelite Monastery Library, Straubing — Restored recently, the library is a magnificent frescoed room in the Carmelite monastery, founded in 1368, which is the oldest building in continuous use by the Order. Two Carmelites left this monastery in 1864 for Louisville, Kentucky to establish the Order in the USA.

Ancient Observance, gave permission for an American foundation by a pair of Germans, Cyril Knoll and Xavier Huber. In 1864, they left the struggling house at Straubing to initiate a Carmelite presence in Leavenworth, Kansas. At a time when so many German immigrants needed every sort of pastoral care, the two friars were welcomed by the local bishop. Cyril Knoll was a solid and hard-working religious, who desperately wanted to make Carmel take root in America. But his ambitious drive to enlist men and found houses at any cost led him into a series of disappointing ventures in Maryland and Kentucky. He had little financial skill, and his human management talents often failed to match his determination. He was overly eager to build a large Carmelite presence in the new world overnight. Some of his early recruits were completely unfit for religious life, but others were superb. Knoll eventually pulled back from his bold plans and humbly allowed others to succeed in his place.

Within a few years, Knoll's colleagues established more successful communities in New Jersey, Pennsylvania, and on the Canadian side of Niagara Falls. There would still be other unsuccessful settlements, but more succeeded than failed. The steady growth in the numbers of diligent ministers bolstered the strength of the immigrant church, but also drew good vocations from it. Vicar general Savini insisted that the American mission communities remain united under a single administration, rather than splintering into widely-separated factions and fragments. By 1890, several of those far-flung houses were united to form an American province, named to honor the Most Pure Heart of Mary. The first provincial was Pius Mayer, a calm and unruffled administrator, and a deeply spiritual man. The new province grew steadily under his leadership, and eventually became the largest in the Order.

About the same time, Archbishop Corrigan of New York asked Carmelites from Ireland to come to his city. His particular interest was in the fine hospital ministry to the poor by the Whitefriars Street community in Dublin. The first Irish Carmelites were entrusted with the care of the sick and the poor at Bellevue Hospital, which they have maintained ever since. In addition to the initial priory on 28th Street in New York City, another house was added in Tarrytown, New York, in 1897. For the time being, both houses remained a part of the Irish province, but the core of a new entity had been solidly begun.

The arrival of Discalced friars in America followed a very similar path. In 1875, friars of the Bavarian province founded a house in Paterson, New Jersey, as a refuge from Bismarck's *Kulturkampf* in Germany. Although this institution did not last, other friars from the same province established a more successful monastery at Holy Hill, Wisconsin, in 1906. The beautiful location was already a very successful pilgrimage site, especially for German-speaking Catholics in the Midwest, and the small band of Carmelites rapidly turned it into a popular and well-served place of prayer and learning. The hard work of Eliseus of the Sacred Heart and his fellow pioneers enabled a steady growth in the years that followed.

Another contingent of friars from Spain, beginning in 1912, established a presence in Arizona, while they worked to restore older communities in Mexico. Their zeal was rewarded with vocations and later houses in Oklahoma, Texas, and Arkansas. Yet another band of friars from Ireland arrived in California in 1924, and staffed several houses with generous numbers of their own men. By the mid-20th century there were three distinct provinces of Discalced friars. The present house of studies in Washington, DC, is also noteworthy as the headquarters for the Institute of Carmelite Studies, an excellent scholarship and publication ministry.

Further Outreach

At the very dawn of the 19th century, a tenuous Carmelite presence came to Australia with some of the earliest deportees to Botany Bay. The Irish Rebellion of 1798 implicated thousands of sympathizers, including two lay Carmelites, who became the center of Catholic worship in the priest-starved land. Periodic visits by Carmelite missionaries were finally validated in 1881 when the bishop of Adelaide made a formal request to the Irish province for a Carmelite presence. A small team led by Joseph Butler was sent from Dublin, and was steadily reinforced over the years by others coming from Ireland. Although the Australian houses would not become an independent province for some time, they represented a solid contribution to the vigor and spirituality of the Aussie church.

Beginning in the 17th century, the Discalced Carmelites had already established a long tradition of service to the Christians in India. Some of the earliest Apostolic Vicariates were entrusted to the Carmelites, with impressive results. Their spirituality was well known and eagerly accepted in that exotic land where ordinary people were sometimes described as being "infatuated" with God. So it came as no surprise that a young Indian priest, Kuriakose Elias Chavara (1805-71) decided to adopt the Carmelite style of prayer when he co-founded a new congregation of priests (1855) within the Syro-Malabar Catholic Church. His Carmelites of Mary Immaculate worked valiantly to prevent a schism within his Church, as they also labored at evangelization, social reform, and free education of children, women, and lower caste people. With the aid of Leopold Beccaro, OCD, Kuriakose founded the first sisters' congregation for native women, also affiliated with the Carmelites as a Third Order family.

Another young woman, a Palestinian, was attracted to Carmel by an unusual path. Miriam Baouardy was born between Nazareth and Haifa in 1846 to a poor family of devout Melkite Catholics. As a young orphan, she was taken to Alexandria in Egypt by her uncle, but refused to accept a marriage which he had arranged for her. She also received a serious wound on her neck when she refused to convert to Islam. Finally, after working as a domestic servant in many places, she found her way to the Carmel at Pau, in southern France. She took the name of Mary of Jesus Crucified, and soon became known for her intense spiritual life. She was sent to India as one of the founders of a house in Mangalore, which grew eventually into a flourishing congregation called Apostolic Carmel. After she returned to France, Miriam helped to organize and establish the first Holy Land foundation in Bethlehem, where she lived out her remaining days. Before her untimely death in 1878, she left some remarkable notes on how the Holy Spirit works in the souls of righteous people.

Thérèse

It seems fitting that the 19th century, which dawned as a near-death experience for the Carmelite family, would culminate in the story of a little one who bore powerful witness to the reality of a loving God in her completely uneventful life. Thérèse Martin was born to a comfortable Norman family at Alençon in 1873. She was the youngest of five daughters, and grew up in a tender, nurturing environment. In 1877, just after her beloved mother died of breast cancer, the family moved to Lisieux. Her uncle Isidore was a pharmacist there, and suggested the move so that he could help look after the family. Thérèse remembered that time as the end of her carefree happiness and the beginning of a period of turmoil and worry. In 1883, she came down with a mysterious illness which only passed after her family prayed fervently for her. Thérèse recalled that in her feverish state she saw Our Lady smile at her, and that her health quickly returned as a result. She would later state that "Mary is more mother than queen."

Wooden sculpture of St. Thérèse of Liseux showing various espisodes from her life. The sculpture hangs on the wall of the chapel in the National Shrine of St. Thérèse of Lisieux in Darien, Illinois. Below the sculpture is a reliquary of St. Thérèse.

Thérèse also spoke of a personal "conversion" in 1886 which enabled her to move beyond her sensitivity and scruples, as she realized that her weakness did not matter to a truly loving God. From that point onward, she was determined to enter religious life in order to use every minute to draw closer to that same benevolent Father. When Thérèse was only 14, she asked to follow her older sisters into the Carmel of Lisieux, but was refused because of her age. She was greatly disappointed, but then took advantage of a pilgrimage to Rome to present her case directly to Pope Leo XIII. The astonished pontiff made no promises, saying only that God's will would be done. As things turned out, she was admitted to the convent in 1888. What followed was the most joyful time of her life.

Although she had less than ten years to live, Thérèse threw herself enthusiasti-cally into the regimen of daily life inside the red brick walls. Her sense of opti-mism and whimsy brightened even the drudgery of scrubbing and laundering. The older nuns found her attitude refreshing, but saw nothing unusual about her following the rules and regulations of convent life. Rules were taken as a matter of course, and young Thérèse was among the best at observing them. She showed no interest in the everyday pettiness or community factions within the convent. Small-minded irritations simply did not matter to her. She just went her way, like a bright, cheerful little sparrow. In 1893, Thérèse was named acting novice mistress, which gave her the opportunity to demonstrate some of the building blocks of what she called her "little way" of love and confidence in God.

Early in 1896, she began to experience the first symptoms of tuberculosis, which would eventually claim her life. After her death, some of the sisters won-dered what they would ever say about someone so ordinary, of one who had been taken from them so quickly. So it came as a genuine surprise when her autobiography was published, and became an overnight success. Thérèse had only written *The Story of a Soul* because her prioress had requested it, but that work disclosed a remarkably mature spiritual journey. The "little way" enabled Thérèse to be free of her faults and weakness, because her benevolent Father saved her from all harm.

When she first professed her vows, it is significant that she took the religious name Thérèse of the Child Jesus. She embraced her status as a child, who rated as nothing in the world's eyes, and yet a child who expected every good thing from a loving Father. Being a child, she had no need to earn a living, but rejoiced in merely gathering flowers and playfully offering them back to God. Her unique way of celebrating the Incarnation was to see Jesus the Redeemer as a child like herself, as a little one. Thérèse rejoiced in the humanity of the Son of God, which blessed forever the individual believer for no good reason at all—except love.

Later in her short life, Thérèse added "and the Holy Face" to her religious name. French piety in the late 19th century included reflection on the face of the suffering Jesus, as portrayed on Veronica's veil, or the newest photographs of the Shroud of Turin. She made this addition because she saw the suffering of Jesus as the maturing of a faithful and committed life. Throughout her own illness and the privations of her austere life, she never sought out suffering for its own sake, any more than Jesus did. But like her Lord, Thérèse accepted whatever pain entered her life as a way to measure and express how great her love really was. She died in 1897.

Pope Pius XI, who canonized Thérèse in 1925, called her the greatest saint in modern times. He felt that her insights could serve as a catalyst to transform and renew all of human society. Countless ordinary Christians have agreed, since they clearly find common ground with Thérèse. Like her, most people admit a lack of sophistication in spiritual theology, but have a shared desire to love and serve God among the pots and pans of daily life. In the end, Thérèse reminds us that a dialogue with the true and loving God was far more significant than the frightful violence of the 20th century, which was just then coming to birth. "Love trumps might." Thérèse understood the strength which Elijah saw in his gentle, whispering breeze, indeed far more powerful than the wind, earthquake, and fire.

A near contemporary of Thérèse was Elizabeth of the Trinity (1880-1906). Elizabeth Catez was born in a military camp where her father was serving as a captain in the French army. Even as a small child she had a volatile temper, but settled down dramatically after receiving her first communion. She was increasingly attracted to prayer and religious matters. By the time she entered the Carmel of Dijon at age 21, her awareness of God's presence was already well developed. Although she died only five years later, her writings leave a clear trail of her rich appreciation of herself as host to the Trinity, a loving community of persons.

Mosaic of Carmelite St. Thérèse of Lisieux on the wall of the tomb of Pope Pius XI in the crypt of St. Peter's Basilica in the Vatican. Calling her the "greatest saint in modern times," Pope Pius canonized her in 1925 only 28 years after her death. She has been referred to as "the star of his pontificate."

Steady Rebuilding

For Carmelites of the Ancient Observance, 1889 marked the end of the long century when general chapters were rare. Angelo Savini had served heroically as vicar general since 1863 during the Order's most desperate years, but was now nearing the end of his life. Representatives of ten provinces met in Rome to elect Luigi Galli prior general in 1889. At the same chapter, they enacted several measures which demonstrated that the period of mere survival was over, and that a true revival had begun. New constitutions were desperately needed, since they had not been revised since 1626, or reprinted since 1766. Thus a complete revision of the legislation was authorized for the entire Order, based on the old principles of the Strict Observance. From that point onward, there would be no internal distinctions between levels of adherence or fidelity, since all friars would necessarily be "observant." Another bad practice, conventuality, also met a quick death. From now on, all friars belonged to a province, and not a particular house. The new version of the constitutions was completed by 1904.

Luigi Galli promoted these measures vigorously, and was reelected at the next chapter in 1896. Under his guidance, free-standing provinces were approved for Spain, Malta, and the United States. An international college in Rome was planned for the education of students from any part of the world, and a symbol of unity among the many provinces. Several new spiritual manuals and liturgical books were authorized, and these appeared gradually over the following decade,

Pius Mayer (center with beard), Provincial of the American PCM Province at the General Chapter of 1896. Six years later he would be elected prior general. Under his leadership the Order returned to countries lost during the very difficult late 1800s, new constitutions were issued, and liturgical books were reformed.

enriching the prayer life of the revived Order. Galli died before the next chapter in 1902. In a symbolic way, he represents the end of the 19th century struggle to survive. Luigi Galli was the last of the many heroic Italians to carry on the mantle of Elijah for the Ancient Observance. The leaders of the 20th century would represent the newer, faster growing provinces. The first of these was Pius Mayer, the capable, German-born pioneer of the new American province, who led the Order until 1918.

Pius Mayer began by consolidating the many small provinces in Italy, while promoting growth there and elsewhere. He clearly saw the need of augmenting vocations and restoring high quality formation in the spirituality and traditions of the Order. From his personal experience, Mayer appreciated how useful it could be to move men and women from one country or culture to another. In effect, he created a "foreign legion" of helpers to go wherever they were needed. This vision of the internationality of the Order lent a sense of "bigness" to his rebuilding efforts, and demonstrated just the sort of association which enriches an intercontinental community. He encouraged the struggling communities in Poland by sending Dutch friars to serve in posts of responsibility. He continued to encourage German and Irish friars to go to America. Since 1894, Spanish volunteers had been working to revive all three of Brazil's historic provinces. But by 1900 it was obvious to the Spaniards that they were unable to carry the entire burden themselves. They asked to concentrate only on the northern part of the country. In 1904, therefore, prior general Mayer asked the Dutch province to help in southern Brazil, specifically the Rio province. They responded generously, and enjoyed very profitable results.

Another successful effort at outreach was the affiliation of congregations of working sisters. Ever since the Enlightenment crusade against communities of cloistered nuns, the growing movement toward apostolic congregations of women demonstrated how well they could play a part in education or social work. One such group, the Carmelite Sisters of Grace, had already been established in 1724 to care for the elderly and teach needy girls in Bologna. Their habit and their spirituality were patterned after Mary Magdalene de' Pazzi. Similar working congregations would represent the new branch on the tree of Carmel. In several cases, local groups of women were established to address a specific ministry, and then affiliated with the Carmelites as regular communities who followed the Third Order rule. The decades of the late 19th and early 20th centuries were a golden age for such congregations, which have greatly enriched the ministry of the Church, while at the same time offering the blessings of Carmelite spirituality to countless humble people.

One such group of women was the Sisters of the Virgin Mary of Mount Carmel, founded by Elisea Olivier Molina in eastern Spain in 1891, primarily to do teaching and nursing work. Since their spiritual care had already been in the hands of the Carmelites almost from the beginning, it was natural to request a formal relationship with the Order. Pius Mayer gladly agreed to their affiliation in 1906. Today these dynamic sisters are active in many parts of the world, including Rwanda and East Timor.

A similar case occurred in Brazil. Mother Maria das Neves established a sisterhood in Rio de Janeiro to do hospital work in 1899, and eventually asked for a legal connection with the Carmelite family. Mayer agreed, and the Carmelite Sisters of Divine Providence were welcomed in 1913. These sisters have subsequently added education, evangelization, and care for the elderly to their ministries. They are active in Brazil, Argentina, and Ecuador.

A similar vigorous congregation was established in 1891 by Anna Marie Tauscher van den Bosch. She began her ministry in Germany when she opened a house for homeless children, and within a short time, other dedicated women joined her. They affiliated with the Discalced Carmelites in 1904, with the name of the Carmelite Sisters of the Divine Heart of Jesus. Headquartered in the Netherlands, they work in many parts of the world today, with a continuing concern for orphans and neglected children.

World War I

Beyond any doubt, the First World War was a dramatic convulsion of the world order. The carnage of that horrid war had a traumatic effect on nearly every country and society where Carmelites lived and worked at that time. But it had little direct impact on the Carmelites, since there were relatively few houses in the areas where most of the fighting took place. The one single exception was Poland, where German, Austrian and Russian forces clashed over a wide swathe of the Eastern Front. The church and priory at Bolszowce were reduced to ruins by a bombardment, but without loss of life. Other houses in the east were damaged during the war and the Polish-Ukrainian fighting which followed in 1920.

Because of the desperate shortage of soldiers in practically all national armies, a large number of Carmelites were conscripted into the armed forces, in spite of their clerical status. Members of the various Italian, French, German, Austrian, and Polish provinces served in their respective military units. Many others served valiantly as chaplains or medical personnel. These individuals undoubtedly endured the physical and psychological effects of that distressing war. But none of them lost their lives, and most returned to their communities after the fighting ended. The new century began with apocalyptic violence, but the worst was yet to come.

+   +   +

Chapter 10

Carmel's New Garden

Manila: 2014. The young mission worker smiled as she dusted the small statue of Mary and Jesus. "What a beautiful home you had together!" she whispered. "I hope we can share some of your love with our poor ones." It would not be long before the beggars and street people began to fill the tiny chapel. She kissed her small scapular, her symbol of dedication, as she smiled even more broadly.

Rebuilding the Framework

Linked with the slow restoration of the Carmelite presence in the world was a quiet but solid rebound in serious study. The new international college of Sant'Alberto in Rome was a strong focus of renewed scholarship and solid formation for the next generations of White Friars. With the loss of so many libraries and archives, Carmelites were in genuine danger of losing their collective memory and heritage. From about the turn of the 20th century, two serious and very talented historians began the agonizingly slow work of reconstructing the self-image of the Order. Both Benedict Zimmerman, OCD (1859-1937) and Gabriel Wessels, O. Carm. (1861-1944) adopted a freshly critical approach to the historiography of the Order. They strained out much of the folklore and pious superstition which had long haunted the credibility of the Carmelite story. Both scholars wrote extensively on the people and texts which had shaped the unique Carmelite spirituality and presence within the Church. Both would be followed by other eager young scholars who spread the same heritage more broadly than ever before in history. Especially noted among these later academics to work in Rome were Silverio de Santa Teresa, Bartholomew Xiberta, and Joachim Smet.

Beginning in 1926, a Discalced house of studies was established in Rome to begin a systematic program of studies for friars from around the world. By

Facade of Collegio di Sant'Alberto, now Centro Internazionale Sant'Albert (CISA), pictured shortly after the reconstruction in 1999-2001. Originally built to house the General Curia and international house of studies when the Order lost Traspontina to the Italian government, the building was dedicated in 1901. A three-story building originally, the fourth floor was added as was the chapel pictured to the left. At its peak year of 1958-1959, the student body numbered 58 with a faculty of 16, besides 16 graduate students attending the universities of Rome. *(Photo courtesy of Carmelite Media)*

1935, it had grown into the Pontifical Theological Faculty of the Teresianum. The success and popularity of that school soon required more space, and led to the move in 1954 to the magnificent Villa Pamphili. And in 1957, the extremely popular spirituality department grew into the international Institute of Spirituality, the only pontifical faculty authorized to grant degrees in spiritual theology for Carmelites and others.

Following the conclusion of World War I, Carmelites of the Ancient Observance held a general chapter in 1919. Elias Magennis was elected prior general, and proved to be a very good choice. Elias was an Irishman who had worked in Australia, and thus brought with him a broad view of the Order's mission, coupled with his own furious energy to help restore it. He was able to build on the foundations of better scholarship and mission outreach that Pius Mayer had laid down. There had been a Carmelite presence in Australia since 1881, and the efforts of the Irish province to establish a sister province "down under" were finally beginning to bear fruit. A free-standing Australian province would finally emerge in 1948.

This longing to restore and expand the Carmelite presence led Magennis to several forceful and courageous measures. He joined various central European jurisdictions in 1922 to reestablish the Upper German province, with Bamberg as its heart. He also encouraged his fellow Irishmen to push ahead with their New

York mission, which developed into the province of St. Elias by 1931. Another Irish project restored a presence in England in 1926. Before the Reformation, English Carmel had consisted of 37 houses with over 1000 friars. By a singular stroke of good fortune, the venerable priory of Aylesford was repurchased in 1949, and lovingly restored. The efforts of the Irish helpers flourished, with aid from some of the other provinces. The historic English province was reborn in 1969.

The Irish Discalced friars followed a similar pattern, sending generous reinforcements to England during the decade of the 1920s. They also made foundations in Australia, beginning in 1948, with enthusiastic hopes for growth. With the demise of the distinct Spanish Discalced Congregation, multitudes of Spanish and Portuguese friars now joined a strong surge of missionaries to Latin America in the years after the war. This period turned out to be another particularly fertile era for the Discalced missionaries.

Rebound of the Missions

Before the storm of the French Revolution, there had been about 50 Discalced stations and communities in mission countries. But many of those had to be abandoned when the home provinces in Europe were extinguished, and were only recovered at a later date with much effort and prayer. Between 1902 and 1914, Cardinal Jerome Gotti was prefect of the Congregation for the Propagation of the Faith, and was well placed to encourage his fellow Discalced friars to redouble their mission efforts. The struggling missions of Syria, Mesopotamia, and the Persian Gulf received a fresh transfusion of friars and helpers from other congregations. The seeds planted in India during the 17th century continued to grow and flourish, to such a degree that today the Discalced missionaries are remembered among the principal founders of India's Catholic presence. Their efforts led to the establishment of several dioceses and the staffing of seminaries for the broader Church. Several large Carmelite provinces today serve people of both the Roman and Syro-Malabar rites. Successful foundations were also made in Japan and the Philippines. Sadly, the Chinese missions did not survive the Communist Revolution of 1951.

Carmelite nuns were blessed with comparable success in the developing mission countries. Back in 1861, the Lisieux community had founded a convent in Saigon, followed by another in Hanoi in 1895. Thérèse had hoped to go to this latter one, but was not allowed because of her declining health. Since then, Vietnamese vocations have proven to be especially resolute, in spite of decades of war and Communist harrying. Women's contemplative communities in Asia have been very successful, particularly in India and the Philippines. Missionary efforts throughout the Order were especially energized by Pius XI's encyclical *Rerum Ecclesiae* in 1926, in which the Pope reminds all Catholics of the duty to evangelize non-Christian peoples, and to foster clerical and religious vocations among them. It is significant that he also stressed the importance of the contemplative life in the mission apostolate, and then punctuated his statement the following year by naming Thérèse of Lisieux the co-patroness of the missions.

In 1930, Elias Magennis sent friars from Spain's Andalusian province to revive the Order in Portugal, intending to reverse the 1834 suppression. Sadly, the process moved more slowly than the general had hoped, despite Portugal's glorious Carmelite past and a strong Third Order presence. The community remained in their Lisbon residence, but without a church or chapel to use as an outlet for their ministry. The political and social turmoil of the inter-war years was too much to allow for the calm and steady growth required. Carmel in Portugal would have to wait until after World War II for a more solid footing.

Magennis discovered that perhaps the finest tool in his hand was the restored Dutch province, which doubled in strength during the decade right after the war. Apart from an impressive growth in numbers, there was also a spiritual and intellectual fire, ignited by a circle of energetic young Dutchmen. The brothers Eugene and Hubert Driessen, Titus Brandsma, and Athanasius van Rijswijck collaborated to translate the works of Teresa of Avila into Dutch. The same men continued their scholarly activity on Carmelite roots and sources, encouraged by their dynamic provincial Cyprian Verbeek. Although the Dutch were already heavily committed to rebuilding the Rio province in Brazil, they also threw themselves into restoring the Lower German province, beginning with the recovery of Mainz in 1923.

And in that very same year, Dutch missionaries opened the first priory in eastern Java, the heart of their Dutch East Indian colony. At first, most of their Catholic parishioners were people of European origin. But the pastoral skills of the Dutch, coupled with a genuine missionary zeal, opened the wider doors to large numbers of native Javanese converts. From this dynamic acorn, planted in the world's most populous Muslim country, a self-supporting Indonesian province would emerge only a few decades later.

Working Congregations

Like his predecessor, Magennis also integrated several congregations of working sisters into the Carmelite family. Some of these had much older histories. The Institute of Our Lady of Mount Carmel, for example, had been established in 1854 by Mother Maria Teresa Scrilli in Italy. She began to do teaching and social work in her home town of Montevarchi, in the province of Arezzo. When the house was suppressed by the anticlerical government five years later, Mother Scrilli made another foundation at Foiano, which was also secularized within a short time. After another fifteen years of waiting, she tried yet again, and brought her old companions together in Florence and elsewhere in central Italy. These resilient sisters managed to outlast the official hostility, and grew steadily as the new century dawned. Their formal affiliation with the Carmelites came in 1929. Today their communities are found on four continents, including one in Israel.

The Congregation of Our Lady of Mount Carmel had yet more venerable origins. In 1826, a French priest assembled a group of Carmelite tertiaries in Tours into a teaching community, drawing upon an even older tradition from 1704. After the revolution of 1830, anticlerical legislation forced Sisters Julie Thérèse Chevrel and Augustin Clerc to flee to Louisiana. There they transplanted their congregation's fine educational tradition to New Orleans in 1833, and began by founding a school for free black girls. During the American Civil War, the sisters lost contact with their support from France, and shared the growing poverty of the defeated Confederacy. In spite of those privations and recurring epidemics of yellow fever, they continued their ministry to the poor and forgotten. These durable sisters extended their calling to many parts of the region. They were recognized as a regular Third Order affiliate in 1930. Today they also have numerous houses in the Philippines.

Another congregation was founded in Sicily because of the inspiration of Thérèse of Lisieux. Even as a young girl, Rosa Curcio developed a love for Carmel by reading the works of Teresa of Avila. She professed vows as a Third Order Carmelite with the name of Sister Maria Crocifissa, and devoted herself to works of mercy, especially among the poor. In 1925, the canonization of Thérèse energized Mother Curcio to establish the Carmelite Missionary Sisters of Saint Thérèse of the Child Jesus as an active congregation to spread God's love to both home and foreign missions. From the very start, she counted on strong support and inspiration from Carmelite friars, especially Lorenzo van den Eerenbeemt. Lorenzo encouraged her interest in foreign missions, and helped move her headquarters from Sicily to the coastal town of Santa Marinella, near Rome. From a solid base of houses throughout Italy, the congregation now serves missions in Brazil, Tanzania, the Philippines, and elsewhere.

A community of a different sort grew out of a civil war in Venezuela. After the failed rebellion of 1901, large numbers of poor, sick, and wounded people had no one to care for them until a band of generous women, led by Mother Candelaria of Saint Joseph appeared on the scene. A local bishop encouraged them to spread their nursing skills to other hospitals and clinics, especially where people were too poor to pay for their own health care. Their association with the Carmelites came in 1925, thanks to a visit by Elias Sendra, who was in the process of founding missions for Spanish friars in both Venezuela and Puerto Rico. Today those sisters have expanded their ministry to the young and the elderly in Bolivia and Brazil as well.

The Corpus Christi Carmelites actually began as Dominican tertiaries in England, but were drawn to Carmel by the practical spirituality of Thérèse of Lisieux. Their foundress was Mother Mary of the Blessed Sacrament Ellerker, who found her own personal path to the Catholic Church as a teenager. She gathered a small community at Leicester in 1908, intending to do social work. Their wonderfully diverse apostolic works included pastoral counseling, motor chapels and dialogue with non-Catholics, pamphlet publishing, parish visits, and care of the sick and elderly. In 1920, they made the momentous decision to found a mission in Port-of-Spain, Trinidad, which subsequently became the motherhouse of the congregation. Although Dominican friars were quite helpful in the early years, Mother Mary decided to aggregate with the Carmelites by 1928. In addition to their vigorous presence in Trinidad, the sisters also run missions today in Grenada and elsewhere in the Caribbean.

Yet another creative ministry got its start in 1929, when Mother Angeline Teresa McCrory envisioned a revolutionary approach to caring for the elderly. She had entered the Little Sisters of the Poor, who do heroic work for the elderly poor who have no resources of their own. But Mother Angeline saw a need to extend care to aging people who were not indigent, but still needed assistance in their later years. By 1931, she had established the Carmelite Sisters for the Aged and Infirm in New York. Mother Angeline Teresa crafted a fresh perspective for the drab "old folks" homes which had been common up until that time. She promoted a cheerful, non-institutional atmosphere in her homes, with flowers, small luxuries, and a great deal of pampering. Her own deeply spiritual core found joy in treating her charges as "guests," not patients, with the same care which Jesus himself would enjoy in her home.

The Spanish Civil War

During the Spanish Civil War, there were many casualties and a shocking amount of destruction for a conflict of the duration of a mere three years. Over one million Spaniards were killed between 1936 and 1939. By the end of the war, nearly 7000 priests and religious had also been killed, including 160 Carmelite friars and 9 cloistered nuns. The bishops and diocesan clergy of the Church, as well as the religious orders, had tended to side with the conservative Nationalist rebels during the war. By contrast, the Loyalist government was strongly anti-clerical, and attempted to reduce the Church's influence in Spanish society. But it was a violent faction within the Loyalist camp which promoted the bloody crusade against religious leaders. That campaign of hatred was orchestrated by a dedicated core of anarchists and Marxists, who were all too aware that they might have only one opportunity to exterminate their ideological enemies. Local hatreds were further complicated by international entanglements. France and the Soviet Union actively supported the Loyalists, while Fascist Italy and Nazi Germany sent aid to the Nationalists. Spain became a grim testing ground for the terror weapons of the next World War.

Lenin had stated in 1920 that Spain would be the arena of the next Marxist revolution. In spite of Spain's good fortune in avoiding the horrors of World War I, the overall weakness of its government and the political polarization of the country did not allow an easy transition to democracy. Spanish Carmelites had made good progress in their recovery from the 19th century troubles, and they were blessed with many young vocations because of the quality of their religious fervor and fidelity to Albert's Rule. But like the victims of the French Revolution before them, their success was seen as a threat to those who were

The Shrine Church at Aylesford, England along with adjoining land was recovered in 1949, having been suppressed in 1538 by King Henry VIII. One of the Order's first foundations in Europe, the restored Aylesford became a frequented Marian shrine and spiritual center. *(Photo courtesy of Carmelite Media)*

motivated by a hatred of religion. Dedicated revolutionaries like Francisco Largo Caballero were able to motivate their followers to the most extreme violence against helpless nuns and friars under the pretext that they were oppressors of the common people. Moderates within the Loyalist bloc seemed helpless to stop them, but were often themselves radicalized by the bitterness of the butchery on both sides.

Many of the Carmelite casualties occurred early in the conflict, before most of the religious knew how dangerous their situation was, and before the battle fronts had solidified. Especially in Catalonia and the eastern parts of Spain, Loyalist forces were stronger, and it was more difficult for religious to find places of safety. Members of the communities in and around Barcelona were dispersed or killed with a particular heartlessness. In nearly every case, their churches were looted and their houses destroyed. The entire community of Tárrega was exterminated, with their dozen bodies burned afterward in a gasoline fire. The Discalced friars of Toledo were also taken directly from their monastery to the wall of their church where they were gunned down by a firing squad. A distressing number of victims were novices or young professed students, who still gave courageous testimony to their love of God and his people. Other casualties in-

Blessed Hiliary Januszewski, prior of the Carmelite community in Krakow, Poland, was imprisoned in Dachau Concentration Camp. This representation hangs in the community room of the Krakow priory. *(Photo courtesy of Carmelite Media)*

cluded distinguished scholars and elderly missionaries who had provided heroic witness to their faith.

Although women religious were generally less likely to be killed than men, there were many frightening incidents. Large numbers of nuns were evicted from their homes. The Discalced nuns from the convent of Cerro de los Angels were loaded into a truck headed for Madrid and a firing squad. The obvious parallel with their sisters of Compiègne a century earlier inspired the nuns to prepare for their impending martyrdom by singing hymns as their truck rumbled along. By the time the truck arrived at the outskirts of the city, the leftist militiamen were so unsettled by the nuns' courage that they set them free. More than a few other sisters were hurt or killed in the shockingly lawless world of civil strife. When the Nationalists finally occupied the last Loyalist strongholds in 1939, General Franco attempted to restore or rebuild the Spanish Church which had supported him so loyally. But such a restoration was not to be done overnight.

Second World War

The Second World War was much more severe on the Carmelites than was the First. There had been warnings of the impending bloodbath, of course, but no one could have imagined the magnitude of the slaughter and devastation which was about to be unleashed. The wartime leader for the Carmelites of the Ancient Observance was Hilary Doswald (general 1931-47), and for the Discalced Carmelites was Peter Thomas of the Virgin of Carmel (1937-46). Both had to continue in office longer than the standard terms because of the impossibility of safely convening a chapter. Both tried valiantly to communicate with their far-flung provinces and missions, and to encourage the men and women to hold fast to the ideals of Albert's Rule, and to the courage shown by so many of their sisters and brothers in former crises. All things considered, the Order performed courageously, despite the almost impossible conditions.

Many residences were destroyed by aerial bombing, mainly in occupied Europe. The venerable Discalced monastery at Würzburg was obliterated by bombs, as was Augustine of the Blessed Sacrament's London foundation in Kensington.

The church in Cagliari, Sardinia, was destroyed by a bomb. In Naples, the ceiling of Carmine Maggiore collapsed under a bombing, and the monastery was damaged. The priories in Pisa, Bologna, and Vienna were all bombed and partially damaged. The Vienna bombing also destroyed the newly completed church, and killed one Carmelite along with several neighborhood people who had taken refuge there. The old historic church in Boxmeer, next to the last-surviving Dutch priory in the 19th century, was destroyed during the German retreat in 1944. It was a tragic loss of a 15th century gem, complete with beautiful wood-carving and stained glass; the tower was blown up by Wehrmacht troops to deny the allies a possible observation post. And the priory at Nijmegen, where Titus Brandsma had lived and worked, was destroyed by a stray bomb. His own personal study, with all his papers and books, had been sealed by the Gestapo after his arrest, and was completely obliterated by the explosion.

A disturbing number of sisters and friars also died in combat, bombings, and concentration camps. Even those religious who were not victims of outright violence or mistreatment had to share the lot of their civilian neighbors through malnutrition, privation, illness, and the complete disruption of normal life. Several German Carmelites were drafted into the army, and died on battlefields far from home. At least six Polish Carmelites were sent to Dachau or other concentration camps, including one who survived to tell the heroic story of the others. One of those who did not survive was Hilary Januszewski, former prior of the community in Krakow. He bravely volunteered to care for victims of typhus in barrack #25, knowing that his chances of survival were very poor. He died after 21 days of unselfish service, only a few days before American troops liberated the camp. Another Pole was killed while serving as a chaplain for the Polish troops storming Monte Cassino in 1944. An extraordinary number of Carmelites from English-speaking provinces also served as chaplains, and some became casualties. At least 30 Dutch missionaries were swept into Japanese prison camps when Java was captured. More than a few friars from many other countries were called up to serve in their respective armed forces, including one very high-profile Frenchman.

Louis of the Trinity was the Discalced provincial in Paris when he was called back to serve in the French navy. He had fought with great distinction in the previous war, but gave up a promising career as a naval officer in 1920 to enter Carmel. Louis quickly built a reputation as a successful retreat master, scholar, and preacher. But when he answered the call to defend his country in 1939, he resumed his identity as Captain d'Argenlieu. After the disaster of 1940, he escaped from the Germans and made his way to England, where he joined General de Gaulle's Free French movement. His personal charm and courage aided the efforts to rally France's African and Asian colonies in support of the liberation forces of the mother country. After his return to London in 1943, he was named commander of Free French naval forces in Britain, and helped plan the Normandy invasion of 1944. As the war came to an end, General de Gaulle walked down the Champs Elysées in liberated Paris, with Admiral d'Argenlieu at his side. After the war, he was named to the difficult post of governor general of Indochina. But in 1947, he retired to his monastery once again, notwithstanding international acclaim and the highest military decorations. For the final 17 years of his life, he attempted to live and work quietly, avoiding all public applause, and attributing all good blessings to God alone.

Already before the 1940 occupation of the Netherlands by German forces, friar Titus Brandsma had locked horns with the demons of Nazi ideology. As a respected professor of philosophy and former chancellor at the Catholic University of Nijmegen, he was extremely well-placed to express his opinions, and have them heeded by a broad cross-section of Holland's well-educated society. He had written and spoken many times of the hidden dangers of the racism and neo-pagan principles not only of the German Nazi party, but of their Dutch counterpart, the NSB. He stressed the long history of toleration and compassion shown by the Dutch people to Jews and nearly every other minority. He denied that Hitler's appeal to raw power and violence had anything to do with authentic German or Dutch patriotism, but was instead a regression from Christianity and indeed all culture which had any human significance. Long before the first paratroopers dropped onto Dutch soil, Titus was a marked man, considered dangerous because he was so persuasive, and because he could not be intimidated by threats or shouted down by the Nazi propaganda machine.

During the first year of occupation, Titus actively supported the courageous stand of the Dutch bishops against any collaboration with the Nazi regime. He used his position as spiritual advisor to the Catholic schools to urge steadfast loyalty to Christian morality and teachings, including fair treatment of Jewish students. He worked mightily to encourage Catholics to maintain their beliefs and strict moral code in the face of growing coercion and brutality. He even pondered a scheme to smuggle Jewish fugitives out of Europe, using the Carmelite missions in Brazil as a safe haven.

But the point of no return came when the Dutch bishops named him as their liaison with Holland's many Catholic newspapers and journals. Nazi administrators had grown increasingly frustrated with the editors' refusals to accept partisan advertisements and news releases for their publications. They announced a new policy to punish any offenders. Titus wrote a strong circular letter to the journalists urging a unified front, and then followed it up with a personal visit to each of them. When the newspapers did not flinch at the Nazi intimidation, Titus was held responsible. The Gestapo came to the Nijmegen priory and arrested him on January 19, 1942. During his interrogation in the prison at Scheveningen, he freely admitted and defended all his actions to the police. He went so far as to write a lengthy explanation of why Dutch Catholics opposed the Nazi regime, quoting from memory a great variety of sources and documents to demonstrate his case. It did not take much time for the Gestapo to understand that this stubborn friar could not be brought to heel by any of the means at their disposal.

During his imprisonment, Titus reached deeply into his spiritual resources and grasped the trust in God which gave martyrs their strength. Like John of the Cross and so many others before him, he drew joy from the isolation which his prison imposed, and grew ever closer to the prayerful ethos of the Carmelite soul. His writings from prison show a growing sense of courage, even an irrepressible cheerfulness, as he contemplated Jesus on the cross. He even attempted to write a biography of Teresa of Avila from memory, using the space between the lines of another book. But by June, he was transferred to the camp at Dachau, from which no one was ever released alive. Despite the privation and horror of that living hell, he comported himself with love, joy, and courage. He lost no opportunity to hearten other prisoners and even reached out in goodwill to his guards. His end came in little more than a month, on July 26, when his frail health finally broke down, and his life was terminated with a lethal injection. His fellow Dutchman, Brother Raphael Tijhuis, survived the camp and told the story of the heroic little friar's last days.

One of the most tragic victims of the concentration camps was Sister Teresa Benedicta of the Cross, known in secular life as Edith Stein. This brilliant woman was born to a devout Jewish family in Silesia, and pursued studies in philosophy at the University of Breslau. She became fascinated with the philosophy of phenomenology, as promoted by Edmund Husserl, and decided to deepen her learning by following his classes at the University of Göttingen. By the time she completed her doctorate with highest honors at Freiburg in 1916, she had become Husserl's personal assistant and a well-respected scholar in her own right. Her well disciplined mind helped Husserl to organize his notes and re-cast his teachings into a more organized and understandable format.

The goal of Husserl's study was to clarify all knowledge, and to discover the most basic foundation of that knowledge, and indeed the essence of being itself. Although Edith had come to consider herself an atheist in the course of her university studies, she was still attracted by the deep spirituality of some of the members of her philosophical circle. Many of those leading philosophers had Jewish roots, as she did, but several had converted to Christianity. Husserl always acknowledged his debt to the clear thinking of Thomas Aquinas, and asserted that the reality of the visible world pointed also to a reality outside of itself. This might well be called the "first cause" or "creator of all." Edith would further develop this presence of power into the loving presence of a caring God.

Edith's philosophical quest expressed itself in her loving concern for her own family, friends, her Jewish people, and all those in particular need. During World War I, she had worked as a Red Cross nurse, caring for ailing and wounded soldiers on the eastern front. All the while, she struggled with her issues of faith and certainty. Her journey reached its critical point when she read the autobiography of Teresa of Avila in a single night. When she finished, she exclaimed, "This is truth!" After a short interval, she was baptized into the Catholic Church. Over the following years, she worked to deepen her spiritual life as she continued to teach, study, write, and lecture on a broad variety of topics. She had thought about entering the Carmelites, but did not do so until 1933, when Hitler closed all university careers to people of Jewish origin. She took her vows at the Carmel of Cologne with the name of Teresa Benedicta of the Cross, and began the happiest time of her life.

Edith's superiors encouraged her to continue her philosophical writings. By this time, her work had taken on a strongly spiritual flavor. She explored the features of Christian existentialism, as she investigated deeper forms of prayer, and she urged women to drive themselves forward toward greater contributions in society. Some of her best work reflected on John of the Cross's insights on suffering and death, in the context of the paschal mystery. The plight of her fellow Jews in Hitler's Germany brought a special note of poignancy to those reflections.

When it became evident that Hitler was planning to eliminate the Jews under his rule, the nuns at Cologne moved Edith and her sister Rosa across the border to the Dutch Carmel at Echt in 1938. Their apparent safety was all too brief, since German troops occupied Holland in May, 1940. Archbishop DeJong and the other Dutch bishops tried valiantly to oppose the harsher measures of Nazi rule. On the day when Titus Brandsma died, the bishops issued a strong and overt protest against the sufferings of the Jews. The Nazis concluded that they had to retaliate strongly. In retaliation, the Gestapo then arrested all Catholics of Jewish origin and deported them to the death camps.

True to her vocation, Edith never stopped caring for other prisoners, especially the children, and encouraging them with her sense of calm dignity. She was able to share her own hope with those for whom hope no longer seemed to exist. Just before she was loaded onto the prison train, she smuggled a short note to her prioress. "I am quite content now. One can only learn the science of the cross if one truly suffers under the weight of the cross. I was entirely convinced of this from the very first, and I have said with all my heart: *Ave Crux, Spes Unica*. (Hail Cross, our only hope.)" Edith and Rosa were ultimately sent to the ghastly camp at Auschwitz, where they ended their lives in the gas chamber. They died just two weeks after Titus Brandsma.

When Edith chose her religious name, Teresa Benedicta of the Cross, she reflected the longing which she felt to come to grips with the mystery of suffering. It is simple to conclude that the millions upon millions of deaths in the Nazi holocaust were meaningless, that the lives of so many hapless victims were just thrown away like rubbish. But like John of the Cross and so many others before her, Teresa Benedicta came to see the Cross as love, which went far beyond mere suffering. She, who began her studies to find the significance of being itself, by a tortuous path, discovered her model in Jesus. It was that same Jesus who died, suffering for others, but whose life was restored by the Father. Far from throwing her life away as worthless, from a sense of guilt, or because she was a nobody, she had come to see herself as God's precious daughter, and she peacefully returned her life to the Father for completion in glory, according to his own timetable.

Yet another victim of the concentration camps was the formidable Père Jacques. Born Lucien-Louis Bunel in 1900, this intriguing man was ordained to the diocesan priesthood, and worked for several years as a teacher. He entered the Discalced Carmelites in 1931, with the religious name of Jacques of Jesus. Because of his educational background, he was quickly named headmaster in charge of a boys' school in Avon-Fontainebleau. During the Nazi occupation of France, he decided to hide three Jewish boys by enrolling them in his school under assumed names. He was quite aware of the danger to himself, but the charade worked successfully until 1944, when the Gestapo came to arrest him. There was still one other Jewish refugee working at the school who was not discovered, since the other boys refused to reveal his presence.

Kilian Lynch, prior general of the Order from 1947-1959, promoted the recovery of lost communities and provinces as well as expansion of the missions of the Order. *(Photo courtesy of the British Province)*

As Jacques was transferred from one prison camp to another, he considered himself to be a friar charged with a new ministry rather than a suffering captive. By the time he reached the atrocious camp at Mauthausen, he had already built a reputation among his fellow prisoners as a tower of hope and prayerful care for all in need. He survived long enough to see his camp liberated by American troops, but died within the month because of his weakened state. Many surviving prisoners gave him the credit for their own courage and resolve.

Post-War Recovery

As the war finally came to an end, the heroic task of rebuilding got under way once again. The valiant struggles of the Carmelites were noted by the outside world, and refreshing numbers of new vocations began to ask for entry to the Order. Many veterans of the armed forces and various charitable organizations had found their faith tested by the violence and inhumanity of the conflict, and decided that a spiritual path was the only way to heal their deep distress. They began to fill the ranks of those Carmelites who had not survived the ordeal.

As with the period of recovery from any crisis, dynamic leadership is an essential element of growth. Carmelites were blessed with some outstanding

Kilian Healy, prior general from 1959-1971, was a member of the Second Vatican Council and moved to implement the changes in religious life, the liturgy, and the Church itself. *(Photo courtesy of the British Province)*

leaders at this very juncture. The Discalced chapter of 1946 elected the exceptional scholar Silverio de Santa Teresa as the new general, whose wealth of academic talent gave him a clear vision of the Order's aspirations. Silverio had devoted his life to charting the story of the Teresian Reform, and to producing critical editions of the works of Teresa of Avila and John of the Cross. Similarly, the 1947 chapter of the Ancient Observance chose Kilian Lynch to resume the process of restoration. Kilian was a powerful and creative force of nature, founded on a solid spirituality and an ambition which never rested. Both of these generals promoted the recovery of lost communities and provinces, and the expansion of the Carmelite presence to altogether new areas. The late 1940s began an unprecedented expansion of missions, as well as completely new foundations for cloistered nuns in the far corners of the world.

Within only a few years of the war's end, former colonies in Asia and Africa began to attain self-governing status, and eventually outright independence. Beginning with the Philippines (1946), India (1947), and Indonesia (1949), a relentless wave of decolonization transformed the developing world. The independence movement which swept through most of colonial Asia then went on to the African dependencies as well. By the end of the 1960s, most of the European colonial empires had conceded free government to their former subjects. For more than a few of the people in Carmelite mission territories, the exhilaration of self-rule was tempered for a time by the typical disruptions that accompany any change of power, and the practical struggles for each new country to become truly independent and self-sustaining.

Perhaps the most significant religious event of the 20th century was the opening of the Second Vatican Council in 1962. Both general superiors of the Carmelites, Anastasio of the Holy Rosary and Kilian Healy, participated actively in all sessions of the Council, as did the many Carmelite bishops from around the world. A substantial number of other theologians and experts in related fields accompanied the council fathers as consultants and technical helpers.

Carmelites were active right from the start making contributions and interventions as the debates proceeded about the best ways to make the Church more faithful to the Gospel and the call of the Good Shepherd.

By 1950 the Tridentine Church had become defined largely by what it opposed, rather than the open-armed appeal of Jesus to be the forgiven friends of God, comfortable with loving conversation at all times. Vatican II revitalized that image with the replacement of the intimidating language of Constantine's court chancery with the appealing idealism more typical of Albert's Rule. Carmelite contributions to the document on religious life were one obvious service. But the two documents on the Church also received a great deal of their attention, especially with regard to the sacraments, to the duties of the hierarchy, and to the place of Mary as model and patroness of the entire Church. Carmelite missionaries were equally vigorous at proposing refreshing ideas for a more effective transmission of the Gospel.

One of the most significant benefits of the Council was the call for all religious institutes to return to their roots. Each religious family was summoned to its origins, to consider what its founding motivation still continued to say to the modern world. Although the Council unleashed a great deal of turbulence in its wake, the Carmelite family gained much from the deep introspection of returning to the primitive Rule and its basic idealism.

And so, in the wake of the Second Vatican Council, the Carmelite world took several vigorous steps forward. In May 1965, only a few months before the Council's solemn closing, Discalced general Anastasio of the Holy Rosary assembled his provincials from all over the world on Mount Carmel. As they visited the ruins of Brocard's newly excavated chapel, they prayed for God's guidance over their plans for Carmel's renewal. This dramatic action served to energize and inspire the leaders for what would happen next.

Since the Council

As Carmelites have followed the Council's mandate to return to their roots, there has been a corresponding renewal of interest in historical research and writing. The Mount Carmel Project, spearheaded by Sister Damien of the Cross, began a scientific re-examination of the wadi Ain es-Siah. Sister Damien, the former Eugenia Nitowski, brought her professional experience as an archeologist to the slopes of Carmel. She led an army of volunteers from both branches of the Order, as well as fellow scholars and ordinary lay people, to take up shovels and brushes, and uncover details of the past. Several expeditions during the years 1987-92 uncovered previously unknown evidence of the earliest hermits, and enriched the systematic study of Carmel's roots.

A new style of Carmelite missionary activity yielded excellent results in many African countries, but especially in India, beginning in 1982. A traditional mission station could take many years of presence and building on the part of a community, and then produced new vocations only after much delay. But the "new missions" followed an entirely unique pattern. German Carmelites of the Ancient Observance visited India to identify young people interested in a Carmelite vocation, but could not remain there themselves because of restrictive laws against foreign missionaries. The Indian candidates were given a solid spiritual formation, first in Germany, then in India itself. The system took advantage of German proficiency and financial support, but allowed the Indians to adapt their learning to their own cultural conditions, with very little ethnic misunderstanding.

Other new congregations sprang up in the mission countries, as the numbers of Carmelites advanced there. The vigorous Handmaids of Our Lady of Mount Carmel were established in 1953 by Bishop Donal Lamont, and continue their ministry in Zimbabwe among orphans and school children. A similar group, the Carmelite Sisters of Our Lady, have worked at teaching and parish retreats in the Philippines since 1982. The sisters of the Carmelite Religious of Trivandrum affiliated with the Discalced family in India beginning in 1925.

In Indonesia, a very unique women's congregation called Putri Karmel was established by Fr. Johannes Indrakusuma in 1982. Falling back on the early Carmelite eremitical tradition, these sisters live in more secluded areas, and work to develop and share a more focused contemplation and spiritual existence. Indrakusuma went on to found a similar group of male hermits in 1986 called Carmelites of Saint Elijah. They also favor remote and beautiful locations, with a ministry of spiritual direction and retreat preaching. Both branches have also founded houses in Malaysia.

The renewed interest in Carmel's eremitical roots has spawned a remarkable spate of small but fervent clusters of male and female Carmelite hermits in many parts of Europe and the Americas. The old desert houses of Monte Oliveto and Bolarque provided an example for the modern quest for quiet reflection in a very noisy industrial and technological world. Thomas of Jesus would have to be very pleased with this new rebound of solitude-seekers.

The "Donum Dei" Missionary Family is another unique blessing to the entire Carmelite world. It began as an informal grouping of young women in France, inspired by Father Marcel Roussel-Galle. They called themselves Missionary Workers, and sought to work with the poorest of the poor, those most in need of the Lord's mercy. Their foundational spirituality was the story of Jesus and the Samaritan woman at the well. Jesus told her that if she were only aware of the gift of God, she could discover springs of living water within her. Beginning in 1950, Renée Prieur extended their ministry into many parts of five continents, beginning with the French-speaking world.

Since much of the group's outreach took place among the desperately poor, a very different source of funding was necessary. In an utterly unique flair of imagination, the missionary women opened fine gourmet restaurants in major cities of the more prosperous countries, and served their own variety of international haute cuisine. Diners are invited to accompany their culinary

Notre Dame de Lumières -- The convent and church of the Carmelites of Nantes. In 1988 the Carmelite Order approved the return of the Order to France for the first time since the French Revolution. The building in Nantes has three components: a conventual church, a convent and a cloister with a library of spirituality. The church is shaped like a pentagon around the altar, as if a great tent with the Christian people gathering around the Lord. Above the church is a 30 meter tower, topped by three flames of fire, symbolic of the mystical quest of Carmel. *(Photo courtesy of the French General Delegation)*

delights with short prayers or scripture reflections, as they were gently made aware of the needs of those who had less than themselves. After her network was already well-established, Renée began discussions with the Carmelites, especially Fr. Redemptus Valabek, about joining the family, an objective realized in 1987.

For friars of the Ancient Observance, many years of hoping and planning came to fruition with a quiet return to France in 1989. The women of the Donum Dei family greatly facilitated the process for an international founding community, as they opened a house in Bourges. That initial house was followed within a few years by a beautiful foundation in Nantes, thanks in great part to the support of the local bishop. Angers and Villefranche followed, with the hope of good vocations among the local people.

In 1989, the general chapter of the Ancient Observance decided to reorganize itself dramatically. Since so much of the creative energy (including most of the vocations) was coming from third-world countries, the structure of the curia was changed to reflect that reality. The four assistant generals would no longer represent major nationalities, but quadrants of the globe, of which two were automatically the mission areas of Latin America and Afro-Asia.

The disintegration of the Soviet Union and the end of the Cold War (1989-91) opened several doors of opportunity. Carmelites rushed to fill the void created by decades of enforced atheism in Eastern Europe. From a tiny postwar presence in Czechoslovakia, dedicated Carmelites had expanded their influence among Catholic men and women to serve as a solid basis for expansion once it was safe to do so. Italians hastened to encourage vocations from Romania, and assist them through formation. Polish friars, who had formed an effective "opposition party" during the Communist regime, now moved into the Ukraine to recover and rebuild lost communities. Other initiatives are under way to share Carmel's unique gifts with the religion-starved people of the former Soviet bloc.

In the mid-1990s the two Carmelite generals, John Malley and Camillo Maccise, acted to draw attention to the concept of the "Carmelite Family" throughout the world. Their policy was to broaden all forms of cooperation and solidarity among all those, whatever their affiliation, who follow the Carmelite approach to their relationship with God. This refreshing attitude reflected and highlighted the renewed cooperation which was already far advanced. Both branches of the Order had joined their vigor in scholarship, missionary efforts and a more solidly established sense of family.

Emblematic of this increased collaboration was an earlier congress on Albert's Rule overlooking the Canadian side of Niagara Falls. Men and women from every branch of Carmel came together in a spirit of prayer and reflection, and parted with the warm glow of the rich fraternity they had experienced. Although it was only a single event, that congress became for many the opening of a newer and more abundant sharing of the gifts of those who seek the face of the living God in solitude.

May that loving interchange ever grow and flourish, in the light of the previous eight centuries!

✝   ✝   ✝

Appendices

Rule of Carmel

[1] Albert, by the grace of God
called to be patriarch of the church of Jerusalem,
to the beloved sons in Christ, B. and the other hermits
who are living under obedience to him
by the spring on Mount Carmel:
health in the Lord and the blessing of the Holy Spirit.

[2] In many and various ways
the holy fathers established how everyone,
whatever his order
or whatever kind of religious life he has chosen,
must live in allegiance to Jesus Christ
and serve him faithfully from a pure heart and a good conscience.

[3] However, because you ask us
to give you a formula of life
in accordance with your commitment,
which you must observe in the future:

[4] The first thing we establish is
that you have one of yourselves as prior,
who is to be chosen for this office by the unanimous assent of all,
or of the greater and sounder part,
to whom each of the others is to promise obedience,
and strive to fulfil his promise in the reality of deeds,
along with chastity and the renunciation of ownership.

[5] *You may have places in solitary areas*
or where they are given to you
which are suitable and convenient
for the observance of your religious life,
as may seem fit to the prior and the brothers.

[6] Furthermore, according to the site of the place
in which you propose to dwell,
all of you are to have separate individual cells,
and these cells are to be assigned to each
by the disposition of the prior himself
and with the assent of the other brothers or the sounder part of them.

[7] *Nevertheless, you are to eat*
whatever may have been given you in a common refectory,
listening in common to some reading of Sacred Scripture,
where this can be done conveniently.

[8] It is not permitted to any of the brothers
to change his appointed place or exchange it with another,
except with the permission of whoever is prior at the time.

[9] The prior's cell is to be near the entrance of the place,
so that he may be the first to meet those who come to that place;
and everything that must be done subsequently
shall proceed according to his judgement and direction.

[10] All are to remain in their cells or near them,
meditating day and night on the Law of the Lord
and keeping vigil in prayer,
unless they are occupied with other worthy activities.

[11] *Those who know how to say the canonical hours with the clerics*
are to say them according to the institution of the holy fathers
and the approved custom of the Church.
Those who do not know them are to say the Our Father
twenty-five times for the night vigil,
except on Sundays and solemnities,
for the vigils of which we establish that the said number be doubled,
so that the Our Father is said fifty times.
And the same prayer is to be said seven times for morning lauds.
Likewise for the other hours the same prayer
is also to be said seven times each,
except for the evening office, when you must say it fifteen times.

[12] *None of the brothers is to call anything his own,*
but everything is to be held in common among you,
and distributed to each according to his need by the hand of the prior,
that is by the brother appointed by him for this task,
taking into account the age and needs of each.

[13] *It is permissible for you, however,*
to have asses or mules, as your need requires,
and some provision of animals or poultry.

[14] An oratory, as far as it can be done conveniently,
is to be built in the midst of the cells,
where you must come together every day
in the morning to hear Mass,
where this can be done conveniently.

[15] On Sundays, also, or on other days when there is reason,
you shall discuss the preservation of order
and the salvation of souls,
and at this time the excesses and faults of the brothers,
if these are revealed in anyone,
should be corrected by means of love.

[16] You are to observe the fast every day except Sundays
from the feast of the Exaltation of the Holy Cross until Easter Sunday,
unless sickness or bodily weakness
or some other worthy reason
suggest the fast be broken,
for necessity has no law.

[17] *You are to abstain from eating meat,*
unless it is taken as a remedy for sickness or feebleness.
And since you have to beg more frequently while travelling,
outside your own houses you may eat food cooked with meat,
so as not to be a burden to your hosts;
but at sea even meat may be eaten.

[18] Because, indeed, a person's life on earth is a trial,
and all who wish to live devotedly in Christ suffer persecution,
and also since your adversary the devil goes about like a roaring lion
seeking whom he may devour,
you are to use every care to put on the armour of God,
so that you may be able to withstand the deceits of the enemy.

[19] Your loins are to be girt with the cincture of chastity.
Your breast is to be fortified with holy thoughts,
for it is written, Holy thought will save you.
The breastplate of justice is to be put on,
that you may love the Lord your God
with all your heart and all your soul and all your strength
and your neighbor as yourselves.
In all circumstances the shield of faith must be taken up,
in which you will be able to quench all the flaming arrows of the evil one,
for without faith it is impossible to please God.
The helmet of salvation also is to be placed on your head,
that you may expect salvation
from the only Savior who saves his people from their sins.
The sword of the Spirit, too, which is the word of God,
is to dwell abundantly in your mouth and in your hearts;
and whatever things you have to do,
let them be done in the word of the Lord.

[20] You must have some sort of work to do,
so that the devil may always find you occupied,
lest because of your idleness
he manage to find some way of entering into your souls.
In this you have the teaching and the example alike
of the blessed apostle Paul, in whose mouth Christ spoke,
who has been appointed and given by God
as preacher and teacher of the nations in faith and truth;

if you follow him you cannot go astray.
In toil and weariness, he says, we lived among you,
working night and day so as not to be a burden to any of you;
not as if we do not have the right,
but so as to give ourselves to you as a model,
so that you might imitate us.
For when we were with you we used to admonish you
that if anyone is unwilling to work, let him not eat.
For we have heard that there are certain people among you
going about restlessly and doing no work.
We admonish people of this kind, then,
and beseech them in the Lord Jesus Christ that,
working in silence, they eat their own bread.
This way is holy and good: walk in it.

[21] The Apostle, in fact, recommends silence,
for he commands working in it;
and also the Prophet testifies, Silence is the cultivation of justice;
and again, In silence and hope will be your strength.
And so, therefore, we decree that you keep silence
from after compline until after prime of the following day.
At other times, however,
although so strict an observance of silence is not kept,
talkativeness is nevertheless to be carefully avoided,
for as it is written -- and experience teaches no less --
In talkativeness sin will not be lacking;
and, The one who is careless in speech will meet with evils;
and again, The one who uses many words injures his own soul.
And the Lord says in the gospel:
For every idle word that people speak
they will render account of it on judgement day.
Let each one, therefore, make a measure of his words
and proper reins for his mouth,
lest as it happens he stumble and fall in his tongue,
and his fall be irreparable and deadly.
Guarding his ways with the Prophet so he does not sin in his tongue,
let him strive diligently and carefully
to observe the silence in which is the cultivation of justice.

[22] And you, brother B.,
and whoever will be appointed prior after you,
should always have in mind and observe in practice
what the Lord says in the gospel:
Whoever wishes to be the greater among you will be your servant,
and whoever wishes to be the first among you will be your slave.

[23] You other brothers, too, honor your prior humbly,
thinking not of him but rather of Christ
who placed him over your heads,
and who says to the leaders of the churches,
Whoever hears you, hears me;
whoever rejects you, rejects me,
so that you will not come into judgement for contempt,
but for obedience will merit the reward of eternal life.

[24] We have written these things briefly for you,
establishing a formula for your way of life
according to which you are bound to live.
But if anyone will have expended more,
the Lord himself, when he returns, will repay him.
Use discernment, however,
which is the guide of the virtues.

This text was prepared for the 800th anniversary of the Carmelite Rule in 2007. Paragraph numbers are in square brackets to indicate that they are not part of the original Rule. They were agreed upon by the General Councils of both Carmelite Orders and published in 1999. Innocentian additions are given in italics.

Selections from *The Flaming Arrow*
(Ignea Sagitta)
by
Nicholas, Prior General of the Carmelites (1266-71)

From the Prologue:

Nicholas, in his poverty, bids all his fellow prisoners health and the counsel of the Holy Spirit forever.

The sight of that devoted mother of mine who conceived me as one dead and brought me forth before my time between her degenerate stepsons on the one hand, and those wrongful prisoners who are her true children on the other, moves me to minister to each, with the help of God's grace, what each stands in need of. ....

I humbly ask these true and lawful sons to restrain their indignation while I roundly rebuke the pride of the stepsons for the shame it has brought upon us; nor would I have the stepsons grow angry for, as God is my witness – who hears wills, not words – it is for their own benefit, for their salvation, to call them out of danger, that I rebuke them.

In this desire of mine, it is my heart's love that goes out to every one of you without exception, for it is a shame common to all of us that I want to do away with. But I know...that this letter, fittingly named *The Flaming Arrow* for its bright, sharp truthfulness, welcomed as it may be by the lawful sons whose faces are toward the light, will seem hateful toward the stepsons, whose ill deeds it will show to be the deeds of those who hate the light.

From Chapter III:

.... Fools! What use is this veneer of apparent truth with which you try to gloss over your protestations? Do you imagine that he from whom no secret lies hidden can be deceived by such nonsense – indeed, such lies? You falsely assure anyone who is ready to believe you ... that you have abandoned your desert life and come into the cities. Let me point out to you that you achieve neither of these aims in the city, while both were fully accomplished in the solitude of your former days.

As long as you persevered in solitude in your contemplations, your prayers and holy exercises, with profit to yourselves, the renown of your holiness wafted abroad like a perfume, far and wide, over city and town, brought wonderful comfort to all those it reached; and it attracted many in those days to the solitude of the desert, edified by its fragrance, and drawn as though by a cord of tenderness to repent of their misdeeds.

But now conducting yourselves as worldlings among worldlings, you profit neither yourselves nor them. Indeed in not profiting you lose, and you offend the people, the very ones you are so anxious to please, by inflicting on them the poisonous stench of your ill fame. ...

From Chapter IV:

Where among you, tell me, are to be found preachers, well versed in the word of God, and fit to preach as it should be done?

Some there are, indeed, presumptuous enough in their craving for vain glory to attempt it, and to trot out to the people such scraps as they have been able to cull from books, in an effort to teach others what they themselves know neither by study nor by experience. They prate away before the common folk, without understanding a word of their own rigmarole as boldfaced as though all theology lay digested in the stomach of their memory, and any tale will serve their turn if it can be given a mystical twist and made to redound to their own glory. Then, when they have done preaching, or rather tale telling, there they stand, ears all pricked up and itching to catch the slightest whisper of flattery. But not a vestige do they show of the endowments for which, in their appetite for vain-glory, they long to be praised. ....

From Chapter V:

Misguided deceivers of your brethren present and to come, the foundation of your argument is false. Be silent for very shame. Let me give you the true explanation. ....

What is this new Order that has appeared in the cities, tell me? Answer me, though you must surely blush as you do so, in what useful occupation are you engaged there? I will spare you the embarrassment of telling the truth, and will answer more truthfully than you would yourselves. Two by two you roam the streets of the city from morning to night, you scurry hither and thither; and your master is he who "prowls about like a roaring lion seeking someone to devour." Thus in you, to your utter disgrace, is the prophecy truly fulfilled; "On every side the wicked prowl."

.... The main reason for your wanderings is not to visit orphans, but young women, not widows in their adversity, but silly girls in dalliances, beguines, nuns, and highborn ladies. Once in their company, you gaze into their eyes and utter words fit for lovers, the downfall of right conducts and a snare to the heart. ....

From Chapter VIII:

.... A professed member of our Order who has been allotted a cell has the obligation, whenever he finds himself out of his cell, of examining his conscience as to whether he is excused by a lawful duty. And if he does not find a reasonable excuse, he is obliged to return to his cell. If he scorns the protests of conscience and declines to return, let him know that he is breaking faith with his profession.

In the cell, however, the less perfect might grow weary of spirit if spiritual employments were prolonged beyond measure, so it has pleased divine providence to add to them, in second place, bodily toil, so that as one duty succeeds another, all our time may be spent to our own profit and our Creator's glory. This further provision reads: "You must give yourselves to work of some kind, so that the devil may always find you busy." Our twofold occupation in solitude, then, engages both body and soul, and while body and soul are busied turn and turn about, the bulwark of our castle – chastity – is fortified, every moment of our time is well spent, and our gain in terms of merit is incalculable.

From Chapter XI:

And now that you have heard the things that lead to damnation, I will tell you some of the wonderful privileges which are ours in the desert. It is unbelievable how much consolation, outward and inward, they bring.

In the desert, all the elements conspire to favor us. The heavens, resplendent with the stars and planets in their amazing order, bear witness by their beauty to mysteries higher still. The birds seem to assume the nature of angels, and tenderly console us with their gentle caroling. The mountains too, as Isaiah prophesied, "drop down sweetness" incomparable upon us, and the friendly hills "flow with milk and honey" such as is never tasted by the foolish lovers of this world. When we sing the praises of our Creator, the mountains about us, our brother conventuals, resound with corresponding hymns of praise to the Lord, echoing back our voices and filling the air with strains of harmony as though accompanying our song upon stringed instruments. The roots in their growth, the grass in its greenness, the leafy boughs and trees, all make merry in their own ways as they echo our praise; and the flowers in their loveliness, as they pour out their delicate fragrance, smile their best for the consolation of us solitaries. The sunbeams, though tongueless, speak saving messages to us. The shady bushes rejoice to give us shelter. In short, every creature we see or hear in the desert gives us friendly refreshment and comfort; indeed, for all their silence they tell forth wonders, and move the interior man to give praise to the Creator, so much more wonderful than themselves. ....

Selections from *Institution* *

Book 1 - Chapter 2 *How Elijah was the first man, under the inspiration of God, to lead the monastic and prophetic eremitical life, and how God communicated to him the way of reaching this goal and the perfection of this life, partly openly and partly in a mystical fashion.*

This prophet of God, Elijah, was the first leader of monks, from whom this holy and ancient way of life took its origin. For he, having reached divine contemplation and filled with the desire for higher things, withdrew far from the cities, and laying aside all earthly and worldly things, was the first to begin to devote himself to following the religious and prophetic eremitical life, which, under the inspiration and command of the Holy Spirit, he initiated and formulated. Then God appeared to him and commanded him to flee from normal human habitation and hide himself in the desert away from the crowds, and thereafter live like a monk in the desert according to the way of life made known to him.

This is all proved by the clear testimony of Holy Scripture, for we read about this in the *Book of Kings*, Chapter 3: "The word of the Lord came to Elijah saying, 'Depart from here and go towards the East, and hide yourself in the wadi Carith, which is over against the Jordan, and there you will drink of the torrent, and I have commanded the ravens to feed you there.'"[46]

Now these salutary commands which the Holy Spirit inspired Elijah to fulfill, and these welcome promises which he encouraged him to strive for, should be meditated upon by us hermit monks word for word, not only for their historical sense but even more for their mystical sense; because our way of life is contained in them so much more fully, that is, the way of arriving at prophetic perfection and the goal of the religious eremitical life.

The goal of this life is twofold.[47] One part we acquire by our own effort and the exercise of the virtues, assisted by divine grace. This is to offer God a pure and holy heart, free from all stain of sin. We attain this goal when we are perfect and "in Carith," that is, hidden in that love of which the Wiseman speaks: "love covers all offences."[48] Wishing Elijah to reach this goal, God said to him, "Hide in the wadi Carith."

The other goal of this life is granted to us as the free gift of God, namely, to taste somewhat in the heart and to experience in the mind the power of the divine presence and the sweetness of heavenly glory, not only after death but already in this mortal life.[49] This is to "drink of the torrent" of the pleasure of God. God promised this to Elijah in the words: "And there you shall drink of the torrent."

It is to achieve both these goals that the prophetic eremitical life is adopted by the monk, as the prophet bears witness: "In a desert land" he says, "where there is no way and no water, so in the sanctuary have I come before you, 0

God, to see your power and your glory."[50] And so, by choosing to remain "in a desert land where there is no way and no water," and so to come before God "in the sanctuary," that is, with a heart purified of sin, he indicates that the first goal of the solitary life which he has chosen is to offer God a holy heart, that is, purified of all actual sin. By adding "to see your power and your glory," he indicates quite clearly the second goal of this life, which is, whilst in this life, to experience or to see mystically in the heart something of the power of the divine presence and to taste the sweetness of heavenly glory.

Through the first of these, that is, through purity of heart and perfection of love, one comes to the second, that is, to an experiential knowledge of the divine power and heavenly glory. As the Lord says in John Chapter 14: "He who loves me will be loved by my Father, and I will love him and will show myself to him."[51] And so God, by what he had proposed to the holy prophet Elijah in all the above words, wanted greatly to persuade him - the first and outstanding leader of monks - and us his followers, that we should "be perfect as our heavenly Father is perfect," "having above all things love, which is the bond of perfection."[52] Therefore, in order that we may be worthy of the perfection urged on us and the promised vision of glory, let us seek attentively to understand clearly and logically, and to fulfill in our actions, the form of life given by God in the above words to blessed Elijah as a way to achieve them.

For, speaking to the holy Elijah, the Lord also says, both in the Old Law and the New, to every hermit monk: "Depart from here," that is, from the perishable and transitory things of this world, and "go towards the East," that is, against the natural desires of your flesh, "and hide in the wadi Carith," so that you do not live in the cities with their crowds, "which is over against the Jordan," that is, so that through love you are cut off from all sins. By these four steps you will ascend to the height of prophetic perfection, and "there you will drink of the torrent." And so that you may be able to persevere in this: "I have commanded the ravens to feed you there."

All this you will understand better if, going through each part separately, we explain them clearly and in order.

[46] I Kings 17:2-4.

[47] The ideas here come from *Cassian Conferences*, 345-6.

[48] Proverbs 10:12.

[49] *cf* also *Cassian Conferences*, 284-5.

[50] Psalm 63: 1-2. The Latin text used here differs from modern versions.

Book 5 - Chapter 2

How Saint John the Baptist was an outstanding member of this Order, and a most perfect imitator of Elijah in the eremitical monastic life.

Therefore, the successors of those holy prophets, the monastic sons of the prophets, who, as was said, dwelt in the solitude of Mount Carmel and in the wildernesses near the Jordan river and in other deserts and towns of the Promised Land, preserved what had been given over the ages by these prophets: that Christ was to become man, to die and gloriously to rise again for the redemption of the human race, him for whom they yearned from the bottom of their hearts, and hoped would come. These, God had thought worthy to instruct, through Elijah and other prophets of the same Order, of the future coming of Christ. And also, he taught of the presence of Christ in the world through his precursor, ordaining that this precursor should go before Jesus Christ "in the spirit and strength of Elijah," and that already in his youth, he would enter their monastic eremitical life established by the prophet Elijah. Which Luke the evangelist does not omit to mention, saying of the precursor: "And the child grew and was strengthened by the Spirit, and he was in the solitary places."[249] It is to be noted that Luke says "in the solitary places" because John stayed both in the solitary wastes of the Jordan wilderness like the sons of the prophets, and in the solitary places of the mountains like Elijah and Elisha.

Jacques de Vitry in the first book of his *History of the East and the West*, Chapter 53 has: "In the solitude of the Jordan, blessed John the Baptist fled from the crowds of men, so that he might freely open himself to God, and from his earliest years, he hid himself there."[250]

Ambrose, in his *Letter to the Bishop of Vercelli*, Chapter 13 has: "From such places came those figures Elijah, Elisha, John and Elizabeth, who, clothed in sheepskins and in goatskins, afflicted and in want, distressed with grief and sorrow, wandered about in deserts among the high and thickly covered mountains, the impenetrable rocks, the terrors of the caves and dangers of the crags, of whose way of life the world was not worthy."[251]

John XLIV bishop of Jerusalem as before:

When therefore "he came" in the sacred "fullness of time," to these monks in the desert, he was that "man sent by God whose name was John," that is, the Baptist, an outstanding member of that eremitical monastic life which was established by Elijah. For both Elijah and John were clothed in rough garments, free from debauchery, eating frugally, living always a solitary life in the desert. Also they were both chosen by God to be the precursors of Christ, John preaching about the first coming and Elijah about the last, as the Lord said: "Elijah will come and he will restore everything, But I tell you that Elijah has already come and they did not know him and they did with him whatever they wanted. Then the disciples understood that he had spoken to them of John the Baptist."[252]

And so the priests and the Levites sent by the Jews from Jerusalem to John, knowing that he followed most faithfully the eremitical monastic life of Elijah, asked him if he was Elijah. For as the angel Gabriel had prophesied of him, "He will come in the spirit and power of Elijah," so following his example, abandoning his father's house and worldly occupations, he lived his life completely in the desert. And like him, "not drinking wine or any strong drink," he wore, in imitation of Elijah, a "coat of camel hair and a leather belt around his waist" as the evangelist Matthew records.[253]

Chrysostom in his *Commentary on Matthew*, homily 10: "The evangelist did not consider it superfluous to speak of John's clothes. For indeed it was a marvellous and strange thing to behold so great austerity in a human frame; which thing also particularly attracted the Jews, seeing in him the great Elijah, and guided by what they then beheld, to the memory of that blessed man."[254]

John XLIV bishop of Jerusalem as before:

Therefore Christ, knowing that John through his life gave witness to the monastic life of the prophet Elijah, said of him to the crowds, "If you are willing to accept it, he is Elijah."[255]

Jerome in his *Commentary on Matthew* has: "John is called Elijah not because of the stupid Pharisees and certain heretics who teach the rebirth of souls, but because, according to another text of the gospel, he came "in the spirit and power of Elijah" and he had the same Holy Spirit or grace or character. For in austerity of life and discipline of mind, Elijah and John are equal; both lived in the wilderness and wore a leather gird1e."[256]

[249] Luke 1:17, 80.

[250] Jacques de Vitry, *Hist. orientalis*, cap. 53.

[251] *cf Heb* 11:37-39; Ambrose, *Letter 63*, 67, (trans.) H. De Romestin, Nicene and Post-Nicene Fathers, Second series, vol. 10 (1896) 466.

[252] Galatians 4:4; John 1:6; Matthew 17:11-13.

[253] John 1:19-21; Luke 1:17, 15; Matthew 3:4.

[254] John Chrysostom, *Homilies on the Gospel of Matthew*, 10:4 (trans.) G. Prevost, (Oxford, 1843) i, 138.

[255] Matthew 11:14.

[256] Jerome, *Commentary on Matthew*, 2 (Matthew 11:15), (no translation has been traced)

Book 5 – Chapter 8

How the Carmelites, having been instructed by the apostles in the teachings of the gospel and the prophecies contained in the Old Testament, preached the faith of Christ throughout Phoenicia and Palestine.

They were "faithful to the teaching of the apostles and in the breaking of bread. With one mind they kept up their daily attendance" praying "in the Temple, praising God with gladness and simplicity of heart."[274] All their days were spent in following their studies and in learning the holy gospels. Also, they had a collection of sacred books and the laws of the fathers, from which they sought an allegorical interpretation. For every old law seemed to them to be like an animal, in that, exteriorly, like the body, it had its text and what was designated by the words; but interiorly in the text, like the soul, there is hidden an invisible and spiritual understanding of some profound divine mystery. This meaning, which they learned from the apostles, they entered into ever more sublimely and nobly as in a mirror, and from the individual elements of the text they drew some amazing aspects of understanding, and they were filled with a divine and more profound knowledge of the sacred books as if from an abundant banquet.

Finally, many of them, sharing with others what they had acquired from the apostles, preached the faith of Christ throughout Phoenicia and Palestine, explaining the dogmas of faith and, by their way of life and monastic vocation, demonstrating the most praiseworthy Church of God.

From the *Roman Chronicles*: "At the time that Jesus Christ was preaching, some brothers came from Mount Carmel to Jerusalem. And some of them in the seventh year after Our Lord's passion, during the reign of the Roman emperor, lived as a community near the Golden Gate in Jerusalem, until the time of the emperors Titus and Vespasian. And during the period that blessed Peter was bishop of Antioch, they preached the Catholic faith in different places throughout the surrounding region."[275]

Joseph of Antioch in his book *On the Exemplary Army of the Early Church*, Chapter 12, writes: "Highly committed men appeared, of the exemplary army of Christ, helpers of the apostles, given to solitary contemplation, followers of the holy prophets Elijah and Elisha, who came down from Mount Carmel and dispersed throughout Galilee, Samaria and Judea, everywhere preaching the faith of Christ. Who, in honor of the Virgin Mary, built a church on the slopes of Mount Carmel where they devoted themselves especially to the Mother of the Savior."[276]

Thus ends the fifth book of the way of life and great deeds of the Carmelites.

---

[270] Acts 3:2; 4:22; 3:2, 3-4, 6-10.

[271] cf Acts 3:11; Acts 3:12 sqq; Acts 3:16.

[272] Acts 3:25-26.

[273] Acts 4:4.

[274] Acts 2:42, 46.

[275] *Roman Chronicles*. This quotation has never been traced; it is probably derived from a Carmelite author, *cf.* Staring, *Medieval Carmelite Heritage*, 73.

[276] Joseph of Antioch, *On the Exemplary Army of the Early Church*, Chap. 12: another untraced quotation, neither the work not the author is known. Probably from a Carmelite source, *cf.* Staring, *Medieval Carmelite Heritage*, 328.

Ribot, Felip, "The Ten Books on the Way of Life and Great Deeds of the Carmelites (including The Book of the First Monks): A medieval history of the Carmelites written c. 1385. Edited and translated by Richard Copsey, O. Carm. Faversham, UK: St. Albert's Press, 2005

For Further Study

Boaga, Emmanuele, and Luigi Borriello, eds. *Dizionario Carmelitano*. Rome: Città Nuova, 2008.

Egan, Keith, ed. *Carmelite Prayer: A Tradition for the 21st Century*. New York: Paulist Press, 2003.

McGreal, Wilfrid. *At the Fountain of Elijah: The Carmelite Tradition*. Maryknoll, NY: Orbis Books, 1999.

Mulhall, Michael, ed.. *Albert's Way: The First North American Congress on the Carmelite Rule*. Rome: Carmelite Institute, 1989.

Payne, Steven. *The Carmelite Tradition*. Collegeville, MN: Liturgical Press, 2011.

Rohrbach, Peter Thomas. *Journey to Carith: The Sources and Story of the Discalced Carmelites*. 1966. Reprinted, Washington, DC: ICS Publications, 2005.

Saggi, Ludovico, and Valentino Macca, eds. *Saints of Carmel*. Translated by Gabriel Pausback. Rome: Carmelite Institute, 1972.

Smet, Joachim. *The Carmelites: A History of the Brothers of Our Lady of Mount Carmel*. 4 volumes. Darien: IL: Carmelite Spiritual Center, 1976-88.

Smet, Joachim. *Cloistered Carmel: A Brief History of the Carmelite Nuns*. Rome: Carmelite Institute, 1987.

Smet, Joachim. *The Mirror of Carmel: A Brief History of the Carmelite Order*. Darien, IL: Carmelite Media, 2011.

Welch, John. *The Carmelite Way: An Ancient Path for Today's Pilgrim*. New York: Paulist Press, 1996.

Recommended Carmelite Websites

For more information about the Carmelites today,
our spirituality and our ministries worldwide, visit:
carmelites.net
ocarm.org
carmelites.info
ocarm-ocd.org

For a listing of Carmelite provinces worldwide, visit:
carmelites.info/provinces

For a listing of Monasteries of Carmelite nuns, visit:
carmelites.info/nuns

For a listing of Carmelite Hermitages, please visit:
carmelites.info/hermits

For a listing of sites about Lay Carmelites:
carmelites.info/lay carmel

For a listing of Affiliated Congregations and Institutes:
carmelites.info/congregations

For more information about our work
with the United Nations, visit:
carmelitengo.org

For more information about other publications
available from the Carmelites, visit:
carmelites.info/publications
icspublications.org

Author's Biography

Leopold Glueckert, O. Carm, was born in Hammond, Indiana on January 1, 1943. His first contact with the Carmelites was at Chicago's venerable Mount Carmel High School, where he admired the priests and brothers there for their verve and zest for life. Although they were well prepared and skillful teachers, there was something more…a stance of joy and enthusiasm at living in God's sometimes perplexing world. His decision that "I've got to be like them" led to his entry to the minor seminary at Niagara Falls, and the subsequent years of formation. He professed his first vows as a Carmelite in 1962, and was ordained to the priesthood in 1968.

Although his ministry since that time has always been teaching history in some form, he never let go of his interest in the 800 year-long saga of the White Friars. His theological studies in Rome awakened an awareness of the "big-ness" of the Carmelite story, and his subsequent history studies at DePaul (MA, 1976) and Loyola (PhD, 1989) Universities of Chicago have strengthened that interest. Since 1980, Carmelite novices in formation have been challenged by his classes in Carmelite history every summer. In 2007, he began teaching the same subject at the Washington Theological Union, as well as periodic lecturing. Leopold believes that story telling, although one of the simplest skills of even the most primitive societies, has the power to energize and motivate humans to their very best accomplishments. Even the youngest children tell stories, and they are very good at it. We neglect this art form at our peril.

Index

www.ingramcontent.com/pod-product-compliance
Lightning Source LLC
Chambersburg PA
CBHW020610270326
41927CB00005B/267